HARD TIMES IN THE HOMETOWN

Hard Times in the Hometown

A History of Community Survival in Modern Japan

MARTIN DUSINBERRE

University of Hawai'i Press
Honolulu

Printed in the United States of America

17 16 15 14 13 12 6 5 4 3 2 1

Library of Congress Cataloging-in-Publication Data

Dusinberre, Martin, 1976–
Hard times in the hometown : a history of community survival in modern Japan / Martin Dusinberre.
p. cm.
Includes bibliographical references and index.
ISBN 978-0-8248-3524-8 (cloth : alk. paper)
1. Kaminoseki (Japan)—History—19th century. 2. Kaminoseki (Japan)—History—20th century. 3. Kaminoseki (Japan)—Social conditions—19th century. 4. Kaminoseki (Japan)—Social conditions—20th century. I. Title.
DS894.79.Y349K363 2012
952'.197—dc23

2011025413

University of Hawai'i Press books are printed on acid-free paper and meet the guidelines for permanence and durability of the Council on Library Resources.

Designed by inari

Printed by Sheridan Books, Inc.

To Asuka

CONTENTS

LIST OF FIGURES AND TABLES

FIGURES

TABLES

NOTES ON TERMS

Japanese names are written in Japanese order, with the surname first, unless the subject is an author who publishes in English.

When transliterating Japanese, macrons indicate a long vowel. For common proper nouns, such as Tōkyō or Ōsaka, I have omitted the macrons unless they appear as part of a Japanese term. This is also the case for Chūgoku Denryoku Kabushiki Gaisha, whose official English name is Chugoku Electric Power Company, Inc.

All references to money are given in contemporary (unrefined) values and, where possible, contextualized for their significance.

The main historical and imperial periods discussed are

Edo period (1603–1868)
Meiji period (1868–1912)
Taishō period (1912–1926)
Shōwa period (1926–1989)
Heisei period (1989–)

ACKNOWLEDGMENTS

This book could not have been written without the generosity of Kaminoseki townspeople. For welcoming me as family, I would like to thank Kawaguchi Kaneji and especially Reiko, and Hamamura Eiji and Yaeko. Kimura Tsutomu; Awaya Shigenori, Kayoko, and Miwako; and the late Nishiyama Hiroshi also offered invaluable support. I am grateful to Mayor Kashiwabara Shigemi and the staff of Kaminoseki Town Office, the Kaminoseki Board of Education (with particular thanks to Kawamura Mitsuo and Akaishi Shūji), Chōsenji temple, the Iwaishima Hōsankai, and the members of Kaminoseki's two local history associations. Many other people gave generously of their time in Kaminoseki and beyond: some appear in the notes, but those not named are not forgotten. Elsewhere in Japan, my grateful thanks to Ben and Kyoko Stainer, the Yamashita family, Kawaguchi Hiroyuki, David Blake Willis and Mika Obayashi, and especially to Yoda Toshio and Kimiko.

Of the many teachers who stimulated my interest in history and in Japan, I would particularly like to thank my doctoral supervisor, Ann Waswo, who first encouraged me to think that my interest in Kaminoseki could turn into a book. Seki Kazutoshi, Judith Brown, Rana Mitter, Roger Goodman, and Angus Lockyer all offered timely encouragement at different stages of the doctorate, as did staff at the Nissan Institute of Japanese Studies, Oxford University. Other friends and colleagues who have generously helped and advised include Daniel Aldrich, Scott Ashley, James Babb, Victor Ban, Andrew Barshay, Harald Fuess, Alan Gamlen, Andrea Germer, Aya Homei, Sachiko Horiguchi, Yuki Imoto, Elizabeth Kramer, Lee Kuribayashi, Ho Swee Lin, Lola Martinez, Kanaya Masato, Aaron Miller, Tosh Minohara, Hideko Mitsui, Dave Morse, Naitō Junko, Tom Nelson, Nishimura Akira, Ōta Chiharu, Stephen Robertson, Osamu Saitō, Paul Scalise, Felix Schulz, Naoko Shimazu, Bill Steele, Tuukka Toivonen, Scott Urban, Tom Williams, Yasui Manami, and especially Naomi Standen and Ben Houston.

I wish to acknowledge the support of various organizations during the preparation of this book. A Japanese Ministry of Education, Culture, Sports, Science, and Technology research scholarship supported my initial fieldwork in 2003–2005. I was also the grateful recipient of postgraduate studentships from the Arts and Humanities Research Council and of grants from the Oxford Sasakawa Fund and the St. Antony's College Research Fund. I would like to thank the Great Britain Sasakawa Foundation and the Newcastle University HaSS Faculty REF Fund for support since 2008. I also appreciate the considerable assistance I received in the archives: from Izumi Tytler and the superb staff of the Bodleian Japanese Library, and from the Japanese National Diet Library, the Diplomatic Record Office of the Japanese Ministry of Foreign Affairs, the Yamaguchi and Hiroshima Prefectural Libraries, the Yamaguchi Prefectural Archives, the Ōshima Museum of Emigration, and the Yanai subbranch of the Ministry of Justice. My particular thanks to Pat Crosby and Stephanie Chun at the University of Hawaiʻi Press and to Susan Stone for patient copyediting. Sheila Severn Newton drew the book's maps. I alone am responsible for any errors in the text.

Colleagues at the School of Historical Studies, Newcastle University, offer daily support in a convivial atmosphere. There are too many individual acts of kindness to note, but particular thanks to Jeremy Boulton and Tim Kirk. My East Asian Studies colleagues in other parts of the university have been equally generous, as have Japanese Studies colleagues within Britain.

Friends and family have supported me in every way imaginable. There is not space to name everyone, but they know who they are and how they have helped, and I hope they also know how grateful I am. My mum and dad, Juliet and Bill Dusinberre, and my brother Ed and his family have been ceaselessly encouraging: this book would not have been possible without their love and good cheer. My wife, Asuka, was with this project from the very beginning, over a coffee in Fukuoka. For her love, fortitude, and infectious laughter in the years since, I dedicate it to her with the greatest thanks of all.

PART I

Good Fortunes in Kaminoseki

1

The Silk Road of the Sea: A Beginning

In days past, visitors to Kaminoseki arrived by boat, sailing into the town's gentle bays on the back of prosperous winds and tides. Kaminoseki was then just another port, one of many that punctuated the journey from Shimonoseki to Osaka through the glorious scenery of Japan's Inland Sea.

My own journeys to Kaminoseki, starting in September 1998, were somewhat more prosaic, involving a train, a bus, and a group of high school students whose early morning inquisitiveness tested my otherwise sunny demeanor. Our route took us twenty kilometers down the mountainous Murotsu peninsula to the southern extreme of Yamaguchi prefecture, where I was to teach English twice a month: a town at the end of a road that felt so remote as to be at the end of the world. Crossing the high bridge that connects the peninsula to Nagashima island, the bus would stop at the high school and then descend to the Kaminoseki seafront. Anxious to record my insights for posterity, I would take out my notebook and scribble down observations both perspicacious and pithy: "traditional Japanese architecture," "a traditional Japanese port," "traditional Japanese people."

On my first visit to Kaminoseki, the principal and an English teacher from the junior high school (111 pupils) drove me up Mt. Kamisakari, a 314-meter peak at the northern end of Nagashima. From a small parking lot, we climbed to the top of an observatory tower that offered a magnificent view—perhaps the only place in Japan where it is possible, simultaneously, to see Honshu, Shikoku, and Kyushu. Directly below us on one side of the tower, stretching twelve kilometers away to the southwest, lay the spine of Nagashima, a "long [*nagai*] island [*shima*]" of forested slopes dropping steeply down to the sea, with two or three small hamlets nestled around sheltered bays. Another four kilometers beyond Nagashima, across waters as still as the land itself, was Iwaishima island, at whose junior high school (four students) and elementary school (five students) I would also be teaching English once a month; and beyond Iwaishima, in the very far distance, rose the hazy mountains of northern Kyushu. To the southeast, it was much the same picturesque scene: in the foreground, the mounded island of Yashima, still inhabited but with an elementary school that had closed many years previously, and beyond it the faint outline of western Shikoku etched onto the horizon. And directly below us on the northeast side of the tower lay the Kaminoseki straits, where the Inland Sea narrows to pass between Nagashima and Honshu's Murotsu peninsula. Kyushu, Shikoku, Honshu: as seen from Mt. Kamisakari, Kaminoseki now seemed not remote but rather at the very heart of Japan.

In 1969, economic historian Thomas C. Smith published a seminal essay on this region. Smith showed how farming families on the Murotsu peninsula, which was known as "Kaminoseki county" in the mid-nineteenth century, derived a large proportion of their income from nonagricultural work such as domestic industry, trade, fishing, or transportation. "By-employments," he wrote, "ready preindustrial people for modern economic roles since they represent an incipient shift from agriculture to other occupations, spread skills useful to industrialization among the most backward and numerous part of the population, and stimulate ambition and geographical mobility." Thus Smith extrapolated from his case study some reasons why, from the late nineteenth century onward, Japan made such a remarkable transition from a preindustrial economy to an industrial economy and why "a long period of premodern growth, extending back at least to the early seventeenth century and possibly beyond, was followed by modern growth."[1]

Elsewhere in the Inland Sea region, the industrial economy was in full view. One overseas visitor, traveling west toward Yamaguchi prefecture from Hiroshima in the 1980s, had "gasped" at the landscape fifty kilometers northeast of Kaminoseki. "Admittedly," she wrote, "it has been decades since the train window here offered an enchanting ink painting of perfectly poised islands, but I hadn't expected, or remembered to expect, the phantasmagoria of Gary, Indiana, with its spherical and cylindrical tanks accentuated by billowing smoke and shooting flames at any hour of the day or night."[2] But if such smoke and flames were industrial manifestations of what Smith called "modern growth," then the quiet islands visible from the Kamisakari Observatory

Tower suggested that his focus on growth was but one theme of modern Japan's history—one not necessarily applicable to Kaminoseki itself.[3] In 1998, the town had no major industries and only limited public transport links, the schools were hemorrhaging pupils, the rice paddies and vegetable fields were increasingly overgrown, and the "traditional" wooden houses were often empty. Even the observatory tower had been constructed using the 100-million-yen "Furusato Fund" through which the Japanese government attempted to boost the flagging economies of rural hometowns (*furusato*) in the late 1980s.[4] Here, in short, was a town that in geographical terms was at the center of Japan and whose nineteenth-century by-employments apparently placed it on the cusp of modern prosperity, yet whose appearance, on the eve of the twenty-first century, suggested periphery and decline.

A large sign next to the straits' bridge wrestled with these contradictions. "Kaminoseki: The Silk Road of the Sea," it proclaimed, with hand-drawn icons depicting fifteenth-century Ming embassies, sixteenth-century trade ships, the Dutch ships and the Korean embassies of the Edo period, and the Chōshū activists who led the revolution in 1868. Multicolored threads from each icon passed through the Kaminoseki straits, in the center of the map, thus weaving the pre-1868 history of the town into a story of rich engagement between Kaminoseki and the outside world. Yet in the same way that Smith took his analysis of Kaminoseki's preindustrial by-employments only up to the mid-nineteenth century, the sign remained silent when it came to Kaminoseki's post-1868 history. Returning to the town in 2003 to start dissertation fieldwork, I was curious to find out what had happened to the "silk road" after 1868 and to the erstwhile farmers, merchants, fishermen, and shippers of Kaminoseki during the period of Japan's "modern growth." If Kaminoseki county could offer historians insights into Japan's early modern history, then I began to wonder whether Kaminoseki's post-1868 story might help scholars also understand the rougher fabric of Japan's modern history.

~

One reason for a book-length study of Kaminoseki is that the town's location highlights an imbalance in the historiography of modern Japan. Not only did Kaminoseki straddle key trade and diplomatic shipping routes, as indicated by the Silk Road sign, but in the mid-nineteenth century it was also situated in one of the nation's most important political domains. From the mid-1850s onward, the Chōshū domain was a major agitator in national politics as the Tokugawa

Figure 1.1. "Kaminoseki: The Silk Road of the Sea," Nagashima, 2004

shogunate attempted to deal with the new threat from the West. In 1868, young radicals from both Chōshū and Satsuma, an anti-Tokugawa ally in the southwest of Kyushu, led the revolution that overthrew the shogunate (an event also known as the Meiji Restoration; see Chapter 3). "Modern Japan Started Here" was the title of a lecture I once attended in Hagi, the former castle town of Chōshū; "Welcome to Hagi, the *furusato* of the Restoration," read a sign in the city center, playing on late-twentieth-century popular discourses of the "hometown."[5]

The significance of the domains and individuals that led the Meiji Restoration was not lost on English-language historians in the postwar period. Much scholarship focused on political or economic aspects of the pre-1868 decades (as with Smith's aforementioned work), or on leading politicians from Chōshū, Satsuma, and the sympathetic domain of Tosa, in southern Shikoku.[6] More recent studies examine Chōshū's Itō Hirobumi ("the man who made modern Japan") or the important contributions of Chōshū men to the development of Japan's Imperial Army; but such analyses ignore the lives of the domain's ordinary people, especially in the post-1868 decades.[7] Thus, in the historiography of modern Japan, "Chōshū" is all too often thought of as an adjective—Chōshū politicians, Chōshū generals, Chōshū cliques—rather than as a proper noun, a place worthy of study.[8] Just as the name "Chōshū" was dropped in 1871, when the domain was renamed Yamaguchi prefecture, so have local residents in many ways dropped off the radar of modern historiography.

The relative absence of Chōshū/Yamaguchi from analyses of modern Japan was exacerbated by the ways in which a new generation of historians reacted to the "positive" agenda of much early postwar English-language scholarship, with its teleological transition from premodern growth to modern growth and its privileging of institutional and political history. One such reaction, "people's history," will be discussed in Chapter 4, but of interest here is the geographical frame of such studies. Neil Waters, for example, offered a new approach to the Meiji Restoration by analyzing "local pragmatists" in Kawasaki, just to the west of Tokyo, while Roger Bowen's study of anti-Meiji rebellions in the 1880s focused on three areas to the capital's north.[9] In the 1990s, studies that challenged the dominance of the nation-state framework proliferated in both the Japanese- and English-language historiography.[10] David Howell examined the complex and uneven transition from protocapitalism to capitalism by focusing on Hokkaido, while Kären Wigen studied the central Japanese Alps region of Shinano so as to explicate "the making of a Japanese periphery." Michael Lewis offered a similarly peripheral view of modern Japanese history by focusing on Toyama prefecture in the period 1868–1945. In so doing, he built on the work of Japanese scholars such as Furumaya Tadao, who analyzed discourses of "backwater Japan" (*ura Nihon*) from the late nineteenth century onward and who urged his readers toward a critical "rethinking of modern Japan."[11] Taken together, these studies and many others have offered historians a rich understanding of the social and economic histories of central and northeast Japan in the modern period. Conversely, despite (or perhaps because of) their political significance in the late nineteenth century, the regions at the vanguard of the Meiji revolution have not been exposed to such analyses.[12] A study of Kaminoseki helps fill that historiographical gap.

A second reason for focusing on Kaminoseki in particular, rather than on southwestern Japan more generally, was provided by a second painted sign that caught my eye during fieldwork, just a few meters down from the Silk Road sign. Atop a grassy hill, a husband, wife, and their young son enjoy a family picnic. Behind them, a new road curls smoothly across the forested slopes of a long island before entering a tunnel in the distance. On the other side of the tunnel, and completely out of scale to the rest of the image, stand two large square buildings, each flanked by a steel-framed tower. "Together with nuclear power," the sign announces, "a lively town."

Figure 1.2. "Together with nuclear power, a lively town," Nagashima, 2004

As I started fieldwork, I noticed several other signs on Nagashima, each referring to the idealized discourse of the Japanese "hometown" (see Chapter 9). In the hamlet of Hetsu, for example: "Bright and rich *furusato*-making through a nuclear power station: [bringing] vitality to young people and comfort to the elderly." In the hamlet of Shidai: "[Through nuclear power,] a *furusato* where young people gather and where we have heart-to-heart communication!" The organization that had erected these signs (but not the Silk Road one) was the Kaminoseki Municipal Town-Making Liaison Committee, a coalition of local civil society associations. The existence of this committee, and its uncompromising support for atomic energy, followed an extraordinary development in the early 1980s, when the Kaminoseki municipal council actively requested the construction of a nuclear power station in the town (Chapter 10).

Such a request flew in the face of the protest movement known as Not In My Back Yard (NIMBY), which has been synonymous with campaigns against the nuclear power industry in postwar Japan.[13] Instead, the council's embrace of a so-called public bad—a nuclear power plant—was an example of Definitely In My Back Yard. As this book argues, pronuclear lobbyists in Kaminoseki viewed nuclear investment as a means of community survival, through which brightness, young people, and vitality might be restored to a hometown that had lost all these by the early 1980s. The story of how silk roads led to nuclear survival in Kaminoseki is therefore a story of hard times and rural decline in modern Japan—one that is counterintuitive and of interest because it occurred in the backyard of the leaders who "made" modern Japan.

But despite the depiction of large nuclear plants on the "lively town" sign, the reality as seen from the Mt. Kamisakari observatory tower was quite different. Even in 2003, almost two decades after the original request, there were no buildings or towers at the western tip of Nagashima. From taking the ferry to Iwaishima past the proposed site, it was clear that even the ground and beaches remained untouched. A sign near the fishing cooperative at Iwaishima indicated why no progress had been made: "Preserve our rich fishing and important *furusato:* absolute opposition to the Kaminoseki nuclear power station!" Centering not only on the pros and cons of nuclear power but also on the discourse of "hometown," a dispute appeared to have divided the town and delayed the start of construction—a dispute so bitter that close friends warned me it was a "no touch" topic.

As Natalie Zemon Davis has observed, however, "a remarkable dispute can sometimes uncover motivations and values that are lost in the welter of the everyday."[14] My friends' warnings notwithstanding, the nuclear dispute was clearly an important episode in Kaminoseki's modern history (Chapter 11): not to write about it would, as Robert J. Smith argued to justify examining a similar controversy, "result in a serious distortion of the record, a kind of falsification by omission."[15] But as I conducted oral history interviews in the town and tried to work out a strategy for broaching a "no touch" topic,[16] I found that the welter of the everyday was in fact key to uncovering townspeople's motivations in either supporting or opposing nuclear power. Moreover, the stories of everyday life that were emerging in interviews—of a sword maker who retrained as a blacksmith, of a sake-brewing emigrant to southern Sakhalin, of a coal shipper in the Inland Sea—seemed to offer new ways of understanding the broader motivations and values of so-called ordinary people as they experienced the extraordinary transformations that Japan underwent since the mid-nineteenth century. As the following chapters argue, far from being just a rhetorical tool in a late-twentieth-century dispute, the everyday hometown was a stage on which ordinary people practiced political, economic, social, and cultural interactions as they both shaped and responded to the exigencies of modern life. To study the hometown community is to understand the motivations and values of ordinary people in modern Japan.

A third reason to focus on Kaminoseki is because of the extraordinary range of sources that the town offers to historians of everyday life—sources not always available to scholars writing about Japan's ordinary people.[17] In addition to material culture evidence—houses, schools, commemorative headstones—and oral history interviews, this book draws on two important sets of documents. The first is the *Bōchō fūdo chūshin'an,* a survey of individual counties and villages initiated by the Chōshū domain in the early 1840s and published in twenty-one volumes in the 1960s. Widely considered to be one of the best sources of social and economic data for mid-nineteenth-century Japan, the survey provides particularly detailed results for Kaminoseki county—hence Thomas C. Smith's essay on preindustrial by-employments. Using the *Bōchō fūdo chūshin'an* to reconstruct a detailed picture of everyday life in Kaminoseki on the eve of Japan's re-engagement with the West allows us to contextualize the extent and impact of social and economic change thereafter (Chapter 2).

The second set of documents, this time unpublished, surfaced with great good fortune in a dilapidated warehouse close to the Kaminoseki seafront. Stored in around eighty cardboard boxes, this was a collection of 2,300 official documents, ranging from the 1870s to the 1960s, which had first been catalogued by the Kaminoseki Town History Editorial Board in 1972. Unfortunately, the board members had written catalogue numbers for each document on a piece of paper that they taped to the original. By the time I opened up the boxes in 2007, the tape had melted, rendering the number all but unreadable in many cases. Moreover, more than a thousand documents, mainly from the 1950s and 1960s, were missing—the victim both of municipal mismanagement and of the collection being hastily moved to the present warehouse from another building severely damaged by a typhoon twenty years previously. Nevertheless, I was still left with more than a thousand unpublished and otherwise abandoned documents, several two or three hundred pages long, that were mostly compiled by the Murotsu village office between the late 1880s and the merger with Kaminoseki village in 1958.

At the most basic level, the Murotsu collection allowed me to check the reliability of the *Kaminoseki Town History* (1988), on which I had hitherto been overly dependent.[18] Written by an all-male committee of esteemed local personages, the 880-page *Town History,* which did not employ footnotes, had very few factual errors (at least in the three hundred or so pages that referenced the documents in question). However, with the warehouse documents, I could now identify absences in the official account—the places where, for example, the authors might have probed the social consequences of the rather dry institutional documents that they had transcribed in large numbers. In particular, the collection revealed a much deeper history of overseas migration in the prewar period than the brief, twelve-page section of the *Town History* might suggest (Chapter 6).[19] Equally important, the rediscovered collection enabled me to follow up on my oral histories bearing a new set of questions. I could thus reconstruct not only individual stories of daily life in modern Japan, in the mold of Simon Partner's *Toshié* or *The Mayor of Aihara,* but also do so across several generations, as in Gail Lee Bernstein's *Isami's House.*[20] If the roadside signs voiced the hopes and fears of ordinary people with regard to late-twentieth-century Japan, oral interviews and the warehouse collection now revealed the complex stories of villagers who, no less than leading Chōshū politicians, helped "make" the new Japan in the mid-nineteenth century.

But local Japan has always spoken in multiple voices, and in Kaminoseki, despite the rich variety of sources, some voices continue to speak louder than others.[21] As far as I could see, the warehouse documents were entirely recorded by men—the bureaucrats of the municipality. Moreover, the types of documents on which I particularly relied in order to tease out the details of individual histories—tax returns or land registers, for example—were recorded in the name of the household head, who was almost always a man. This limitation in the written evidence was exacerbated by my experiences during interviews. Being a male researcher and having originally told people in Kaminoseki that I was studying Japanese history (*Nihonshi*), I was first directed to those "knowledgeable" elders who were considered best equipped to answer academic questions: men. Even after I softened my language—I was now interested in talking to people about "the past" (*kako no koto*) and about "everyday life"—the majority of my interviews were still with men.[22] Consequently, the voices of individual women are not as prominent in the pages that follow as I would wish, or as some other scholars have achieved in their work. For better or for worse, this is a history mainly of Kaminoseki's men—of their achievements, difficulties, and human foibles.

During my first period of fieldwork in Kaminoseki, I read an interview with the American novelist Philip Roth. "People prepare for life in a certain way and have certain expectations of the difficulties that come with those lives," he said, "[and] then they get blindsided by the present moment; . . . 'History is a very sudden thing,' is how I put it. I'm talking about the historical fire at the center and how the smoke from that fire reaches into your house."[23] For many months, and no doubt influenced by Roth's novels, I wondered about the ways in which the smoke from the center had drifted into the households of the Kaminoseki periphery. How had the Meiji Restoration come to the town? How did townspeople react to Japan's new engagement with the outside world? In short, how were townspeople objects of change in modern Japan?

But all these questions assumed that historical change occurs only in the exceptional realm of the "noneveryday," in the historical fire at the center. By contrast, scholars of German *Alltagsgeschichte* (everyday life history) rejected such an assumption. Ordinary people, Alf Lüdtke argued, were not just the objects of history, but also its subjects: their everyday motivations and values were thus worthy of study. Lüdtke and his colleagues attempted to do this for modern German history, partly as an attempt to understand "fascism's everyday face" and thus to acknowledge (once again using the metaphor of blindness) that "the historical actors were (and are) more than mere blind puppets or helpless victims."[24]

That the realm of everyday space can be a site for historical change has concomitant implications for the framing of historical time. As Ulrich Herbert suggested of modern Germany, what historians generally consider to have been "good times" and "bad times" do not always match the lived realities or the memories of interviewees as they recount their life histories.[25] Indeed, a characteristic of histories focused on the "human tradition" is that individual life stories do not necessarily match the temporal and thematic structures of macrohistorical accounts.[26] As a consequence, the chapters in this book, although roughly chronological in order (at least within each part), do not necessarily follow themes that a reader of modern Japanese history might expect. For example, I have not devoted a chapter exclusively to the Second World War—"hard times" if ever there were. Meanwhile, the 1930s—the "time of crisis" analyzed by Kerry Smith in his village study of Sekishiba (again in the northeast of Japan)—are discussed more in terms of the hometown's dependence on overseas communities than in terms of rural distress (Chapter 7).[27] This is partly because a number of excellent studies have recently been published on rural suffering in the 1930s and on the role of ordinary people in the war years,[28] and I wanted to focus on other stories that arose from the archives and from oral history interviews. Another reason was that the single most traumatic event for the communities of Kaminoseki occurred on the last full day of conflict—14 August 1945—and therefore the community memories of "war" spill into memories of hard times in the immediate postwar years (Chapter 8).

Instead of seamless transitions from one transformative event to another, this book patches together alternative narratives and timelines from "the hodgepodge character of personal experience."[29] Thanks to the work of previous scholars, we already know about the views of ordinary people vis-à-vis the Meiji Restoration, their role in the establishment of the new Meiji state, their experience of mid-twentieth-century dislocations and wartime defeat, and their struggles during the years of postwar growth.[30] My focus on Kaminoseki allows us to go one stage further, to see how the same community—the same households across several generations—experienced historical change. In this way, it becomes possible to connect otherwise disparate themes in the history of modern Japan: we can begin to understand the relationship between Edo period economic growth and the subsequent Japanese empire, or between political practices in the late nineteenth and late twentieth centuries, and more besides.

The "guiding threads" that hold this patchworked history together are the names of households and of individuals that appear and reappear across generations of Kaminoseki daily life.[31] Yet this fact alone raised a difficult dilemma. To name individuals whom I knew were involved in less salubrious aspects of the nuclear dispute risked going against the ethics of fieldwork, which privileges anonymity. Equally, to change their names would entail changing also the names of their ancestors, thus distorting the historical record.[32] As several chapters argue, family and household names convey a range of specific historical meanings in Kaminoseki (as elsewhere in Japan). To alter the names in the documents meant losing these meanings as well as undermining one of the greatest contributions of history from below—the naming of the otherwise nameless. As a result, I decided to use almost no pseudonyms in this book: I interviewed townspeople on the understanding that I would use their real names and thus be able to draw connections across three or four generations of hometown history, and I have anonymized interviewees only when explicitly requested to do so or when the political or socioeconomic context seemed, in my opinion, to demand it.

The questions raised by *Alltagsgeschichte* have thus been one major influence on the structure and themes of this book. A second, related influence has been the practice of microhistory.[33] Like their colleagues in the social history and "history from below" movements, the first Italian practitioners of microhistory in the 1970s sought to move beyond teleological analyses of the rise of the nation state and modern economic development—analyses not dissimilar to those of Thomas C. Smith in his work on Kaminoseki. To this end, they criticized quantitative history and abstract typologies that reduced ordinary people to mere exemplars and case studies of macrohistorical trends: such studies, they argued, relegated the "lived experience" of ordinary people to history's margins.[34] Instead, they proposed a microhistorical analysis on a reduced scale, which would permit "a reconstitution of 'real life' unthinkable in other kinds of historiography."[35] By altering the scale of observation in this way, "phenomena previously considered to be sufficiently described and understood assume completely new meanings.... It is then possible to use these results to draw far wider generalizations although the initial observations were made within relatively narrow dimensions and as experiments rather than examples."[36] In other words, reducing the scale of analysis to a hometown community or even to a single unknown individual would not, they emphasized, lead to less historiographically ambitious research. Rather, the reduced scale of microscopic analysis would conversely force a reconsideration of the macrohistoriographical picture.

Because of the extraordinary empirical detail of microhistorical studies—the result, more often than not, of the chance survival of a document or a collection—the question then arises of their "typicality." But, as Carlo Ginzburg asks of Menocchio, a sixteenth-century miller who could read and write, "typical of what?"[37] That is, to start with a question of typicality implies a "big picture" framework that is already fixed, in which the individual or community story will serve merely as historical detail. This is one reason that microhistorians tend to reject the designation of their work as case studies: "a case study," according to one definition, "pursues more narrowly-defined objectives, such as the testing of particular generalizations.... Case studies rarely seek to pose wholly new questions or to assert original interpretations."[38] Thus, this book does not offer the story of Kaminoseki as "typical" of any particular trend in modern Japanese history or as a "case study": the town's privileged location in the Chōshū domain, its high incidence of prewar overseas migration, its escape from physical wartime damage, its high poverty rate in the 1950s, its role as location for a famous television drama in the 1970s, and not least its candidacy for a nuclear power plant make it an extremely unusual community in many ways—unusual as well in its combination of all these trends. As a result, a microhistory of Kaminoseki does not segue seamlessly into macrohistorical narratives of modern Japan.

But that, arguably, is the significance of my account. In three different ways, I propose, the history of Kaminoseki forces us to rethink dominant narratives in the history of modern Japan. First, economic decline is a major theme that runs throughout this book. On the eve of Japan's reengagement with the West, in the mid-nineteenth century, Kaminoseki was one of the most prosperous towns in one of the most prosperous domains in the whole country. Thereafter, the town's economy collapsed; the silk road of the sea, to the extent that it survived, now bypassed Kaminoseki, mainly owing to the transformed political order in Japan—a transformation that townspeople helped bring about in the 1860s—and to the introduction of new technologies from the West. Understanding how ordinary people lived with decline in their everyday lives, especially in the traditionally "advanced" regions of the southwest,[39] will contribute to a rethinking of post-1868 Japanese history that is still to a large extent interested in questions of modern growth.

To focus on the theme of decline is not simply to highlight the costs of modernization. The individuals portrayed in this book did not just wait for change to be imposed from on high but devised ways to make their everyday lives better. In so doing, they helped shape the modern state, in particular the country's engagement with the outside world in the late nineteenth and early twentieth centuries, and its recovery from defeat after 1945. By reconstructing these everyday life stories, I secondly offer new evidence that the ordinary people of modern Japan exercised individual agency in their lives. Henceforth, these individual "micro" decisions and motivations need to be better integrated into the "macro" analyses that historians undertake of modern Japan.

A third theme concerns space and borders. Although the scale of my microhistory is reduced to the current municipality of Kaminoseki, a town of just thirty-five square kilometers, it ties the histories of townspeople to ambassadors from Ryūkyū and Korea, dentists in Hawai'i, hoteliers in San Francisco, sake brewers in Sakhalin, merchants on the Japan Sea coast, coal miners in northern Kyushu, energy bureaucrats in Tokyo, and a multinational utility company based in Hiroshima. To this extent, *Hard Times in the Hometown* is not just a local history, narrowly framed by administrative boundaries; the hometown, I argue, was also a site of global history, in which the lived experiences of the townspeople regularly traversed the borders of municipality, region, or nation.[40]

A town that to my untrained eyes first appeared "traditional" and yet whose nineteenth-century employment practices were considered harbingers of "modern growth," a town momentarily in the political heart of Japan and yet marginalized by economic and political change, a town in which individual stories of growth and success were framed by long-term economic decline: Kaminoseki mediates between the paradigms of tradition-modernity, center-periphery, and growth-decline that have often been used to frame Japan's extraordinary transformations between the mid-nineteenth and late twentieth centuries. By focusing on individual experiences, I hope if not entirely to reject such polarities, at least to show in significant new detail what Japan's modern transformations meant for the everyday lived realities of all but unknown people in an all but unknown hometown.

2

Edo Period Riches

In December 1860, the Scottish botanist Robert Fortune (1812–1880) found himself on a steamship heading westward through the Inland Sea. Japan had only been "opened" by the West some six years previously, and the *England* was one of the first foreign commercial vessels allowed to navigate these waters.

Southeast of Kaminoseki, as the *England* headed into the Bungo Suidō channel, a storm struck. In his *Narrative,* published three years after the event, Fortune maintains a calm tone as he describes how Captain Dundas turned the ship away from the storm and sought shelter. Yet the relief at what captain and crew found is still palpable:

> As we approached the land there seemed to be no shelter except an open bay, protected indeed by the land on the west, but fully exposed to the eastward. On nearing the shore, however, we observed an opening on our left, not more than sixty yards wide, which . . . led into a beautiful land-locked harbour. We steamed through this narrow passage, and anchored in thirteen fathoms of water.
>
> The place in which we now were had all the appearance of an inland lake, and was protected from the wind in all directions. On each side of us two small towns were observed, pleasantly situated on the banks of the lake, and forming little crescents along its shores. The houses had white-washed walls, and appeared to be clean and comfortable looking buildings. Little temples also appeared on the hillsides, surrounded by pine-trees; and Buddhist priests were seen about the doors. Hills filled the background, well-wooded in some parts, and terraced in others all

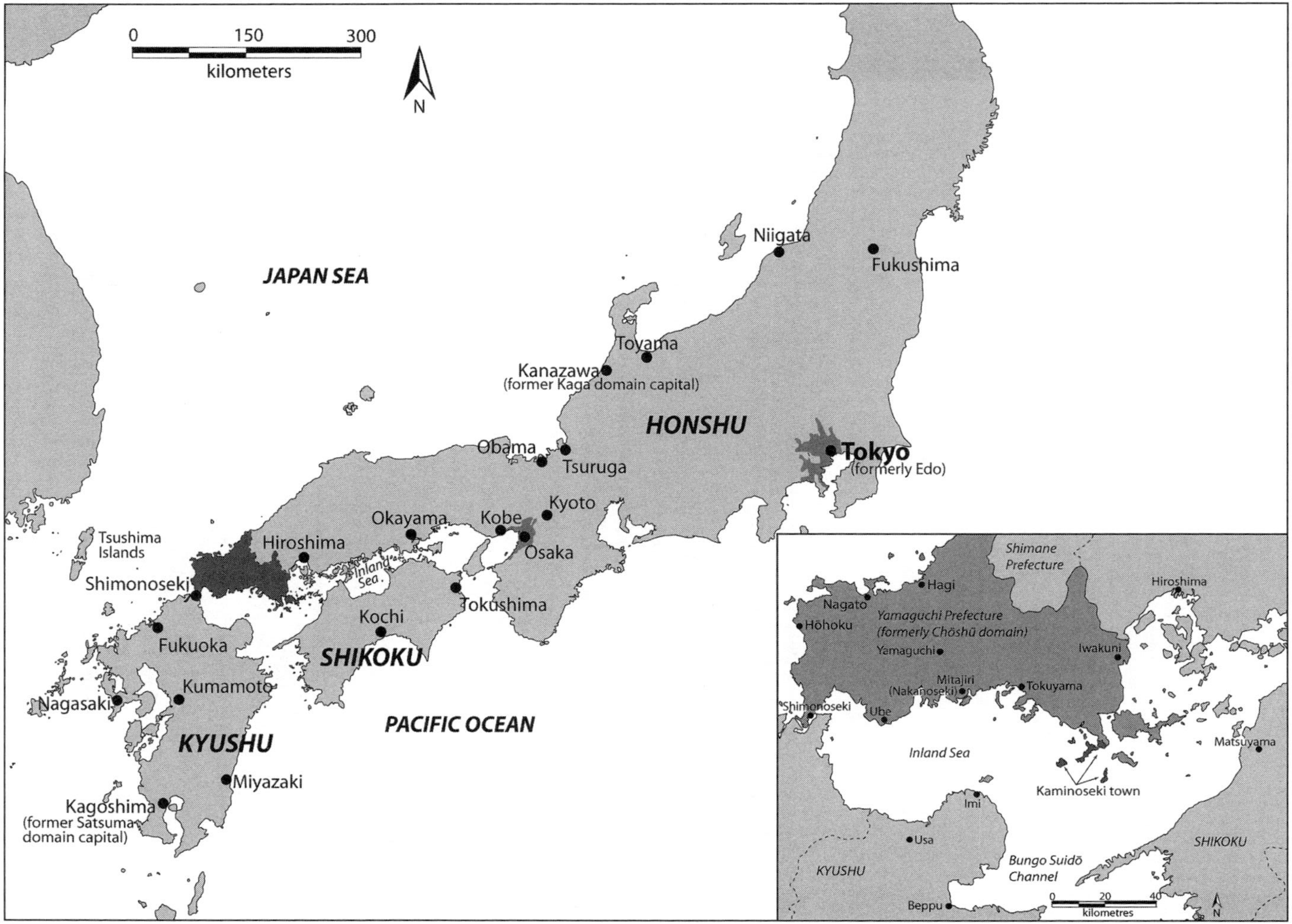

Figure 2.1. Map of Japan and Yamaguchi prefecture

the way up to their summits, showing that here the soil was fertile and productive.[1]

Fortune was merely the latest in a long line of visitors to praise this natural landscape. In 1776, the Swedish botanist, Carl Peter Thunberg (1743–1828), wrote in his diary that the area's "mountains in several places resembled beautiful gardens."[2] One millennium earlier, envoys traveling from Nara to the Korean kingdom of Silla not only praised but even prayed to the land, thus recording the earliest surviving written description of Iwaishima: "Praying for safety / of people traveling on / pillowing the grass / How many generations / has Iwai Isle remained?"[3] The poem perhaps reflects the ambassadors' sense of apprehension as they left behind the isles of the Inland Sea and set out across the exposed waters of the Suō channel for northern Kyushu, some fifty kilometers away: no steam engines for these men, should a sudden storm descend.

The poems of the Silla ambassadors, which form part of the larger *Man'yōshū* collection (759), remind us of the ancient roots of local place reverence in Japanese literature.[4] But reverence, admiration, or plain relief were the emotions of outsiders: how did the local people view their own landscape? Fortune notes that as the *England* chugged toward the straits, villagers "came out of their houses to look at the strange *He-funy* [*hi-fune*], or fire-ship."[5] But though they may have been surprised by the sight and sound of steam engines, the people of Kaminoseki and Murotsu, the "two small towns" on either side of the Kaminoseki straits, were used to ships coming their way—sometimes hundreds of large and small vessels in a single day.[6] They knew, as did Fortune, that "this [was] a most extraordinary anchorage, and well worth the attention of those who navigate this sea," and they appreciated that where the ships anchored, certain services would be required—food, water, shelter, and recreation. After all, as in the case of Carl Peter Thunberg, prevailing winds and tides might conspire to force "the disagreeable necessity of staying almost three weeks before we got a good and prosperous wind to carry us on our voyage."[7]

In other words, in addition to revering their landscape according to Shinto practice, the people of Kaminoseki and Murotsu also saw, in the "beautiful" harbor that formed to the west of the straits, an opportunity. Their landscape could generate money, and by the time of Fortune's unexpected visit in 1860, the villagers had perfected a complex money-making system.

The Awa-ya Household

Making money in Kaminoseki depended, first, on the decentralized political structures of the Tokugawa shogunate.

In October 1600, Tokugawa Ieyasu (1543–1616), leader of the largest military clan in Japan, won a famous victory at the Battle of Sekigahara and began the long process of imposing his authority on a country riven by warfare for much of the previous century. As an early political reform, he had himself appointed shogun and established a military government (*bakufu*) in Edo, in his eastern Japan heartland. Tokugawa allies among the daimyo (feudal lords) at Sekigahara were rewarded generously with land and with positions in the new administration; Tokugawa foes, among them men such as Mōri Terumoto (1553–1625), were punished in a variety of ways. Before Sekigahara, Terumoto had been the second wealthiest daimyo in the realm, controlling a vast swath of territory in western Japan from his base in the province of Aki (the western half of present-day Hiroshima prefecture). But after Sekigahara, the Mōri clan was banished to the western extreme of Honshu and forced to establish a new castle town in the remote Japan Sea village of Hagi, well out of harm's way—or so the Tokugawa hoped. This new domain, known as Bōchō or Chōshū, produced just a quarter of the clan's previous wealth.[8]

The Mōri clan's problems were not just limited to their new status as "outside" (*tozama*) daimyo, denied government positions in the *bakufu*. Within the Chōshū domain, the clan controlled only around a third of the land at the beginning of the Edo period, with the rest divided into private fiefs run by samurai overlords.[9] To redress this balance, a domain survey revised the division of the fiefs in 1625, and much of the Murotsu peninsula and Nagashima, including the ports on either side of the straits, was brought under the direct administration of the Hagi government. This extension of Mōri authority within Chōshū suggests that Hagi officials recognized the strategic maritime importance of the straits. Indeed, since the early sixteenth century, Kaminoseki had been a base for one branch of the Murakami Suigun, a sea militia that ruled most of the Inland Sea and that was closely allied to the Mōri. From a castle they built overlooking the straits, Murakami soldiers had special dispensation to levy private customs on passing ships and to maintain the security of shipping lanes. Although "pirates" were outlawed in 1588 and the castle demolished, several former Murakami admirals retained their fiefs in Nagashima and Iwaishima even after the 1625 revisions, almost certainly as compensation for their long service to the Mōri clan.[10]

The Kaminoseki straits gained further importance from a second element of the post-1600 political settlement. To discourage rebellion, the *bakufu* tried to bind non-Tokugawa daimyo—especially hostile "outside" domains such as Chōshū—to the regime by forcing them to maintain a residence in Edo. The lord's wife and children had to live there permanently, effectively as hostages of the Tokugawa, while the daimyo himself took up residence every other year—a system that was formalized as alternate attendance in 1635. In central and eastern Japan, particularly on the roads branching out from Edo, daimyo compliance with alternate attendance was monitored through a central network of *sekisho*. These barriers, some fifty-three on the central highways alone, blocked the roads and enabled armed officials to guard against the smuggling of guns into Edo and the illegal passage of high-ranking women out of the city.[11] A similar network of *sekisho* was also maintained by the domains. Thus, as their names indicate, both Kaminoseki ("upper barrier") and its sister port of Shimonoseki ("lower barrier," the westernmost port in Chōshū) maintained regional security and shipping lanes for the Mōri daimyo. As such, Kaminoseki received substantial investment from the Hagi government. In 1643, for example, a domain-owned official guesthouse (*o-chaya*) that overlooked the straits was expanded. Spreading over an area the size of a soccer field, it now included dining and entertainment buildings, kitchens, baths, outhouses, storage space, and living quarters for staff. Just to the north, a smaller complex—still some three thousand square meters—accommodated middle- and lower-ranking officials.[12] In 1711, moreover, the domain moved its local administrative office (*bansho*) to a prominent location on the Kaminoseki waterfront. Sliding back the building's outer doors, Chōshū officials could seat themselves in one of the tatami-matted rooms—two sets of longbows lined up behind them as a symbol of authority—and survey the straits.[13]

Kaminoseki's facilities catered not only to the Mōri daimyo on their way to alternate attendance, but also to those from several domains in Kyushu.[14] Meanwhile, the workers necessary to host such large retinues were provided by a system of corvée labor, which the Hagi authorities formalized in 1686. Along with three other communities in eastern Chōshū, Kaminoseki and Murotsu were designated "privileged" fishing ports (*tateura*). This gave them monopoly rights, such as fishing with sardine nets in specified areas. In return, the fishermen had to welcome the daimyo and unload his ships, and they also shouldered the more general maritime responsibilities of providing assistance to drifting ships.[15]

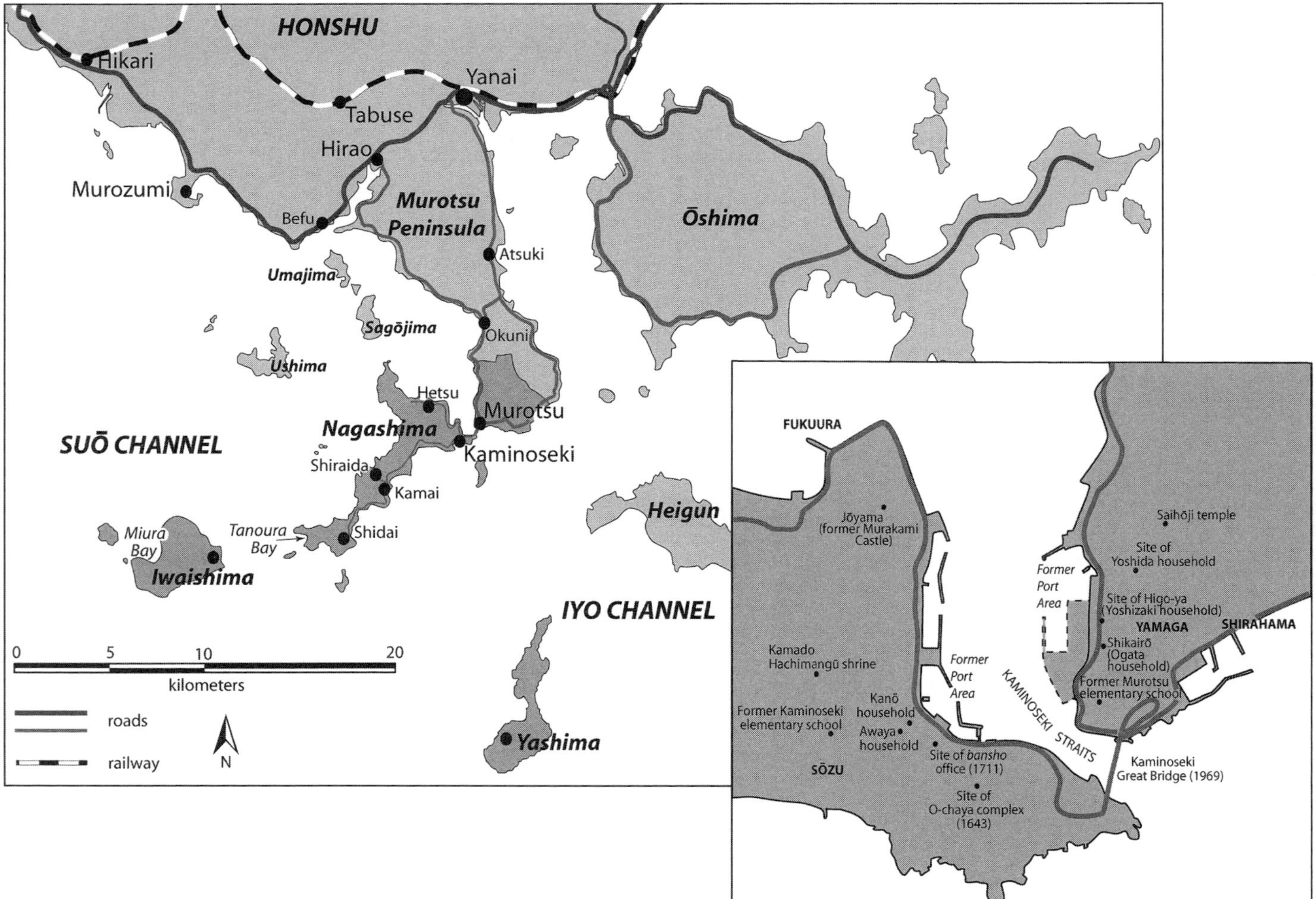

Figure 2.2. Map of Kaminoseki town and the straits communities

The system of alternate attendance thus directly affected the daily lives of Kaminoseki's residents. The protected harbor, which had already attracted the attentions of the Murakami militia in the sixteenth century, created a natural breaking point for the frequent long-distance journeys that daimyo and their officials were now required to make throughout the western Inland Sea. As the Chōshū government organized and improved its services to such distinguished guests, the people of Kaminoseki were coopted to provide labor and hospitality. As the seventeenth century progressed, moreover, their guests became ever more exotic, or so it must have seemed. From many days' sail to the southwest of Kyushu came the ambassadors of the Ryūkyū kingdom, dressed in Chinese-style ceremonial garb, accompanied by their overlord, the daimyo of the Satsuma domain. From the Dutch enclave of Dejima, in Nagasaki, came fair-skinned Europeans including Engelbert Kaempfer (1651–1716), Carl Peter Thunberg (1743–1848), and Philipp Franz von Siebold (1796–1866), all of whom wrote passing descriptions of Kaminoseki. Perhaps most spectacular of all were the Korean Embassies (Chōsen Tsūshin-shi), which came to Japan twelve times during the Edo period and which stayed in Kaminoseki on all but the occasion of the final embassy, in 1811.

As Ronald P. Toby has argued, the Korean Embassies served as a tool of domestic legitimation for successive Tokugawa shoguns. They were an opportunity for the *bakufu* to show the daimyo, samurai, and even the common people that Japan's political order was accepted by the outside world, even as it cut off contact with all the European nations save the Netherlands.[16] But quite what the common people of Kaminoseki and Murotsu made of such spectacles we can only guess. In 1711, when the domain's administrative office was newly relocated to the waterfront, the embassy comprised 569 people, including doctors, musicians, craftsmen and scholars; in addition, there would have been scores of accompanying officials from the Tsushima and Chōshū domains.[17] By contrast, the population of Kaminoseki district in that year would have been less than one thousand people, living in approximately 140 households.[18] In one of the hillside temples noted by Fortune, an 1821 painting depicts an embassy from sometime in the eighteenth century. It shows a procession of more than one hundred boats approaching the straits, led by a guard ship flying the historic flag of the Murakami Suigun militia and a vessel carrying the daimyo of the Tsushima domain, who served as official guide to the missions. The ambassadors themselves sailed in three thirty-meter-long junks, each ship bearing a scarlet and gold coat-of-arms; their staff and cargo

Figure 2.3. The coming of the Korean Embassy: retrospective painting, 1821 (Courtesy of Chōsenji temple, Kaminoseki)

followed in three smaller ships, surrounded by tugs and small rowboats. In the upper half of the painting we see the streets of Kaminoseki port: the vast official guesthouse complex, the domain office on the waterfront, the Buddhist temples, and the white-washed walls of the houses with ceremonial curtains hanging from certain doorways.

One residence that welcomed guests on the occasion of the Korean Embassies was the Awaya household, which survives to this day on the main street of Kaminoseki port. The current Awaya surname is a homonym, with different Chinese characters, of "Awa-ya," the family's Edo period household name (*yagō*)—Awa being a province in what is now Tokushima prefecture, eastern Shikoku. Nobody knows when the Awa-ya was first established in Kaminoseki or whether it was connected in any way to Shikoku, but local records show that the household head, Tokusaemon, hosted a Hagi official during the 1764 embassy. Indeed, officials from Tsushima and Chōshū stayed in almost every household on Kaminoseki's main street and in several Murotsu residences too. As with the hosting of daimyo on alternate attendance, households such as the Awa-ya thus found the diplomatic policies of the Tokugawa shogunate intruding into their very living space.[19]

Ultimately, however, it was not the political structures of the Tokugawa state—the domain system, alternate attendance, foreign policy—that had the greatest effect on the everyday life of the Awa-ya family members. Instead, economic changes in the eighteenth century, in particular an increase in trade through the Inland Sea region, led to new prosperity for the household, and confirmed Kaminoseki's status as a strategic port for the Chōshū domain.

Inland Sea trade was stimulated in two ways. One was the development of an alternative freight route by which domains in rice-intensive northern Japan could transport their produce to the commercial powerhouse of Osaka. Previously, cargo was unloaded in the Japan Sea ports of Obama or Tsuruga and then carried by horse one hundred kilometers south to Osaka. In the late 1630s, however, a samurai in the rich domain of Kaga (present-day Ishikawa prefecture) demonstrated that, despite the longer distances involved, the sea journey from Tsuruga west along the Japan Sea, past Hagi, and then east through the Inland Sea from Shimonoseki was three times cheaper than the overland route. This so-called western circuit was formalized in 1672 with the construction of lighthouses and the provision of charts, trained pilots, and rescue services of the sort offered by Kaminoseki and Murotsu's corvée labor. Thereafter, the amount of freight transported throughout the Inland Sea expanded rapidly—in the case of Kaga-grown rice, from 80,000 *koku* in 1682 to 200,000 *koku* in 1691.[20] Equally, the number of Osaka wholesale agents (*ton'ya*) processing the purchase of rice and other cargo also increased as a result of the western circuit, from just below 400 in the 1670s to more than 5,500 in the 1710s.[21] Through these merchants, local administrators either purchased goods not produced within their own domain—goods that they then shipped home through the Inland Sea—or they purchased silver, which was used to pay for their growing expenses. By the mid-eighteenth century, for example, the Mōri clan needed silver to pay for over two thousand samurai maintaining the Chōshū residence in Edo.[22] Faced with such financial burdens, the domain encouraged other domestic industries: the shallow estuaries of the villages to the north and west of Murotsu were developed as salt fields from the early eighteenth century, while striped cotton manufactured in southeastern Chōshū began to reach the Osaka markets from around the 1730s onward—again, along the western circuit.[23]

A second stimulus for Inland Sea trade concerned the ownership of the ships using Osaka's port in Sakai. Until the late eighteenth century, domainal cargoes to Osaka still consisted largely of tax payments, but the first known case of private enterprise and transportation on the western circuit occurred in 1778.[24] In the Inland Sea, these private ships came to be known as the *kitamae*-ships. Unlike freight ship proprietors, the families that owned the *kitamae* made their money not by charging to transport other peoples' cargo, but by buying that cargo themselves, on the assumption that they could sell it for a profit in Osaka. Lacking modern communications, neither ship owner nor producer in a distant domain such as Kaga could know the central market price at the time of purchase, nor predict what it might be roughly fifteen days later when the *kitamae*-ships sailed into Sakai. In the summer of 1858, for example, rice sold in the Osaka and Kyoto markets for 15 to 20 percent more than in Kaga.[25] Equally, goods bought in Osaka were likely to sell at considerably higher prices in the north, especially if demand was high for products not native to the domain—such as Inland Sea salt, which could be used to preserve fish caught off the Japan Sea coasts or in Hokkaido. With small crews (around seven, including the captain) and relatively large capacity by Japanese standards (between 1,000 and 2,000 *koku,* or 65 to 125 gross tons), this system of "speculative transport" offered tremendous potential for profits.[26]

But the risks were also considerable. *Kitamae*-ships sailed relatively fast, but they found it difficult to tack against a headwind.[27] If, like Carl Peter Thunberg in 1776, they were "under the disagreeable necessity of staying almost three weeks" in one of the Inland Sea ports, there was a good chance that Osaka prices might fall during that period, rendering their cargo loss-making. As owners picked up news of market fluctuations from passing boats, what they needed was a place to store such cargo temporarily and a flow of capital with which they could purchase alternative goods.

In 1763, the Chōshū domain sought to exploit this need with the creation of a separate account within the main domain budget. Among a number of long-term investments made by the account, the most important was the development of the *koshini-gata* system.[28] The basic idea of the *koshini-gata* was to establish domain-managed wholesale agents in the main ports of the Inland Sea, starting in Shimonoseki and then spreading east to Murozumi in 1793 and Kaminoseki in 1794.[29] These agents would offer warehouse space, and the cargoes they stored then functioned as collateral for a loan from the agent to the ship owner. With this new capital, the *kitamae* owners could purchase other goods—either from local producers (such as salt makers or cotton dyers) or from other ships passing through the ports. Interest on the loans enabled the domain to reinvest in the system or to alleviate poverty caused by poor harvests or low fish stocks. Equally important, the interest could be used to pay off spiraling domain debts caused partly by the expense of alternate attendance.

Although the theory was good, for the first couple of decades the system faltered in Kaminoseki because the domain's original capital investment was too low. But in 1819 Chōshū issued a new law that introduced sufficient capital to the system. This stimulated not only the domain agent's business but also that of the port's three teahouses, which doubled as brothels. Kaminoseki's private shipping agents, who worked independently of the domain, were also probably lent capital as part of the *koshini-gata*'s revised budget.[30] Such was the success of the new system that the 1819 law was renewed every ten years until the end of the Tokugawa shogunate, and in 1837, following a plea to the domain authorities from the senior headman of Kaminoseki county, a new *koshini* branch office was established across the straits in Murotsu port.[31]

By the mid-1820s, the primary function of Kaminoseki port had shifted from political to economic. Symbolic of this transformation were the two-storied, white-washed houses newly constructed on the main streets of both Kaminoseki and Murotsu—the "clean and comfortable buildings" noted by Robert Fortune.[32] The Awa-ya residence, for example, was rebuilt in around 1826. Befitting the household's status as one of around a dozen private shipping agents (*ton'ya*) in the port, the new building included a large warehouse for *kitamae*-ship cargoes at the back of the main residence. The Awa-ya primarily stored salt and marine produce, whereas other agents specialized in different commodities—timber for the Kaga-ya household, kelp for the Nagasaki-ya, and sake for Murotsu's Higo-ya.[33] These four household names, four provinces ranging from western Kyushu to eastern Shikoku to northern Honshu, may reflect the extent of commercial ties between Kaminoseki and other parts of Japan.[34]

The Awa-ya and most other local agents also doubled as innkeepers for the *kitamae*-ship owners. Thus we may imagine the Awa-ya's quiet inner guestroom, with its *fusuma* doors sliding open onto an interior garden, as the venue for negotiations over loans and storage. According to the Awa-ya's rare surviving *Customer Register* (*O-kyakuchō*), dozens of such transactions took place each month between the 1830s and the 1860s.[35] The Awa-ya agent, kneeling on the tatami mat with his abacus before him, might offer to sell goods on behalf of the ship owner and take a commission, or he might purchase the goods outright—the agreements stamped with both men's seals. But, particularly during long winter nights, both parties might have come to a more complex arrangement: the ship owner would offer an additional fee, enticing Awa-ya to buy his entire cargo on condition that he could buy the goods back the following spring at the original price. If the market value rose over the winter months, the ship owner would make a profit when he himself then resold the commodity—depending on the price of his original fee to the Kaminoseki agent.[36]

It is therefore likely that, as the *England* steamed through the straits in December 1860, at least some of Kaminoseki's and Murotsu's residents glanced out of their houses not just in curiosity at the new technology on display, but also in anticipation of deals to be done, money to be made. A "fertile and productive" landscape indeed.

Port and Inland Households in 1842

In his account, however, Fortune actually wrote that the *soil* was fertile and productive. By contrast, the prosperity of a shipping agent household such as the Awa-ya was dependent on the sea—specifically on the "extraordinary anchorage" that the crescent, sheltered bays of northern Nagashima and the southern Murotsu peninsula offered to passing ships. Indeed, despite appearances, the soil was not particularly productive on either side of the straits, a fact that led to increasing disparities of wealth within both Kaminoseki and Murotsu. By the mid-nineteenth century, these disparities could be mapped onto the landscape in the form of an Edo period administrative distinction between the "port areas" (*ura-kata*) and the "inland areas" (*ji-kata*) of both settlements.

The port areas of Kaminoseki and Murotsu were the busy commercial districts of each "town": the branch office of the domain's *koshini-gata* agent was here, as were the houses of private agents such as the Awa-ya, Kaga-ya, and Nagasaki-ya. In Kaminoseki's case, the administrative offices of the domain (*bansho*), which oversaw the lending and storage activities of the domain agents, were also located in the port area, along with several large warehouses. The port's two resident samurai, the Yasumura and Hayashi households, lived close to the *bansho,* and the residence of senior village headman Odamura could be found on the main street of the port district, adjacent to the Awa-ya. Turning away from the main street and heading toward the Amidaji temple, a short walk across the aptly named Bridge of Consideration would bring one to the Edo-ya and the Kaneko-ya, two of Kaminoseki's teahouses, where "ladies of pleasure" offered multiple entertainments.[37]

The inland areas—a ten-minute walk up the hill, in the case of Kaminoseki's Sōzu district or Murotsu's Yamaga district, or several kilometers away, in the case of a number of other hamlets (see Figure 2.2)—varied somewhat: by the mid-nineteenth century, communities located closer to the harbor were more like small suburbs of the port areas, whereas those a considerable distance away (particularly in the case of Murotsu) were self-contained villages. Nevertheless, in general terms, the inland areas were primarily agricultural communities. Yet the topography that protected the straits' harbors from strong winds actually undermined the agricultural development of these inland areas. The hills, though only several hundred meters high, were generally too steep for rice planting, and, in the case of Nagashima island, there was a relative lack of fresh water for paddy field irrigation.

Given the unpromising terrain, it therefore seems surprising that the inland areas of both Murotsu and Kaminoseki recorded a population increase of 232 percent and 182 percent respectively in the century between 1738 and 1842.[38] In itself, such population growth was not unusual: all of the districts that comprise the post-1958 municipality recorded significant increases in the same period.[39] In this way, they exemplified the main demographic trend of the later Edo period, by which there was major population growth in many rural areas, particularly in the southwest of Japan. This was counterbalanced by significant population decline in castle towns and urban centers, thus creating little movement in the country's overall population figures, which stagnated at around thirty million people.[40]

Within Kaminoseki's general population growth, the most notable increase was in the number of landless laborers (*mōdo*). In the Kaminoseki inland area, for example, 31 percent of all households owned no land in 1738, a figure that increased to 79 percent in 1842. In absolute terms, there were nine times as many landless households as landowning households in the Kaminoseki inland area by 1842 and more than six times the number in the Murotsu inland area.[41] Such a concentration of landless households in the mid-nineteenth century was somewhat unusual: across the Chōshū domain as a whole, landowning households outnumbered their landless counterparts by more than two to one. The Kaminoseki statistics thus raise the question, how did the members of these landless households eke out a living?[42] It would be tempting to assume that they did so simply as tenant farmers. But as we have seen, the topography of Nagashima island and the Murotsu peninsula was ill suited to intensive rice farming on the scale required to feed an increased population. So while the members of these landless households may have tended a small vegetable patch high above the Kaminoseki straits on Mt. Ōza or Mt. Kamisakari—Fortune described terraced fields climbing all the way up to the mountain summits—they would also have had to turn to by-employments in order to survive.

Historians of Chōshū are lucky to be able to analyze these by-employments in some detail because of a comprehensive survey carried out by the domain in the early 1840s, the *Bōchō fūdo chūshin'an* (Reports on the Customs and Economy of Suō and Nagato Provinces; hereafter *Reports*). Indeed, Thomas C. Smith's seminal study of by-employments in early modern Japan uses data from the *Reports* in order to discuss the case study of Kaminoseki county, one of seventeen counties (*saiban*) that composed the Chōshū domain and one of the counties that provided the most detailed set of answers to the domain's survey questionnaire. Smith's starting point was an important discrepancy in the data: 82 percent of households in Kaminoseki county were farming households (the average across the Chōshū domain as a whole was 80 percent) but only 45 percent of the county's total income was generated by agriculture. In other words, 18 percent of the county's households appeared to be generating more than one-half of the county's income—a highly unlikely phenomenon unless one assumes that farming households were also generating some nonagricultural income through by-employments (commerce, small crafts, wage remittances, and so on). Smith then used a formula to impute the approximate value of that nonagricultural income.[43] His results for Murotsu village were particularly noteworthy: although 44 percent of households were farmers, only 17 percent of the village's income was generated by agriculture. Instead, by far the most important source of income was trade (48 percent). This was the highest such figure for any village in the county and is consistent with economic specialization throughout the region. Thus the villages of Sone and Ogō, both coastal settlements engaged in salt production, boasted high proportions of income from industry; the village of Befu, whose residents particularly specialized in shipping locally produced salt throughout the Inland Sea, made 69 percent of its income from transport;[44] and the outlying islands of Yashima and Iwaishima, had they been included in Smith's analysis, would have shown a high proportion of wage remittance income from off-season work in the whaling and sake industries respectively.[45]

But in discussing "Murotsu," Smith failed to distinguish between the port and inland areas of the village, and he thus underestimated the economic significance of the port to the wider region. In absolute terms, the reported (non-imputed) income from the port area was more than three times that of the inland area, even though the number of households in both areas was roughly equal. Moreover, 98 percent of the port's households were nonfarmers, and the port's reported income was entirely generated by nonagricultural activities, of which trade (72 percent) was the most important.[46] The same was true of the Kaminoseki port area, which in absolute terms generated even more money than that of Murotsu. Fully one-quarter of Kaminoseki's annual reported income in 1842 was generated by the three "teahouses" alone, which employed fifty-four female prostitutes (*yūjo*) and five male "clerks" (*tedai*).[47] Shipping agents such as the Awa-ya household generated another 13 percent; bathhouses, inns, hairdressers, and fishmongers together generated 9 percent; brokers and shops, 6 percent. Thus more than half of the port's total income was created by businesses directly serving the commercial and recreational needs of the *kitamae*-ships and their crews. The only other economic sectors that came close to generating similar proportions of income were cotton dying (7 percent) and sardine fishing (5 percent).

By the mid-nineteenth century, the commercial ports of Kaminoseki and Murotsu were therefore dominating the village and regional economies, and it seems highly likely that they provided by-employment opportunities for nominally "agricultural" households in the inland areas too. This is illustrated by the account—a somewhat functional account, it must be admitted—of an Edo traveler, who passed through Kaminoseki in 1801: "I went ashore and entered a shipping inn [and agent] called Sakura-ya, where I drank sake. I ate bream and striped mullet sashimi, and bream poached with salt, and I drank. The sake and fish cost 320 *mon,* and then I had a bath, returned to my ship, and sailed after midday."[48] A large number of people worked behind the scenes to make such transactions possible. The men who ferried the traveler from his ship to the dock in tiny *yobi-sen* rowboats;[49] the fishermen who caught the bream and mullet; the fish, sake, salt, and soy sauce merchants; the porters who delivered food and firewood for the Sakura-ya's kitchen; the water carriers, cooks, and maids in the inns and bathhouses: all these villagers and many others were economically dependent on the arrival of outside ships to Kaminoseki. Moreover, judging by the Awa-ya's *Customer Register,* ships docked in the port throughout the year, thus providing a steady source of income to all these related workers (unlike sake brewing, for example, which was concentrated in the winter months).[50]

The economic dynamism of the port areas appears to have supported the dramatic increases in the landless population of the inland areas of Kaminoseki and Murotsu that occurred between the mid-eighteenth and mid-nineteenth centuries. Indeed, the fact that the rate of household increase in Kaminoseki and Murotsu outstripped the rate of population increase—a demographic phenomenon not seen in other parts of Nagashima, Iwaishima, or Yashima—suggests that the ports may have served as some kind of economic magnet in the mid-nineteenth century, enticing poor families from other parts of the Inland Sea region to set up new households in the town and make a living as nonagricultural laborers.[51] Such a hypothesis is consistent with the number of landless households rising fastest in the inland areas of Murotsu and Kaminoseki, where rent would have been cheaper than in the commercial port districts.

The Kaminoseki and Murotsu data thus add to our understanding of why urban populations decreased relative to rural ones in the later Edo period. As early as the 1780s, one basic reason for this urban-rural disparity was identified by a magistrate in the castle town of Okayama, several days' sail to the east of Kaminoseki. Cargo ships, he noted, were increasingly putting in at country ports so as to avoid doing business with the town's higher-charging shipping agents: the number of ships docking in Okayama had dropped by a third since the middle of the century.[52] The growth of private wholesale agents such as the Awa-ya, Kaga-ya, Nagasaki-ya, and Sakura-ya households in Kaminoseki helps explain the attraction of the smaller country ports: as the range of goods being stored in those households' warehouses increased, Kaminoseki became not just a place of transit but a marketplace to rival the cities, thus attracting the business of ever more *kitamae*-ships. By 1842, any of the main produce shipped east along the Inland Sea (including rice, silk, lacquer, kelp, fertilizer, timber, sugar, and charcoal) or west (including tea, cotton, salt, and paper) could be stored in or bought from Kaminoseki warehouses.[53] And as the business of the ports expanded, so did the number of economic migrants to Kaminoseki and Murotsu.

But to explain the demographic trends of the *Reports* is not to suggest that life was smooth sailing for the towns' new landless residents. Where Fortune observed what he assumed to be fertile and productive soil, the village headman of Kaminoseki's inland area gave a different perspective on the same landscape. Because the land here is cramped, he wrote in the *Reports,* fields are cultivated to the crest of the ridges and the depths of the valleys; but that land itself is difficult to farm, and the rice fields are insufficient for people's needs.[54] If such a statement spoke of an overstretched community teetering on the edge of food poverty (indeed, all villages in the county needed to import food by the mid-1840s),[55] then the qualitative evidence of the *Reports* further underlined the growing economic disparity between port and inland areas. In both Kaminoseki and Murotsu, for example, most houses in the commercial district of the town had tiled roofs—as did the new Awa-ya residence—whereas the majority of houses in the inland area had cheaper thatched roofs.[56] This gap between rich and poor became even more marked the farther southwest one ventured from the straits toward the hamlets of Nagashima and the outlying islands of Yashima and Iwaishima. In 1842, the average household income in Kaminoseki's port area was nine times greater than that of Yashima.[57]

To a local person's eye, the socioeconomic landscape of the "two small towns" was thus far more variegated than Fortune could have guessed in 1860. The sea may have brought visitors exotic and entrepreneurial through Kaminoseki, but it also generated very different levels of wealth for households within the community.

In 1842, a villager needed only to stroll along the street from the Awa-ya to the Nagasaki-ya or take note of the engraved memorials recording donations from Toyama, Harima, and Osaka in the village's Kamado Hachimangū shrine to appreciate that Kaminoseki boasted a richness of connections that went beyond the borders of the Chōshū domain. To borrow Fernand Braudel's characterization of another great inland sea, the waters flowing through the straits served not to divide Kaminoseki from the mainland, but rather to link the port communities to other regions and to the world outside Japan.[58] But the problem, in the summer of 1842, was that the world outside Japan was rapidly changing. As the roustabouts on the pier loaded and unloaded cargo, as the Awa-ya and Sakura-ya inns prepared for more guests and more business transactions, and as the village headmen of Kaminoseki and Murotsu compiled their *Reports* for the domain authorities, little can they have known about a peace agreement being negotiated between Great Britain and China in far-off Nanking. The treaty brought to an end the first Opium War (1839–1842), but it equally marked the beginning of a new phase of Western imperialism in East Asia. With foreign governments exploiting the new "treaty ports" in China, Japan also became the object of Western commercial ambition.

The unexpected arrival of the *England* on 21 December 1860 may have been one of the first opportunities local people had to see this new East Asian reality in the flesh, but only the most extraordinarily sharp-eyed agent might have guessed that the episode forewarned of severe economic problems. This was not because of Robert Fortune per se, or Captain Dundas, or any other passenger, but rather because of the *England* itself—the "fire-ship" in which they traveled. The technological prowess of such steamships had first been experienced in Japan, at close hand, in July 1853, when Commodore Matthew Perry sailed four US Navy warships to the southern tip of Edo Bay and demanded a new diplomatic relationship. As if his smoke-belching vessels—the Japanese called them "black ships"—were not sufficient to impress his wary hosts, Perry also offered gifts to underline Western technological superiority: three miles of telegraphic lines (with a demonstration of usage), a quarter-sized locomotive train, and 370 yards of track.[59]

In the short term, such technologies appear not to have affected daily life in the straits. Indeed, the ports appear to have profited from the economic instability triggered by enforced reengagement with the West. Although the communities and the wider region did not produce commodities such as silk or tea, which could be sold to the foreigners, Chōshū's *koshini* system and the *kitamae*-ships nevertheless thrived on market volatility and regional price differentials, both of which intensified in the 1850s and 1860s.[60] In the long term, however, new technologies would have catastrophic consequences for *kitamae*-ship businesses and thus for the communities on either side of the Kaminoseki straits. This was because speculative transport depended, ultimately, on the physical distance between producer and market, and on the former's lack of up-to-date information about price movements in the latter. Thus, once the telegraph network began to spread throughout the country, starting in 1872, market information could be instantly communicated and discrepancies in price between different regions never again reached the 15 to 20 percent seen only a few years earlier between Kaga and Osaka.[61] Ship owners lost the margin against which they could speculate for profit—a change that became acute from the mid-1880s onward.

Moreover, ship owners faced competition from steamships that could carry more than ten times the volume of goods at higher speed and against the wind. In the Japan Sea port of Niigata, for example, only eighteen foreign steamers docked in the whole of 1869, compared to almost three thousand Japanese vessels; but the foreign ships nevertheless accounted for 26 percent of Niigata's imports from other Japanese regions, and they further transported a quarter of the port's rice shipments.[62] In neighboring Toyama, the first major protests against these changes occurred in May 1878, when *kitamae*-ship crews and dockworkers demonstrated against a government plan to sell 60,000 *koku* of rice to China—to be transported there by thirty-four steamships.[63] Although *kitamae* owners could themselves invest in steamships, the required level of capital meant that individual shipping businesses were always likely to lose out to major corporations such as Mitsubishi. As a result, there followed a precipitous decline in the number of small *kitamae* owners, from 418 in the Japan Sea coast prefectures in 1880 to just 47 in 1911.[64] In the Kaminoseki county village of Befu, a short sail west of the straits, competition from major corporations led to the collapse of the local shipping industry by the 1880s and to the first exodus of villagers seeking new business opportunities on the Korean peninsula.[65]

The nascent decline of Kaminoseki and Murotsu as an entrepôt of trade and commerce was further exacerbated by the impact of domestic political reform and international trade on the local economy. With the abolition of the domains in 1871, the transportation of rice tax along Inland Sea routes to Osaka was rendered unnecessary (tax was now to be paid in cash rather than in kind). Domain monopolies and monopsonies on particular goods were also abolished, thus exposing local industries to international competition. In what was now southeastern Yamaguchi prefecture, salt and cotton production was particularly hit by cheap imports from the West in the 1860s and 1870s.[66] Changes in agriculture in the regions east of the straits further affected the demand for fertilizers not only from the north of Japan, but also from small-scale producers of dried-sardine fertilizer in Kaminoseki.[67]

Some businesses in the straits did profit from these transformations, especially inns that targeted passengers traveling on the new steamship services, which made scheduled stops at both ports from 1873 onward and whose landings peaked locally in the 1880s. Moreover, the port facilities remained attractive to owners of hybrid Western-style sail ships, whose numbers nationwide increased by a factor of nineteen between 1880 and 1911.[68] The suitability of the ports for these hybrid ships further stimulated what brothel proprietors perceived to be a "dramatic increase" in the numbers of prostitutes, especially in Murotsu, where there were twelve brothels by 1919.[69] For enterprising businessmen—be they innkeepers, brothel owners, ship repairers, or even ship owners—there was still money to be made in the ports, as subsequent chapters will show: decline was not a linear process in Kaminoseki. But Western-style sail ships notwithstanding, the growth of a national freight sector that was moving toward bigger and faster steamships (eventually too big to dock in the crescent harbors) would cause problems for the straits economies, as would the development of overland transportation routes that bypassed the Murotsu peninsula.[70]

Given the scale of economic change, it is difficult to date the beginning of the ports' decline with any precision other than to say that the *kitamae*-ships were themselves in terminal decline by the late 1880s. Indeed, by the turn of the new century, the phrase "backwater Japan" (*ura Nihon*) had been coined to describe the Japan Sea prefectures in which ship ownership had formerly been concentrated.[71] Kaminoseki itself was not yet a backwater, for some new opportunities would present themselves to the people of the town. Nevertheless, compared to the heyday of the mid-nineteenth century years, the waters that flowed into the straits would never again bring such riches.

PART II

Living with a Changing Polity

3

Murotsu and the Meiji Revolution, 1868

In February 1864, three men attacked the *Katoku-maru* as it lay in port in Befu, to the west of the Kaminoseki straits. The men beheaded the ship's principal merchant, a Satsuma native by the name of Ōtani, and set fire to his cargo. As the ship burned the attackers returned to their base in Murotsu. Later, two of the men traveled on to the Minami-Mido temple in Osaka, where they displayed Ōtani's head for all to see and then committed ritual suicide. The third made his way to Saihōji temple in Murotsu, where he too disemboweled himself.[1]

In the wider history of the unrest that preceded the overthrow of the Tokugawa *bakufu* and the "restoration" of the young Meiji emperor in 1868, the *Katoku-maru* incident is no more than a minor episode. But it is nevertheless significant in that it allows us to identify a network of Chōshū men, active at the level immediately below that of better-known leaders such as Kido Takayoshi, Takasugi Shinsaku, and Ōmura Masujirō, who supported and contributed to the Meiji Restoration. In turn, this is important because it is possible to consider the Meiji Restoration—a revolution without a popular uprising—as an event that simply "came" to the Japanese people from on high, driven by court cliques and a small number of samurai based primarily in the Chōshū and Satsuma domains.[2] But the *Katoku-maru* incident suggests that the revolution did not just "come" to the villages of Murotsu and Kaminoseki. Rather, it was agitated for by certain elite households, through their encouragement of radical ideology, their offer of clandestine lodging and money, and their service as soldiers of the revolution. The evidence of such active participation in anti-*bakufu* politics by local men forces us also to ask what might have motivated them to risk their lives and livelihoods in the 1860s. By exploring the actions and motivations of Murotsu's Yoshida,

Yoshizaki, and Ogata households, this chapter adds to a body of scholarship that has reconsidered the history of the Meiji Restoration from the "bottom up" perspective of its unlauded participants, opponents, and general bystanders, and that has demanded further research about the loyalism of local elites to revolutionary ideals.[3]

The Yoshida Household (Ita-ya)

The *Katoku-maru* was owned by Maeda Eizō of Befu. The Maeda household was similar to dozens of others in Befu in making its money in the marine transportation sector of the regional economy. In addition to its ship-owning business, the Maeda household owned one of the Hirao salt fields, from which salt was shipped north to the Hokuriku region and even up to Hokkaido and southwest to Kyushu.[4] Eizō was therefore a highly successful businessman in 1864, and he would have been on familiar terms with many of the other business elites in Kaminoseki county. Indeed, such was his connection with Murotsu wholesale agents that in 1879 his third son, Shūzō, became the eleventh-generation head of the Yoshida household in Murotsu.[5]

The Yoshida residence was located in the heart of the Murotsu port area, between the narrow main street and the tutelary Kamo shrine. Its white-washed walls, which marked off the property from the outside world, were a sign of status normally forbidden to ordinary peasants in the Edo period.[6] Beyond the formal entrance gate, a carefully tended rock garden led to the main house, a two-storied rectangle winged on its short sides by large warehouses. At the rear of the residence were small outhouses and another garden—a luxury in Edo period Murotsu, when land near the booming harbor was at a premium.

The size of the Yoshida complex attests to the household's prosperity from at least the mid-eighteenth century. By the turn of the nineteenth century, when the house is thought to have been built, successive heads of the Yoshida household had already served as one of the port elders (*uradoshiyori*) for nearly two hundred years. Yoshida was the official residence for the daimyo of Satsuma when the lord and his retinue passed through on their way to and from alternate attendance in Edo, and since 1759 it had been a private shipping agent, specializing in the sale of sake.[7] The Yoshida household thus had a vested interest in the success of the Chōshū domain's *koshini-gata* system, and indeed the eighth-generation household head was probably influential in lobbying for the domain to establish a *koshini* branch office in Murotsu in 1837. Through their political and

Figure 3.1. The Yoshida residence (formerly Murotsu), Shōtōen, Hiroshima, 2007

economic activities, the livelihoods of the Yoshida and other leading households in Murotsu—such as the Yoshizaki, who served as headman of the inland area and who was also a sake shipping agent—were therefore increasingly tied to the political and economic fortunes of the Chōshū domain.

A number of scrolls hung on the inner walls of the Yoshida residence. These were collected by Yoshida Kenzō, the ninth-generation household head (died 1870), and they offer an insight into the range of Kenzō's political connections.[8] There was, for example, a scroll written by Murata Seifū (1783–1855), who had been appointed Chōshū's minister of reform in 1838. On assuming power, Murata initiated a massive survey of the domain (the *Reports,* discussed previously) in order to determine its wealth and assets. In addition, he introduced a program of austerity—which included the abolition of commercial monopolies on wax, cotton, sake, salt, and paper—and the expansion of the lucrative *koshini-gata* system.[9] Murata was deposed in a power struggle in 1844, and for the next twenty years Chōshū internal politics swung, pendulum-like, between a radical reforming faction represented by Murata and his followers, on the one hand, and more moderate, conservative cliques, on the other. In 1858, the reforming faction once again took power, now under the leadership of Sufu Masanosuke (1823–1864). Sufu was a protégé and distant relative of Murata and has been called "the most important single figure in Chōshū during the Bakumatsu period"; one of his written scrolls also hung in the Yoshida household, as did ones composed by stalwarts of the Sufu faction, Maeda Magoemon (1818–1864) and Nakamura Kyūrō (1828–1864).[10]

Sufu's administration coincided with the emergence of a radical branch of "revere the emperor, expel the barbarian" (*sonnō jōi*) ideology in Chōshū, articulated in particular by a charismatic young samurai scholar called Yoshida Shōin (1830–1859; no relation to the Yoshida household in Murotsu).[11] Shōin was concerned above all else with preserving the sovereignty of the Japanese nation, especially in the wake of Qing China's defeat by Britain in the First Opium War and the imposition of the Treaty of Nanking (1842). Yet his was no simple redneck xenophobia: under the influence of Dutch scholar Sakuma Shōzan (1811–1864), Shōin recognized that Japan must learn from the West so as to strengthen its defenses.[12] To this end, Shōin even attempted to convince first the Russian Admiral Putiatin in Nagasaki and then Commodore Perry himself in Shimoda to smuggle him out of Japan. Both attempts, in 1853 and 1854 respectively, were unsuccessful, and for the latter crime he was imprisoned in Edo and then in the domain capital of Hagi.[13]

His time in Hagi's Noyama prison gave Shōin a chance to read copiously—more than six hundred volumes in less than two years—and to hone his talent for teaching on his fellow inmates. On his release, at the end of 1855, he returned to his uncle's house in Hagi, where he quickly established a private academy called the Shōka Sonjuku, the School under the Pines, at which he taught until his rearrest in 1858. Although the majority of Shōin's ninety-two students during this period hailed from samurai households, their curriculum in the new academy was a far cry from that offered at the domain's regular school, the Meirinkan. Shōin's vision melded Confucian loyalty with Western military training and nationalistic reverence for the Japanese emperor; he urged meritocracy in education and further retrenchment by the daimyo; he emphasized the practical application of learning; and, above all, he inculcated his students with traditional Chōshū hostility to the Tokugawa clan.[14] Shōin's vision was a potent brew: the majority of his students were inspired to action in the battles of the 1860s, and many of those that survived went on to lead the new Meiji regime.

To judge by the Murotsu collection, Yoshida Kenzō appears to have been a strong supporter of "revere the emperor, expel the barbarian" and anti-Tokugawa ideology. For example, a letter survives that shows he was in personal correspondence with Yamada Akiyoshi (1844–1892), a graduate of the School under the Pines and a key commander—nicknamed "Little Napoleon"—in the proimperial forces during the Bōshin War (1868–1869).[15] Yoshida also owned a scroll written by another School graduate, Nomura Yasushi (1842–1909), who, like Yamada, would go on to hold Cabinet office in the administrations of their classmate Itō Hirobumi (1841–1909). And Yoshida also owned two paintings by the artist and Chōshū native Mori Kansai (1814–1894), who was renowned for his antiforeigner radicalism. Local tradition in Murotsu has it that Yoshida used to invite Mori Kansai to lodge at his house during the 1860s in order to provide artistic cover for the radical activists who also often visited. To avoid arousing suspicion among the Tokugawa secret police, they kept up the pretense of gathering to appreciate new paintings—much in the same way that leading plotters in the central Chōshū town of Yamaguchi met under the guise of enjoying the traditional tea ceremony.[16]

Yoshida Kenzō is thought to have known other key politicians and ideologues in the Chōshū domain,[17] and it seems likely that some of the many scrolls, letters, and paintings that he owned were composed as tokens of appreciation by activists as they passed through the Kaminoseki straits and enjoyed brief hospitality in the Yoshida household's peaceful gardens. Such penmanship was certainly how Yoshida Shōin himself expressed his gratitude when he came to Murotsu and stayed in the Ogata household, in 1858. As a token of thanks, he penned a poem on the wooden sword of his host, Ogata Ichiuemon, farmer, former elder of Murotsu port, and long admirer of "expel the barbarian" ideology.[18] Unfortunately, anyone looking for insights into the finer nuances of that ideology will be sorely disappointed by Shōin's poem, which reads

> [Ogata Ichiuemon] is fifty-three years old; he drinks like a whale.
> The doctor says he shouldn't drink every day.
> How can you live without listening to the doctor?
> So Ogata has cut back: it only takes half of what he used to drink
> to make him feel like the King of the World.[19]

The Yoshizaki Household (Higo-ya)

In addition to the Yoshida and Ogata households, there was a third household in central Murotsu at which radical activists and ideologues were welcomed in the 1850s and 1860s: the Yoshizaki (household name, Higo-ya;

see Figure 4.1). In April 1871, for example, Chōshū-born Kido Takayoshi (1833–1877), one of the most important domain leaders in the Restoration and a leading Meiji statesman until his death, passed through the Kaminoseki straits on government business and took a trip down memory lane: "In the spring of 1868, I departed from Yamaguchi before the Battle of Osaka broke out; and when, en route, I heard about the threatening situation in the Kyoto region, I was feverish with excitement, but the winds prevented my going; so I stayed in this house [the Higo-ya] for several days. . . . When I called the past to mind tonight, my heart was filled with deep emotion."[20]

The reason that both Murotsu and Kaminoseki ports hosted increasingly "feverish" guests between 1858 and 1868—including leading activists from outside the domain, such as Tosa samurai Sakamoto Ryōma in the fall of 1865—was the volatile political situation in the nation as a whole and the new role in national politics that Sufu Masanosuke and his faction were attempting to engineer for the Chōshū domain in particular. The catalyst for both developments was the new US-Japan Treaty of Amity and Commerce, negotiated from 1856 against the backdrop of the Second Opium War in China and eventually concluded in July 1858. Although the treaty differed from the Treaty of Nanking in the crucial respect that it did not allow the import of opium into Japan, it included other clauses that were anathema to "expel the barbarian" radicals such as the young men being trained at Yoshida Shōin's School under the Pines. Five Japanese ports, for example, were to be declared "open" to foreign trade; in each port, foreigners would be allowed to reside in settlements that were outside the rule of Japanese law (so-called extraterritoriality) and in which they could practice their own religions freely. Equally galling for the Hagi students, the *bakufu* signed the 1858 Treaty of Amity and Commerce without the approval of the imperial court in Kyoto—behavior considered intolerable by those whose creed also included "revere the emperor."

Following the Treaty of Amity and Commerce and similar treaties signed in subsequent months between Japan and the other Western powers, the *bakufu,* under the leadership of Ii Naosuke (1815–1860), attempted to shore up its position by initiating a purge of its enemies. For his part, Shōin decided to assassinate a Tokugawa emissary in Kyoto—a plan that alienated even his closest supporters and that led to Sufu ordering Shōin's rearrest in an attempt to protect the domain from the worst of the so-called Ansei Purge. From Hagi, Shōin was eventually transferred to Edo, where he was executed in November 1859. In contrast to Shōin's forthright plan of action, Sufu started a campaign to strengthen Chōshū's ties with other procourt domains and thus to raise the domain's profile on the national stage. In 1861, after Ii (the instigator of the Ansei Purge) had himself been assassinated, Sufu backed a proposed policy of mediation between the *bakufu* and the court in which the trade treaties between Japan and other Western powers were recognized as necessary, but which also called for greater imperial glory to be afforded to the court.[21] Although Sufu later withdrew his support for mediation under pressure from Shōin-inspired disciples radicalized by the "martyrdom" of their teacher, the policy succeeded in raising the profile of Chōshū both in Edo and in Kyoto.[22] Unfortunately for Chōshū, this provoked a response from the Satsuma domain, which also desired a leading role in post-1858 politics: the subsequent bitter rivalry between the two domains would eventually inspire radicals based in Murotsu to attack the *Katoku-maru* and its Satsuma cargo.

But the Murotsu attackers were not, as far as can be known, local men. Rather, they were part of a militia group that had been newly established in Kaminoseki in 1863 and whose origins can be understood by considering the domain's unusual location. Shaped roughly as a rectangle, only one of Chōshū's sides (the east) was a land border: to the north and the west, respectively, the domain faced the Japan Sea, while the southern limit of Mōri territory was marked by the Inland Sea. This was a wonderful location as long as the coastal waters were peaceful: despite its distance from Osaka, Chōshū found itself at the heart of domestic trading routes in the second half of the Edo period, and the domain was able to construct a sophisticated warehouse network, the *koshini-gata,* that exploited the daily business needs of the passing ships. In this way, Chōshū used its fortuitous topography as successfully as Satsuma exploited a subtropical climate that gave it a virtual monopoly on sugar production. As Albert Craig has pointed out, it is no coincidence that the two domains that led the Meiji Restoration had both made significant (though contrasting) financial reforms in the 1840s and could both generate significant profits that could be used for the purchase of Western weapons.[23]

But Chōshū's topography looked considerably less fortuitous if, on three sides of the domain, it was exposed to hostile and aggressive acts by foreign ships. In the summer of 1860, for example, a British vessel docked unexpectedly in Shimonoseki, demanded fuel and food, and coerced a local guard to accompany the ship back to Nagasaki. Although the domain protested to the *bakufu,* whose protest to the British consul resulted in the release of the guard, the *bakufu* denied Chōshū radicals the right to use force against the presence of foreign shipping in Shimonoseki. Venting his frustration, Yamagata Aritomo (1838–1922), another of Shōin's students, wrote: "The ugly English barbarians behaved with extreme disorder and uncontrollable uncouthness."[24] Thus because of its location and the necessity of foreign vessels based in the "open" port of Nagasaki to pass through the Shimonoseki straits on their way to the open ports of Kobe or Yokohama, Chōshū officials perceived the domain to be particularly vulnerable to foreign intrusion. Moreover, the Tsushima Incident of 1861, in which Russian ships attempted to establish a base in the group of islands located halfway between Chōshū and Korea, only to be thwarted by the British navy, was an example of Western imperial rivalries threatening to erupt in Chōshū's backyard.[25] (The capital of Hagi, on the Japan Sea coast, was considered to be particularly vulnerable, and in 1863 the domain administration was moved to the inland town of Yamaguchi.)

As far back as 1849 and in line with other domains throughout the country, Chōshū officials had recognized that military defenses needed to be tightened.[26] In that year, they established a reserve army of farmer conscripts, the Nōheitai, to back up the regular domain army (staffed by samurai). The Nōheitai's establishment was part of a heightened security campaign following the sighting of foreign ships off the Japan Sea coast of Chōshū. Although Hagi administrators concentrated at first on deploying the reserve army on the northern side of the domain, defenses were strengthened in the Inland Sea ports as well—a defensive battery high above the Kaminoseki side of the straits also dates from the late 1840s.[27] In the summer of 1863, however, two events occurred that accelerated the restructuring of domain military capabilities.

First, under pressure from "expel the barbarian" radicals in both Chōshū and the court, the *bakufu* agreed to the official expulsion of the foreigners from Japan—a highly unrealistic proposition but one that indicated the extent to which the *bakufu* was caught between the demands of Western powers, on the one hand, and loyalist extremists, on the other. That date came, in June 1863, and Chōshū activists opened fire first on the US steamer *Pembroke,* as it passed through the Shimonoseki straits, and subsequently on French and Dutch ships too. Predictably, the United States soon retaliated, while 250 French marines temporarily occupied the Shimonoseki fort of Dan'noura, provoking a military crisis within the domain.

The second crisis occurred a month later, when Satsuma leaders engineered an unexpected coup against Chōshū forces stationed in Kyoto. Domain supporters, including seven reformist nobles from the court, were forced to flee westward for their lives. On their way to regroup in Mitajiri (otherwise known as Nakanoseki), five of those seven nobles sheltered in the Higo-ya, the ancestral home of the Yoshizaki household in Murotsu.[28] In a time of assassinations, court coups, and divisions within the domain, the fact that the Chōshū-sympathizing nobles stayed in the Yoshizaki residence suggests that Murotsu, with the sympathetic Yoshida and Ogata households only a stone's throw away from the Higo-ya, had established a reputation as a safe haven for procourt, antiforeign activists.

There was, moreover, a Murotsu connection to the defeat of Chōshū forces by Western powers in the summer of 1863: Ogata Kenkurō, adopted son of the oft-inebriated Ogata Ichiuemon, had been a volunteer during the original attack on foreign shipping. By witnessing at first hand the strength of foreign arms, he had realized, as had Takasugi Shinsaku (1839–1867), another graduate of the School under the Pines, that a new type of army—indeed, a completely new way of thinking—would be necessary. Under Takasugi's leadership, an initial corps of three hundred volunteers, the Kiheitai ("extraordinary unit"), was established in Shimonoseki in August 1863. This was a new type of militia group (*shotai*), different from the domain's aforementioned Nōheitai in three respects: first, the command of such groups was outside the direct control of the domain; second, they were privately funded, mainly by rich peasants and merchants; and third, they were staffed by a mixture of samurai, merchants, and peasants—a revolutionary idea previously advocated by Yoshida Shōin.[29] By the end of 1863, four further *shotai* had been established in the domain: in Mitajiri (500 members), Yamaguchi (100 members), Ogōri (50 members), and Kaminoseki (50 members).[30]

The Kaminoseki group was called the Giyūtai and was set up by Akira Atsunosuke, a samurai retainer in the village of Atsuki, on the eastern side of the Murotsu peninsula. Akira had been good friends with the Yanai-based priest Gesshō (1817–1858), who was an important promoter of Japan's maritime defense in the 1850s.[31] The Giyūtai's official purveyor and one of its significant financial backers was Yoshida Kenzō, and one of the volunteers was Ogata Kenkurō himself.[32] Although the Giyūtai was originally billeted in Kaminoseki, at the beginning of 1864 its headquarters were transferred to Saihōji temple in Murotsu—the temple that housed the ancestral graves of the Yoshida, Yoshizaki, and Ogata households.[33] Both the base and the type of local supporters in Murotsu were thus indicative of the wider coalition of local samurai, merchants, rich farmers, and priests who joined together throughout Chōshū in the early 1860s to fund and lodge radical militia groups.

It was members of this militia, the Murotsu-based Giyūtai, who carried out the *Katoku-maru* attack early in 1864. Their actions exemplified Chōshū radicalism to that point. The ship was flying under a Satsuma flag and carrying a cargo—ginned cotton, sake, and soy sauce—that some suspected was part of a contraband trade between Satsuma and Western powers. To its attackers, it thus represented both the "barbarians" and the Satsuma domain, Chōshū's great rival in national politics. Moreover, the attack was apparently spontaneous and carried out with no direction from other *shotai* units or from radicals in Hagi—proof that there was still much work to be done before "Chōshū" could be considered a unified fighting force capable of taking on either Satsuma or the *bakufu,* let alone expelling the Western powers.

Those closest to the attackers may have had mixed feelings about the incident. After all, Yoshida Kenzō, who was partly financing the Giyūtai, was presumably aware of the losses that his business counterpart in Befu, Maeda Eizō, had sustained as a result of the ship's sinking, and the Yoshida household itself had a long history of offering hospitality to Satsuma officials on their way to alternate attendance. Indeed, the *Katoku-maru* incident appears to have caused some officials in the Chōshū domain severe embarrassment. An official was immediately deployed to Kaminoseki to prevent any more "difficulties" (*sashitsukae*) occurring in domain waters, while ships were temporarily ordered to stop docking within the Kaminoseki jurisdiction.[34] According to the detailed obituary that appears on his gravestone, Murotsu's Ogata Kenkurō was additionally deployed by the commander of Kiheitai forces to try to repair the damage with Satsuma.[35]

Yet the violence perpetrated by Kenkurō's more radical colleagues was merely a foretaste of another summer of unrest. In mid-1864, a militia force of five hundred men, supplemented by extremist imperial loyalists who had fled to Chōshū the previous year, marched back to Kyoto. Although some domain leaders urged restraint, such was the momentum among both troops and other radical leaders to regain Chōshū's influence at the court that an attack on Kyoto became unavoidable. Once again, the domain was roundly defeated and this time was declared an "enemy of the court." Thus had Chōshū radicals succeeded in burning their bridges with the one institution they professed to revere. Ogata Kenkurō, for his part, was not present in the capital; instead, he appears to have been redeployed after his Satsuma mission to the original Kiheitai forces in Shimonoseki. There, just two weeks after Chōshū's capitulation in Kyoto, the domain came under the sustained attack of a fleet of seventeen French, Dutch, British, and American warships and two thousand allied troops—Western governments having finally been driven to comprehensive action by constant Chōshū harassment of foreign shipping in the straits.

Helpless in the face of Western military prowess and humiliated in Kyoto, surviving leaders, such as Kido Takayoshi and Ōmura Masujirō, and a younger generation of School under the Pines graduates, including Takasugi Shinsaku, Yamagata Aritomo, and Itō Hirobumi, appear to have realized the limits of uncontrolled antibarbarian radicalism. Some, like Itō and Inoue Kaoru (1836–1915), both of whom had the chance to study clandestinely in England in 1863–1864, appear to have come to this realization even earlier.[36] As a coalition of *bakufu* forces threatened the eastern borders of the domain during the First Chōshū Expedition, these men went into hiding, and, during the winter of 1864–1865, control of the domain was briefly lost to the conservative faction, which promptly executed reformist leaders such as Sufu Masanosuke. But when the younger radicals daringly fought their way back into government in the Chōshū Civil War of early 1865, they enforced both military realism and a new policy not of expel the barbarians, but of "overthrow the *bakufu*" (*tōbaku*). Using some of the profits generated by the *koshini-gata* system, Kido ordered Itō Hirobumi and Inoue Kaoru secretly to purchase Western guns and steamships in Nagasaki through British arms dealers: in this they were supported by the powerful Satsuma domain, with which relations were mended.[37] In eastern Chōshū, independent *shotai* militia groups, such as the Kaminoseki Giyūtai, were rationalized into a much bigger force. Known as the Second Kiheitai, this unit was under the overall leadership of Takasugi Shinsaku, who regularly passed through the Kaminoseki straits and is known also to have stayed at the Higo-ya residence of the Yoshizaki household.[38] Ogata Kenkurō was one of thirty-five staff officers (*sanbō*) in the Second Kiheitai, whose executives also included at least seventeen samurai retainers (*baishin*), five priests, and three ronin (leaderless samurai).[39] By the summer of 1866, the Second Kiheitai was ready to take on the *bakufu* forces that had once again gathered to put down the rebellious domain.

For the people of Kaminoseki, the Second Chōshū Expedition commenced with an attack on the ports that must have been as terrifying as it was short-lived: at around 10:00 a.m. on the seventh day of the sixth month—a sunny day, according to a samurai diarist in nearby Atsuki—a *bakufu* steamship rounded the eastern side of the Murotsu peninsula and opened fire on the Murotsu districts of Shirahama, Shiraura, and Seto. Domain officials reported to Hagi that two shells had caused damage to the roofs of townhouses in Seto; another appears to have landed in one of the Kaminoseki graveyards, while two more crashed into the sea. Ultimately, it was a fairly harmless attack, but it indicated the strategic importance of the straits to both sets of combatants and also the distinct danger that port residents might find themselves in during a protracted war.[40]

The attack on Kaminoseki appears to have been a prelude to the *bakufu* occupation of parts of Ōshima island. Within a few days, however, the Chōshū government ordered the deployment of the Second Kiheitai to the front, and once more port residents watched as a foreign-built steamship—the *Heiin-maru,* purchased by Takasugi in Nagasaki—passed through the straits to engage the Tokugawa forces.[41] After a short campaign on Ōshima, in which Ogata Kenkurō saw action, *bakufu* forces were forced to withdraw on the twentieth of the month. But as fighting opened on Chōshū's other fronts, the domain government sent a warning to its port officials: "At this time," it began, "marauding sea militia have gradually begun plundering our local waters. There are militia who board Japanese-constructed ships, others who are indistinguishable from merchant ships and thus lie easily at anchor, and others who even if they sail close to the shore are hard to distinguish." Stop every merchant ship entering Chōshū waters, the warning continued, and take particular care to check nondomain ships carrying arms, ammunition, or food—especially the ships of Tokugawa-allied daimyo.[42]

With the final, humiliating defeat of *bakufu* forces in the Four Border War, the shogunate's days were numbered. But for Chōshū leaders such as Itō Hirobumi and Yamagata Aritomo (although not for Takasugi Shinsaku, who died of tuberculosis in 1867), success as militia commanders would be the springboard to national eminence in the new Meiji government.[43]

~

The *Katoku-maru* attack of February 1864 represented a precise moment in Chōshū history, a moment before peace was made with Satsuma, before "expel the barbarians" ideology was superseded by "overthrow the *bakufu,*" and before semi-autonomous militia groups came under a more centralized command. In the absence of any evidence, it is difficult to know whether the heads of the Yoshida, Yoshizaki, and Ogata households continued to support this purer version of Chōshū revolutionary ideology or whether they came to terms with the realist policy that led to military success in 1866–1869. National eminence did not beckon for them as for Kido, Itō, and Yamagata. As Chapter 4 shows, Yoshida Kenzō, his adopted son Shūzō (né Maeda), Ogata Kenkurō, and Yoshizaki Eijirō (the seventeenth-generation head of that household, died 1884) would spend the rest of their days living and working in Murotsu.

Why, then, did these men offer their homes, their money, and their service to the Chōshū revolutionaries? One reason may have been the potential for personal recognition. The status of the Yoshida household, for example, was raised from farmer to samurai in the mid- to late 1860s in recognition of Kenzō's contributions to the domain.[44] Ogata Kenkurō, who was classified as former samurai (*shizoku*) by 1893, also had his status raised, probably sometime between 1865, when he was still officially of farmer ranking, and the immediate aftermath of the Restoration, when he was rewarded in other ways by the new government.[45] Another factor that may have spurred elite Murotsu households to support the revolutionaries was the extent to which each of them was involved in the *koshini-gata* system—as attested by the huge volume of early- to mid-nineteenth-century correspondence and financial transactions in the surviving papers of the Yoshida and Yoshizaki households. Perhaps, as they compared business with other elites in the region (Befu's Maeda household, for example, which would soon be tied to the Yoshida household by adoption, or the Nukushina household in the Tokuyama domain, into which Ogata Kenkurō had originally been born), the Murotsu elites realized that the introduction of Western technology would eventually undermine the complex system of speculative transportation on which the *koshini-gata* was based. By this reasoning, they might have been drawn to Yoshida Shōin's antibarbarian rhetoric by a desire to protect and preserve their livelihoods.

Yet it would have taken a highly prescient mind to predict, in the late 1850s and early 1860s, the later decline of the ports. If anything, the instability in goods and markets triggered by the arrival of Western traders increased the kind of price volatility on which the *kitamae*-ships thrived. Perhaps, therefore, the main reason that these Murotsu households supported Chōshū's radical activists was not the economic threat posed by the West, but rather a sense of physical threat—not just personal but to the village community as a whole. The construction of a defensive battery above the Kaminoseki straits in the 1840s; the intellectual climate of 1853–1854, when not only the foreigners but the foreign ships themselves could be portrayed by Japanese artists as devils;[46] the outrage at the "uncouth" behavior of the British and other Western ships passing through the Shimonoseki straits; the perceived treachery of the Satsuma domain; the danger of being in the firing line; and the warnings about "marauding sea militia" all made an unambiguous "expel the barbarians" ideology and the prospect of an armed local militia attractive to local leaders in the port of Murotsu. Through their support of the Giyūtai and their offer of village facilities to lodge the militia and subsequent groups, Yoshida Kenzō, Yoshizaki Eijirō, and Ogata Kenkurō appear to have prioritized the maritime defense of their hometown, their domain, and ultimately their country. To this extent, they are likely to have shared the concerns of many other local elites in southeastern Chōshū who were influenced by Yoshida Shōin and other radical teachers and who maintained close ties with each other through intermarriage and shared commercial interests.[47] In this sense, the specific histories of the three Murotsu households help us understand the wider concerns of local elites in this part of Japan in the volatile 1860s.

In other words, it seems that the Murotsu elites may have had multiple motivations for offering to aid the leaders of the revolution—some ideological and some more practical, to do with the everyday welfare of their businesses and of the wider community.[48] This is important because historians often assume a uniformity of "Chōshū" experiences in the 1860s. Indeed, a critique of the "Chōshū-centered" view of the Meiji Restoration, particularly on the occasion of centenary celebrations in 1967–1968, was one starting point for a group of scholars to offer a new, "people"-centered view of Japanese history that focused on regions far away from Chōshū and Satsuma.[49] But the fragmentary evidence of this chapter suggests that the "people" of Chōshū—loyal local elites such as the Yoshida, Yoshizaki, and Ogata households—also need to be heard in our account of the Meiji Restoration.

What we cannot know, at least from Kaminoseki and Murotsu, is the extent to which "ordinary" villagers, those below the level of the elites, also supported the revolutionary stance of their village headmen. Much recent scholarship on local political and economic elites (the so-called *gōnō,* or "rich farmers") has emphasized their role as conduits of urban cultural pursuits to the countryside—as exemplified, perhaps, by the literary and artistic evidence that survives from the Yoshida household.[50] Whether the local elites also served as conduits for the flow of revolutionary ideology from Kyoto teahouses to Kaminoseki townhouses is unclear, but the fact that there was no rebellion against authority in Kaminoseki or Murotsu suggests that "ordinary" villagers at least tolerated the revolutionary forces who gathered in their temples and whose presence offered protection for the hometown against marauding militia or hostile gunboats. Equally, the lack of rebellion within Kaminoseki suggests that local leaders had become adept in maintaining their political, social, economic, and cultural influence over their fellow townspeople even in times of great instability. How they could do so is the focus of the next two chapters.

4

The Political Culture of the Meiji Village

In the summer of 1968, as universities throughout Japan were gripped by unrest, a team of students led by the historian Irokawa Daikichi discovered an extraordinary set of late-nineteenth-century documents in a derelict storehouse in Fukasawa hamlet, some sixty kilometers west of Tokyo. The documents included "a draft of a people's constitution consisting of 204 articles." In addition, "we discovered a petition urging the early establishment of a national assembly; . . . we found several hundred books that showed how excited the people [in Fukasawa] were about learning and politics. . . . Through these materials we learned that the village leaders and the men who drafted that constitution, hitherto unknown to history, were without exception family men: farmers, merchants, and school teachers—in other words, 'commoners' with deep ties to the life of the people."[1]

Together with criticism of the Chōshū-centered narratives of the Meiji centenary and the student protests of 1968–1969, Irokawa's discovery and subsequent bestselling book *Meiji no bunka* (The Culture of Meiji Japan) propelled "the people" (*minshū*) to the fore of postwar historiographical debates in Japan. So-called people's historians took issue with a teleological view of Japan's post-1868 modernization—a story of growth and success broken only by the "dark valley" of the 1930s and early 1940s. For example, Irokawa questioned the assumption that the prewar emperor system, which he claimed had "penetrated the minds of the Japanese" by the 1910s, was in any way inevitable and instead argued that the late Edo period and early Meiji years were "surprisingly rich in possibilities."[2] The emphasis that he placed on the "people" (*min*)—as opposed to the "elites" (*kan*), or the nation state—carried distinctive echoes of Yanagita Kunio's native-place studies.[3] But while Yanagita argued that the "common people" (*jōmin*) were carriers of an indigenous Japanese culture, people's historians considered the *min* to be champions of grassroots democracy.[4] Thus Irokawa argued that if the People's Rights movement—a grassroots campaign of political education and protest against the new Meiji government in the 1870s and 1880s—"had continued without setback for another ten or more years, the formation and constitution of the Japanese intellectual class would most certainly have been different. . . . In reality the failure of the People's Rights movement largely doomed the effort for creation of a new culture from Japan's grass roots."[5]

Although people's history was a groundbreaking development in forcing historians to consider nonelite lives through non-Tokyo sources, one problem with Irokawa's conflation of political "possibility" with the People's Rights movement was that "the people" tended only to be studied in regions where anti-Meiji protests had occurred in the late nineteenth century. As Neil Waters pointed out, regions where "nothing happened" were thus ignored,[6] and people from the former domains of Chōshū and Satsuma, whose leaders dominated the new Meiji government, became the "arch-villains of people's history in the Meiji period."[7] Moreover, there was a danger, which Irokawa himself acknowledged,[8] that generic "village leaders" came to be seen as synonymous with the common people and that those leaders were assumed to be intent on creating a "new" culture and democracy that was in opposition to the Meiji state.

As we have seen, however, the village leaders of Murotsu and the surrounding locality were not opponents of the new Meiji regime but rather men who helped establish it. Moreover, as this chapter argues, they were not nascent grassroots democrats but men who grasped the political opportunities created by the new state to maintain their oligarchic authority over hometown life for decades to come. The rediscovered village records of both Murotsu and Kaminoseki thus offer a very different portrait of the political culture of the Meiji period than that suggested by the Fukasawa storehouse documents—a culture that can be understood, at its most basic level, by entering the first building in Kaminoseki municipality to be designated a national Cultural Asset in 2005.

The Ogata Household (Sawa-ya)

In 1879, Ogata Kenkurō, soldier of the revolution, paid a small fortune to construct a uniquely shaped building at the heart of Murotsu port. Known as the Shikairō, it was four stories (*shi-kai*) and more than eleven meters high—twice the height of any other seafront house—and, as such, an

Figure 4.1. The Higo-ya (Yoshizaki household), with the Shikairō on the far right, c. 1913 (Courtesy of Takeuchi Sachiko)

imposing landmark for ships passing through the straits. With three-fingered arabesque dragons ornamenting each corner, fretwork peonies carved over the second floor, and stained glass windows on the top floor—the vivid blues, reds, oranges, and greens directly imported from the workshops of the Saint Gobain company (better known for its Hall of Mirrors at Versailles)—the Shikairō was a bold statement of its owner's cosmopolitan aspirations.[9] It was also a bold statement, twelve years into the reign of Emperor Meiji, of Ogata's continued wealth and political influence in the village.

Ogata had retired with honor from the Second Kiheitai in 1869, rewarded for his service to the Chōshū domain with promotion to samurai status and a one-time payment of 25 *koku* of rice—enough to cover his family expenses for several years.[10] Thereafter, he worked in Murotsu as a shipping agent, taking advantage of the fact that, after 1873, Murotsu became a scheduled stop on one of the earliest steamship routes between Osaka and Shimonoseki. In addition, he was active in a company called the Jun'ekisha, managed by Yoshida Shūzō (1854–1939). Shūzō, who was the adopted son of revolutionary sympathizer Kenzō, was the eleventh-generation head of Murotsu's Yoshida household, and from 1892 he served as the first postmaster of the Murotsu Post Office. From the few records that remain, it appears that the company—whose characters connote "prosperity" and "profit"—was a financial institution that lent money to passing shippers and thus inherited the functions of the Murotsu and Kaminoseki *koshini* branch offices, which had been abolished in 1873.[11] That business was indeed profitable is suggested by Ogata's construction of the Shikairō at the end of the decade. The total costs of the building amounted to a stunning 3,000 yen—just under ten times the combined village income raised through local levies, education fees, and festival levies in the following year.[12] Ogata planned to recoup some of his investment by promoting the facility as an upper-class inn for steamship captains during their overnight mooring in port; he was thus banking on being in a position to exploit the boom in Inland Sea steamshipping that would occur over the following decade.[13]

The extent of the Yoshida and Ogata households' economic success can be gauged by examining tax records from the new municipality of Murotsu village, which combined the Edo period port and inland areas. Unfortunately, no documents survive concerning the local administration of the national land tax—a deeply unpopular levy on individual landowners first introduced in 1873 and calculated as a fixed percentage of land value. But there are some detailed records relating to the Rules on Local Tax (*chihōzei kisoku*), promulgated in 1878.

One element of these local taxes was the "household tax" (*kosūwari*), which was set by individual villages.[14] According to records from the 1890s, Yoshida Shūzō was consistently Murotsu's highest taxpayer, followed by Yoshizaki Naosuke (1838–1898), the eighteenth-generation head of the Yoshizaki household; Ogata Kenkurō and a man called Matsumae Matsunosuke were the only households levied in band 3 of the household tax. There were thirty-one such bands by the early 1890s, and the difference in rates between the top handful of households and the forty or so that were consistently ranked in the bottom band reveals the huge disparity of wealth in late-nineteenth-century Murotsu. In October 1891, for example, Yoshida Shūzō paid 2,540 times more household tax than his fellow villager Yamada Hatsugorō. Between them, just four households out of the 538 taxed that year—Yoshida, Yoshizaki, Ogata, and Matsumae—contributed 9 percent of the total tax levy. This was equivalent to the tax returns of the bottom 230 households.[15]

A second element of the 1878 local tax system was business taxes (*eigyōzei*) and miscellaneous taxes—which in Murotsu and Kaminoseki's case were used to levy tax on fishermen (*gyogyōzei*). The business tax records from Murotsu reveal the relatively high number of trade brokers and shipping agents that remained in the port even as *kitamae*-ship business started to decline.[16] By the turn of the 1890s, however, that decline was beginning to affect even Murotsu's richest households: of twelve business bands, Yoshida Shūzō dropped from band 2 in 1887 to band 4 in 1893, Ogata Kenkurō dropped from band 2 to band 3 in the same period, and Yoshizaki Naosuke dropped from band 4 to band 5.[17] It is surely not coincidental that the same period saw a sudden decrease in the number of steamships stopping in port;[18] indeed, these changed conditions may have been a factor in Yoshizaki Naosuke's decision, in 1892, to stop selling sake and thus end 150 years of Higo-ya household tradition.[19]

The lower ranking of the Ogata, Yoshida, and Yoshizaki households in the business category of the local tax thus suggests that the main source of income for all three came from their landholdings. Fragmentary records indicate that the value of the Yoshida household's total landholdings in 1893 was a little over 1,700 yen; the second-richest landowner was the Yoshizaki household, at nearly 1,100 yen; and Ogata Kenkurō was the fourth-richest landowner in the village, at nearly 500 yen.[20] To put this in context, the average annual income for a five-person farming household in Kumage county in 1891 was just under 50 yen.[21] Such land assets were considerably lower than those of comparable village elites in other parts of Japan: the Aizawa household in the village of Aihara, on the Kantō Plain west of Tokyo, owned farmland and woodland of much greater value in the same period.[22] But the Murotsu figures tell us nothing about other sources of income for the village's leading families—from moneylending to their poorer compatriots, for example, or from charging rent to their tenants. A survey of buildings in July 1892 does reveal that in addition to Yoshida Shūzō's large ancestral residence—three houses totaling 146 *tsubo* (481 square meters), plus five warehouses totaling seventy-four *tsubo*—he also owned at least another thirty-one residential properties for rent throughout the village. For his part, Ogata Kenkurō was landlord of another twenty-four properties; Yoshizaki Naosuke, eight; and the aforementioned Matsumae Matsunosuke, sixteen.[23] By contrast, the size of the poorest households in the "inland" districts of the village was four *tsubo* (thirteen square meters)—a single room with a cheap thatched roof.

These numbers give quantitative substance to the bleak scenes of rural inequality depicted by Nagatsuka Takashi in his 1910 novel *Tsuchi* (The Soil), set in Ibaraki prefecture, north of Tokyo. In the novel, the daily suffering of the protagonist, Kanji, is contrasted to the affluence of East Neighbor (otherwise known as the Master).[24] Yet East Neighbor's economic position brings with it certain social responsibilities: he provides work to impoverished farmers such as Kanji;

his wife, the Mistress, doles out food and money when Kanji is lacking; and both the Master and the Mistress intercede to resolve disputes between villagers. In these instances, fiction surely reflected fact: thus, in late-nineteenth-century Murotsu, those households at the apex of village society, such as Yoshida, Yoshizaki, and Ogata, would have performed similar roles to that of the Master.

Moreover, village leadership brought with it significant fiscal responsibilities. As central government increasingly dictated the types of general budgets on which local tax revenues should be spent—police expenditure, epidemic prevention, bureaucratic administration, and so on—there was less money for village authorities to invest in major projects that might benefit only their own individual municipalities, such as new school buildings or new headquarters for the village office.[25] By the early 1900s, the Home Ministry was actively urging that more private contributions for such projects be solicited from local elites and even from ordinary villagers.[26]

In this duty, the Murotsu elites were magnificent in their beneficence. In 1904, for example, Yoshizaki Eisuke (1878–1952)—adopted son of Naosuke and nineteenth-generation head of the Yoshizaki household—gave the elementary school 22 yen for an electricity generator. In March 1910, he donated four hundred books to the children's section of the village library, including a series on world history; Eisuke would continue to give most generously to the school over the next two decades, including 250 yen for furnishings and equipment in 1934.[27] Yoshida Shūzō, for his part, also contributed toward the improvement of school facilities: he gave 6 yen toward the purchase of a violin in 1902, 22.75 yen for an extractor fan in 1908, and 30 yen toward furnishings and equipment in 1922. But he also made more significant investments for the welfare of the village: 350 yen toward the construction of the new village office in 1914 (around a third of the total budget), 300 yen for the establishment of a telephone network in 1928, and 50 yen toward road repairs in the hamlet of Shida in 1932. In 1918, he also joined with Yoshizaki Eisuke in making respective donations of 100 yen and of 50 yen toward an emergency fund set up to subsidize the local price of rice during a period of nationwide riots, and both men gave the same amounts toward the upkeep of the village police in 1920.

The above list is by no means an exhaustive account of elite largesse to the village. Men like Yoshida, Yoshizaki, Ogata, and other bureaucrats and village councillors made additional, much smaller donations of 1 or 2 yen on an almost annual basis. In this they were often joined by the nonelite majority, especially when it came to benefactions to the school. Moreover, until around the end of the nineteenth century, many of the most senior local bureaucrats contributed to the village by working for free. In Kaminoseki, for example, with one exception the village mayor did not draw a salary between 1889 and 1946; one of the two positions of assistants to the mayor (*joyaku*) was also an honorary post up until the Second World War.[28] Although this phenomenon reminds us that public office for much of the post-1868 period was effectively limited to men of independent means, it is nevertheless another example of elite largesse.

Thus in donations and honorary work, as in many other aspects of post-Meiji village life, economically prosperous households led the way, and both Murotsu and Kaminoseki municipalities would have been significantly poorer without them.

The Rules on Local Tax had been introduced in 1878 as one of the so-called Three New Laws by which the Meiji government completely overhauled the organization of local government, establishing a system of counties (*gun*), towns and villages (*chō/son*), and prefectural assemblies (*kenkai*). In 1880, a fourth law was introduced on rules for city, town, and village assemblies, the selection of which was to be determined by local authorities. In both Kaminoseki and Murotsu, the first elections under the new system were held in April 1889. The electorate comprised male household heads, aged twenty-five or above, who had been resident in each respective village for at least two years previously and who paid 2 yen or more in national land tax. In total, this meant that there were 938 eligible voters in Kaminoseki (to elect eighteen councillors) and 228 voters in Murotsu (to elect twelve).[29] Although no statistics on the contemporary population of both villages remain, from tax data it seems probable that just over a third of Murotsu household heads were enfranchised at the time of the first election for the village assembly.[30]

By any standard, this marked a significant increase in the number of men directly participating in the political process from the handful of key households that had been active during the turbulent 1860s and among whom the key administrative positions of the Edo period—village headman, port elder, and so on—had been shared. Yet the result of the Murotsu elections seemed in many ways to confirm the status quo: Yoshida Shūzō, Yoshizaki Naosuke, and Ogata Kenkurō numbered among the first twelve village councillors elected in 1889 along with Matsumae Matsunosuke, the fourth-highest taxpayer in the village. Six of the twelve councillors, moreover, were merchants and the other six farmers.[31]

Such occupational representation was significant because of the nature of some of the disputes that village leaders were called upon to mediate. In 1894, for example, four prominent merchants wrote to the Murotsu authorities to complain about the behavior of village fishermen. The liberalization of fishing rules after the collapse of the Tokugawa *bakufu* had led to considerable numbers of outside fishermen sailing their boats to the once "privileged" waters of Kaminoseki, Murotsu, and nearby Murozumi.[32] For Murotsu brokers, more fishermen meant more fish to sell and thus greater profits: by 1894, seafood was the single most important export from the village, with 70 percent of sales made to markets in Kobe and Osaka, and the remaining 30 percent to those in Hiroshima.[33] Moreover, as the petition explained, the "two or three hundred" large vessels that docked in the port each winter were "exactly like an ordinary family on the land" and as such supported the wider port economy.

For obvious reasons, Murotsu fishermen appear to have felt differently about so many boats trespassing (as they might have seen it) on "their" waters. Although the petition gives no details, the merchants explain—with remarkable myopia—that "for some unknown reason the fishermen of our village joined together to resist these outside fishermen and finally forced them to leave the port. . . . [Concerning this matter,] we appealed to the fishermen of this village to stop denying the entry of outside fishermen. However, not only did they equivocate and state that they could not do this; they also said that our petition was unfair and would cause them to lose out." The merchants appeal to the "wise and fair judgment" of village administrators to "free the merchants from their difficulties."[34] The outcome of this particular petition is unclear, but seven years later a survey of fishing vessels in Iwaishima waters during the month of September discovered that 13 percent of the 3,400 boats came from outside Yamaguchi prefecture and 55 percent from outside Kumage county.[35] From a fisherman's point of view, outsiders were still a problem.

A major industry was thus politically disenfranchised in Murotsu village—and, we may assume, in Kaminoseki village as well. It may be that some merchants on the village assembly occasionally put aside their own commercial interests in order to support the fishermen, but the late-nineteenth-century composition of the assembly meant that when disputes arose over how to exploit the sea as a natural resource, the voices of the fishermen were less likely to be heard.

TABLE 4.1

Next-door neighbors among the Kaminoseki political elites, 1896

Name	**Household Name (*yagō*)**	**Status in 1896**	**Address (*banchi*)**
Kuniyuki Kazuo	Kogome-ya	mayor	479
Suzuki Torasuke	Tosa-ya	councillor	500
Akimoto Shukutarō	Hano-ya	village clerk	501
Sakata Tasaburō	unknown	councillor	503–504
Futami Yasaburō	Futagami-ya	councillor	511–514
Odamura Magosaburō	unknown	councillor	515–516
Tominaga Isaemon	Abura-ya	former councillor	520
Kanō Sauemon	Kaga-ya	councillor	547
Nagai Jūkichi	Nagasaki-ya	councillor	563–566

Source: Based on a wooden panel listing the Kaminoseki village office ceremony attendees, discovered by the late Nishiyama Hiroshi and announced in *CS*, 3 November 2007, p. 28. I am grateful to Mr. Nishiyama for showing me the original panel. Other data from KYM 66; *TD* (Nagashima); Tanizawa, *Setouchi no machinami*, pp. 75, 85; Yamaguchi-ken Monjokan, *Kaminoseki-chō Kuniyuki-ke monjo, Sakuraya-ke monjo, Yoshizaki-ke monjo*, p. 6.

Note: There was another village councillor, Kōchiyama Kanesuke (or Kensuke), who was descended from a port shipping agent, the Daikoku-ya, whose address I have been unable to trace.

The Izuta Household (Izumo-ya)

In Kaminoseki, results of the village assembly elections underlined political and social continuities to an even greater extent than in Murotsu. In July 1896, a new village office was constructed on land previously owned by a former senior village headman of the county, the Odamura household. The names, titles, and addresses of nine of the attendees to the opening ceremony are shown in Table 4.1. Other than Mayor Kuniyuki, who lived a two-minute walk to the west, and Councillors Kanō and Nagai, who lived a two-minute walk to the east, four of Kaminoseki's eighteen village councillors, plus one former councillor, were next-door neighbors. Their houses, moreover, were clustered in a district known as Ebisu-machi, which had been the commercial heart of the port area during the Edo period and which boasted the highest land prices in the whole of the municipal village (including Iwaishima and Yashima) well into the twentieth century.[36] In other words, three decades after the downfall of the Tokugawa *bakufu,* a clique of Edo period elites—many of them, judging by their household names, descendents of shipping agents—still formed an oligarchy of political power in Kaminoseki.

In order to understand how there was such continuity of village elites, even under the new electoral system, we can examine the career of another village councillor present at the 1896 ceremony, a man by the name of Izuta Masakichi (1833–1910), who represented Iwaishima. Izuta also served as "honorary assistant to the mayor" (*meiyō joyaku*) between 1893 and 1909, and until the construction of the new village office, his private Iwaishima house had served unofficially as the administrative center of the island. Thus in 1891, when Matsumoto Bukichi and his wife decided to seek work in Hawai'i (see Chapter 5), they went along to the "village office" (*yakuba*) within the Izuta household in order to complete their paperwork.

It is unclear exactly how the Izuta family had come to be so prominent by the late nineteenth century. The household, the Izumo-ya, is not thought to have performed the role of village headman (*shōya*) during the Edo period, although oral tradition on Iwaishima remembers it as being very rich.[37] Masakichi himself apparently had a business as a pawnbroker, which would have placed him at the hub of a network of financial transactions throughout the island.[38] If we further assume that he was involved in moneylending—as with the Yoshida and Ogata households in Murotsu—then he would also have found himself at the hub of a network of social obligations.[39] In addition, Masakichi was apparently entrusted with surveying and drawing up the first village property maps of the modern period.[40] Again, this position placed him at the heart of island society as a mediator in disputes and a judge in the complicated process of converting oral ownership claims into written form.

Although there is no evidence to suggest that Masakichi himself abused such influence, stories are told in Kaminoseki of particular prewar mayors and village councillors swindling less powerful landowners out of property deeds—stories that indicate the political and social significance of Masakichi's role.[41] As for his own landholdings, surviving records from the 1890s show that Masakichi held the rights not only to land in Iwaishima, but also to what had previously been the ceremonial heart of Kaminoseki port, namely, the area leading up to the domain-owned official guest complex.[42] That Masakichi came to own this land after 1868 suggests close ties between the Izuta household and domain authorities in the late Edo period, even if the household never actually became Iwaishima headman.

In other words, Izuta Masakichi was the face of local government, a man to whom you would go for help with paperwork or to settle a problem with your neighbor, a man who knew the power of the written word and whose business could offer you money if land taxes or rents became unmanageable in a period of deflation. He was, in short, a man whom it would be wise not to cross.

Izuta Masakichi was also the chief electoral officer (*senkyo gakarichō*) of Iwaishima in both 1889 and 1895—the two elections when he was elected councillor.[43] More precisely, he was an election official for the so-called Second Tier elections, held in most parts of the village on the day before the First Tier elections but in Iwaishima on the same day. Under the first elections for the village council, eligible voters were split into two tiers. This division was made by drawing a line at half the total value of national tax (*kokuzei*) contributions of the village as a whole: those electors who together had contributed the upper 50 percent were deemed First Tier and able to elect nine councillors (six in the case of Murotsu), while those electors who had contributed the remaining 50 percent also elected nine councillors. But since tax contributions were graded according to wealth, rich landowners or merchants who paid a large amount of tax were fewer in number than smaller landowners who contributed less. Thus in Kaminoseki's first village council election of 1889, there were 220 electors in the First Tier compared to 718 electors in the Second Tier, yet the electorate of each tier was given the powers to elect nine councillors.[44] This meant there was one councillor for every 24.4 voters in the First Tier compared to one for every 79.8 voters in the Second Tier: the richest elite in Kaminoseki thus effectively wielded three times the voting power of smaller landowners and merchants.

Despite this imbalance, we might expect that voters in the Second Tier would have elected one of their kind to represent their interests, ensuring at least a semblance of economic diversity on the village council. In fact, however, electors could vote for "candidates" in either rank so that someone like Izuta Masakichi—whose tax payments qualified him as a First Tier voter—was in fact returned as a Second Tier councillor for his two six-year terms, 1889 to 1901.[45] A similar situation occurred in Murotsu, where Yoshida Shūzō, Yoshizaki Naosuke, and Ogata Kenkurō were elected as Second Tier councillors in 1889 and where all three men also served as election officials, thus monitoring the very elections in which they themselves ended up being successfully elected candidates.[46]

At the end of Nagatsuka Takashi's novel *The Soil,* a fire razes Kanji's humble dwelling and that night spreads its destruction to the house of East Neighbor. The next morning, a large crowd gathers to help: "Their attention focused on the master," writes Nagatsuka, "less out of gratitude for what he had done for them in the past than out of concern for the future. The night before they had been invisible. In the light of day they knew they would be seen by the master's family and their contributions noted."[47] In this sentiment, we might speculate, lies the key to understanding why electors in the 1890s voted into office the village's traditional elites. Those elites—the Yoshida, Yoshizaki, and Ogata households in Murotsu; Odamura and Kanō in Kaminoseki; Izuta in Iwaishima—had contributed to the wider community as businessmen, taxpayers, donors, moneylenders, landlords, and administrators. But elections were a time when the "contributions" of the voters could be noted—even though the ballots were meant to be secret.

The bureaucrats and leaders of Meiji period Kaminoseki and Murotsu were thus rich merchants and farmers whose prosperity in the late Edo period carried over into the post-Restoration years. Even as the new nation state centralized and regulated power through new structures of local administration, local elections, and infrastructure such as schools and roads, the Yoshidas and Yoshizakis of this world were able to turn those new structures to their advantage and use them to maintain their traditional grip on local power. They were able to do so not only because of their huge wealth relative to other villagers, but also because of their social influence in the community.

But such influence would not last forever. True, the mayor of Murotsu village municipality between 1913 and 1925, and again between 1929 and 1930, was Yoshizaki Eisuke, nineteenth-generation head of the Higo-ya household and thus a descendent of an Edo period village headman and wholesale agent. Meanwhile, his counterpart in Kaminoseki between 1919 and 1927 was also descended from an agent household, the Sakura-ya (see Chapter 2).[48] But the fact that Yoshizaki Eisuke sold the Higo-ya residence in 1934[49] and moved out of central Murotsu indicated that family fortunes were on the wane by the mid-twentieth century. In the case of the Ogata household, moreover, there was no family connection to the village at all after the death of Kenkurō's son Naoto in 1928, while the Yoshida family also moved away from Murotsu sometime after the death of Shūzō in 1939. As the influence of the traditional elites began to wane, new types of village councillors began to appear—men who had made their money neither in village farming nor in commerce, but sometimes in business ventures much further afield. By the 1960s, moreover, the streets of Kaminoseki that had been home to the port's political and economic elites took on a new residential character: a significant number of fishing households moved down from their former dwellings in the "inland area" to buy properties vacated by departing merchant households. In this way, they could live closer to their boats—boats now moored in waters that were once crowded by passing *kitamae*-ships.[50]

And yet old community structures died hard. During the five-year period that I intermittently spent on Iwaishima conducting fieldwork, the district head (*kuchō*) of the island was Mr. Izuta Tasuku, the great-grandson of Izuta Masakichi.

From a set of official village records such as the Murotsu collection, it is impossible to tell how the Yamada Hatsugorōs of the late nineteenth century felt about their political and economic superiors. But we can be certain that people such as Yamada, men or women who lived with their families in rented, drafty, one-room huts and who were charged 0.002 yen a year in household tax (whether they could pay is a different matter), would have been well aware of their marginal position in village affairs compared to the elite households. In this sense, Ogata Kenkurō's four-storied Shikairō, which was restored at great expense between 1999 and 2001, stood above the village community in more ways than one: it was also symbolic of a political structure in which great power was concentrated in the hands of a minority at the expense of many other village constituencies.

Indeed, for the members of one small group within the village, marginal status was explicitly branded onto their everyday interactions with other villagers. This was the *tokushu buraku* group—a term translated by some historians as "village ghetto" or "outcaste community." In 1842, the Chōshū domain had noted that there were thirty-two hereditary outcaste households (*eta,* literally "much impurity"), numbering 131 people, in Kaminoseki county.[51] At the time, these people had no surnames: indeed, only a few non-samurai elites, such as the Yoshizaki, Ogata, and Yoshida households in Murotsu, were granted such a privilege. But from the early 1870s, the new Meiji government began to allow all commoners to use a surname, and by 1875 this had become a requirement so that the authorities could officially register each individual household (the *koseki* system).

For some people, this was a straightforward process: the characters needed to be easy to write, given that many rural villagers were still illiterate, and if they additionally gave some indication of a household's occupational or geographical roots in the village, all the better—hence the nationwide proliferation of surnames such as Western Mountain (Nishiyama), River Mouth (Kawaguchi), Middle-of-the-Rice-Paddy (Tanaka), or Mountain-Paddy (Yamada). It may be that men like Yamada Hatsugorō or his father had some choice in the matter of their own names, but household heads often appear, in the understated words of the *Kaminoseki Town History,* to have first "consulted with priests or with village leaders [*mura no yūshi*]."[52] Such consultation was probably encouraged so that poorer, marginal villagers did not inadvertently upset village hierarchies by choosing a name above their station.[53] But for the households of Murotsu's outcaste community, the assigned surname reminded the wider world of an Edo period status division that appears to have continued in daily practice even though it was abolished by an 1871 law: the characters of the surname mean "Outside of the Village" or simply "Outside Village." Such nomenclatural discrimination, which is often overlooked in the scholarly literature on the "outcaste" community, was an example of Edo period social prejudices continuing to affect everyday interactions in Murotsu well into the twentieth century.[54]

As the outcaste surname demonstrates, there were no generic "common people" in the late-nineteenth- or early-twentieth-century village. Instead, Murotsu and Kaminoseki were hometowns in which inequalities abounded—in the political, economic, and social spheres and also, as the next chapter details, in terms of ritual. The late-nineteenth-century documents rediscovered in a Kaminoseki warehouse may not be draft constitutions or political tracts, but they show a vitality and ruthlessness to everyday politics as significant for our understanding of Meiji Japan as the documents recovered in Fukasawa in 1968. As the village records reveal, the "people" in Murotsu and Kaminoseki—the leaders of the villages—molded a Meiji culture that was a good deal less democratic, though no less rich and complex, than that depicted by Irokawa Daikichi.

5

Ritual Culture and Political Power

August 1948, and the islanders of Iwaishima are preparing for a festival. Not the annual autumn celebrations that start at the Miyato Shrine and spill down onto the main beach, where the excitable youths of East Hamlet and West Hamlet charge their portable shrines into each other and the day ends up with (fairly) good-natured fisticuffs; rather, the preparations now taking place under the blazing summer sun are on an altogether bigger scale.

In the fallow fields of East Hamlet, men gather to construct a temporary shrine, some twenty meters by seventeen. Under the supervision of a master carpenter, they bind the roof's bamboo cross-slats with vines gathered from the forests of the island's uninhabited interior. In the shade of the village's narrow alleyways, the women work in neighborhood groups to weave thatched matting from *kaya* grasses cut and dried some months previously, to be laid on top of the roof. In the Ujimoto residence, not far from the temporary shrine, twenty-three-year-old Kuichi, who has just been adopted as heir to the Ujimoto household, is finalizing which young men will row in the twelve-boat parades, to be held on the first and last days of the festival. In the Matsumoto household, a ten-minute walk up from the beach, the women are undertaking one final cleaning: this is where the visiting priests will be staying during the week-long celebrations.

For this is no ordinary event: the *kanmai* is a set of rites held roughly once every four years, when priests from northern Kyushu sail to Iwaishima and perform a weeklong program of sacred dances (*kanmai* itself means "dance of the deities"). Except that four years previously, Japan was in the midst of war and it was no time for sacred dances. Indeed, for reasons that are unclear, 1948 is the first *kanmai* to be held since 1933, and while there is a tradition that

Figure 5.1. Iwaishima's *kanmai* festival, 1948 (Courtesy of Morita Shigeo)

bachelor villagers working in the far-off cities of Kobe or Osaka usually try to return home at least once every four years for the *kanmai*, this year sees the participation of returnees from much farther afield: in the case of Ujimoto Kuichi, from the seas north of Hokkaido, where he had been on naval duty in anticipation of a Soviet invasion; for Matsumoto Takeji, from the Imperial Palace, where he had been part of an elite corps protecting the emperor from no-surrender radicals in the army; in the case of many others, from the bloody battlefields or prisoner-of-war camps of the Southeast Asian archipelago. And of course there are scores of young men and women, some 116 from Iwaishima alone, who have not returned at all.[1]

Yet amongst all this bustle and activity, daily life continues. The months between mid-July and late September are the height of the lucrative sardine-fishing season, so most days teams of boats manned by young men row forth and extend large nets into the stretch of sea, some four kilometers wide, that divides Iwaishima from western Nagashima. From the surface of the water it can be difficult to spot the shimmering ripples that indicate a shoal of passing sardines, so older children in the elementary school grounds, above the Matsumoto house, guide the nets from a distance, using flags to communicate to the boats out at sea. When they are later signaled the extent of the catch, these same children will run back down into the village to tell their mothers and grandmothers so that vast pots of water can be put on to boil in advance of the nets' return. Though nobody knows it, these years in the late 1940s will be the zenith of the sardine-fishing industry, and decades afterward elderly villages will recall the 1948 *kanmai* and the sardine nets in the same breath, as if to mark some kind of connection between livelihood and ritual.

The connection between livelihood and ritual, and between ritual and politics is the focus of this chapter. For "politics" in modern Kaminoseki was never simply a matter of bureaucratic administration, council elections, or aggrieved petitions: politics seeped into the spaces in which people gathered, the shrines at which they worshipped, the land that they tended, and even the person that they married.

The Ujimoto Household (Daidai-ya)

In the dense forests above Miura Bay, on the western side of Iwaishima, two stone relics mark the dwelling place of Kōjin, the Shinto deities who are generally worshipped in Japan's fields and mountains. According to the oldest surviving document concerning the *kanmai,* a letter to Chōshū domain authorities dating from 1697, the Kōjin shrines were formally dedicated on the third day of the eight month in the Year of the Rat, during the reign of the emperor Rokujō (1168). The priests who made such a dedication were from the village of Imi, fifty kilometers west of Iwaishima, on the northern coast of Kyushu:

> The origin of the rites is as follows: when priests from Betsugū Hachiman shrine in Imi village, in the Kunisaki county of Bungo, went to the Imperial Capital [Kyoto] to receive their shrine's dedication, they anchored in Miura Bay in Iwamijima [Iwaishima] on their return journey. Although there were until that time just two or three houses in Miura in which people were living, the tutelary deity Kōjin was not being worshipped. For this reason there was no grain harvest: people spent their mealtimes eating only the fruits of the trees and the roots of the plants in season. Given these circumstances, tradition says that the islanders asked the Bungo priests and *miko* [shrine maidens] to dedicate the two Kōjin shrines. But because the islanders were eating only fruits and

> roots, they had nothing to offer the deities; and so they made a votive offering of the fruits of a hackberry tree. Thus even today we offer so-called hackberry cakes once every five years, on the occasion of the *kagura* [dances]. Because of these origins, the most important priests and *miko* of each generation come from both Imi and Noda villages, and thus the tradition of the *kagura* has been established.[2]

There were thus three key elements to the oral traditions of the *kanmai:*[3] (1) many centuries ago, there was no proper food supply in Miura because the Kōjin deities were not being revered by the two or three households then resident in the bay area; (2) thanks to the Imi priests, the Kōjin shrine was properly dedicated in 1168; (3) as a result of the Kōjin deities being properly worshipped, the harvest of the island dramatically improved. This last point is not explicitly stated in the 1697 document, but, both historically and in the present day, Iwaishima villagers have come to consider the *kanmai* as an "oral tradition of the island's development" (*shima no kaihatsu denshō*).[4]

The *kanmai* was thus a story of the birth and growth of an agricultural society, a narrative inextricably tied to the historical identity of the island as a whole—much as the identity of Oberammergau, in southern Germany, continues to be tied to the story of why the village's famous passion play was first performed.[5] And central to Iwaishima's foundational narrative was the notion that islanders owed two debts of thanks. One, externally, was to the priests from the Imi shrine in Kyushu. Thus the 1697 document states that in addition to the quadrennial *kanmai* rites that the Imi priests performed on Iwaishima, the islanders themselves made a reverse pilgrimage to Imi in the third month of each year to receive a talisman (*fuda*) with which to continue worshipping at the Kōjin shrines. This was an annual ritual that came to be known as the *tane-modoshi,* the "returning of the grains."

But the other, internal debt of gratitude was to the "Miura Three"—the three bay households that eventually (so oral tradition has it) transmitted knowledge of the new cultivation techniques to the island as a whole. In the Edo period, these households were known as the Yakushi-ya, the Shima-ya, and the Daidai-ya. In terms of literal meaning, Yakushi, a proper noun, suggests a ritual connection to the Buddha Yakushi. *Shima* (island) may refer to the second household's position as one of Iwaishima's founding fathers, while *daidai* is an orange tree that particularly grows in Miura Bay.[6] In the early 1870s, when commoners were allowed for the first time to take surnames, the first two households became, respectively, Yakushi and Shimanaka (Island-Middle), and their names alone may reflect the high regard—at least in ceremonial terms—in which they were held by islanders as a whole. But it was the surname adopted by the third Miura household that truly underlined the power of the *kanmai* oral traditions: the name Ujimoto, unique to descendents of the Daidai-ya on Iwaishima, means "origin of the clan."

The influence of the Ujimoto household was not merely reflected in its name. Along with two other (non-Miura) households, the head of the Ujimoto household served as hereditary lay priest for the Kōjin shrines, whose deities were removed from the Miura mountaintop to the grounds of the main village shrine, the Miyato Hachimangū, sometime in the nineteenth century.[7] Moreover, the household head also served as hereditary elder (*sōdai*) to the main Miyato shrine, thus supporting the ritual work of the shrine's full-time priest, the Moritomo household.[8] (Priest Moritomo, it appears, was not part of the original *kanmai* oral tradition, but it was nevertheless he who summarized that tradition in the 1697 letter to Chōshū authorities: the Moritomo priests therefore played a sponsorship and organizational role in the rites from a very early date.) The high status of the Ujimoto household also extended into the economic life of Iwaishima, both in terms of sardine net financing (below) and landownership. Thus, when Kuichi (1922–2006) was adopted into the household in 1948, he became heir to the largest landholdings of any single household on the island, including some of Iwaishima's only rice fields, in Miura Bay. His adopted father, Ujimoto Sōtarō, was joint top taxpayer on the island in that year—just as Sōtarō's own grandfather, Toyosaku, had been one of only five individuals to make the top donation of 85 *sen* toward the costs of the *kanmai* festival in 1896.[9]

Not surprisingly, the Ujimoto residence was one of the biggest in the village. As such, it was a natural place for members of the island Youth Association (formed 1913) to gather and socialize in the evenings. There were five such meeting places, spread throughout the village, including not only the Ujimoto household, but also the main Shimanaka household—another of the Miura Three. Here, as in Ujimoto, thirty or forty people at a time would squeeze into a couple of rooms to discuss village issues, share news from the outside world, plan for the next sports day or shrine festival, and once every four years decide on the teams of rowers for the so-called *kaidenma* boats that formed the *kanmai* welcoming parade.

There is nothing in the written records to suggest that the ritual, economic, and social status enjoyed by generations of Ujimoto was an inevitable consequence of the household's close connection to the *kanmai* rites as one of the Miura

Three. The Shimanaka household, for example, appears not to have been a major landowner in Iwaishima, and neither Shimanaka nor Yakushi were hereditary lay priests to the Kōjin shrines. Nevertheless, the ceremonial role played by Ujimoto every four years—the head of the household, dressed in a formal crested kimono, would officially welcome the Imi priests to Iwaishima by offering sake and poached bream—certainly bolstered the political leadership roles to which Ujimoto Kuichi aspired. By 1949, Ujimoto had become head of the Kaminoseki Village Combined Youth Association; and in his early fifties, he was elected to two prominent positions in island society: from 1972 to 1981, he served as head of the Iwaishima Farming Cooperative; and from 1970 to 1982, he was one of Iwaishima's three representatives on the Kaminoseki municipal town council.

The written and oral traditions concerning the origins of the *kanmai* were therefore one key to understanding the complex structure of Iwaishima's political, economic, ritual, and social networks in the twentieth century—networks that, as evidenced by Ujimoto Kuichi's multiple roles within island society, remained influential in the daily lives of islanders well into the postwar period. But the *kanmai* not only reaffirmed the status of individual households; more generally, it also underlined the fundamentally agricultural identity of island society. For although the point was not explicitly made in the 1697 document, islanders interpreted the *kanmai* traditions as a story in which knowledge of new crops had been introduced to a society that had "no grain harvest" but whose harvests thereafter grew substantially. Consequently, households that owned and farmed land came to be implicitly celebrated by the rituals. In the eighteenth century, moreover, there appears to have been very little chance to move from landless to landowning status. Although the number of households on the island more than doubled between 1738 and 1842, the increase was entirely in the landless sector: the number of landowning households remained constant, at seventy-six, for the whole of this period.[10] Thus, for all the splendor of the *kaidenma* parades at sea, and although the festival commemorated a connection between Iwaishima and northern Kyushu that was facilitated by the sea, power on the island came to be as much rooted in the land as the grains that the Imi priests had taught the Miura Three to cultivate.

The Matsumoto Household (Matsu-ya)

On the pebbly eastern beach of Iwaishima village, there once stood a huge pine tree (*matsu*), affectionately known to islanders as the "Thousand-Year

Pine." Children played in its shade, fishermen mended their nets under its canopy-like branches, and those households that could afford a camera posed next to its gnarled, ancient trunk for a family portrait.

In the spring of 1917, an Iwaishima native living in San Francisco, Matsubara Daikichi, paid for the erection of two stone monuments at the foot of the Thousand-Year Pine. The first, an obelisk on a three-stepped plinth, was engraved "A Monument in Honor of our Ancestors" (*shūso-hi*). The inscription recorded that Matsubara had crossed to the United States sixteen years previously, but such was his ongoing concern for his home village (*kyōdo*) that he had decided to erect a memorial to honor 750 years of his ancestors' souls. Matsubara thus dated Iwaishima's ancestral history to 1168—the year, according to the 1697 document, that the *kanmai* rites began.[11] The second stone was a cylindrical pillar with a rounded peak on which a large bronze eagle once spread its wings—until it was blown down by a typhoon in September 2004. This "Monument to the Loyal Dead" (*chūkon-hi*) listed soldiers from the island who had died in the Sino-Japanese (1894–1895) and Russo-Japanese (1904–1905) wars. Although Matsubara Daikichi's name was engraved on the base of the memorial, the eagle was a benefaction from Matsuoka Jinta, whose father had left Iwaishima in 1900 to start a new life in Korea.[12] Today, the two monuments have been joined by a third: a plain concrete cenotaph (*irei-hi*) dedicated to the twenty children from the island who lost their lives in a US bombing raid on Hikari city on 14 August 1945, less than twenty-four hours before Japan surrendered. But the Thousand-Year Pine is no more: the 1948 *kanmai* was to be its last, as it too was blown down by a typhoon in October 1951.

The Matsubara and Matsuoka households were members of the same landowning subgroup on Iwaishima. Such groups, some fifty in all, composed the *kabu-uchi* system.[13] The *kabu,* literally meaning "share," was a privately owned unit of land that could include both forests and fields. In a few cases, the *kabu* was managed within a single family, but the more common pattern was for the land to be distributed between up to half a dozen households, who together formed the *kabu-uchi* (the "inner *kabu*"). Each *kabu-uchi* was thus a basic team of landowning farming households whose members would help each other at harvest time or when it came to the clearing of new mountain land for cultivation.[14]

These practical, work-based partnerships were replicated at the ritual level: members of the *kabu-uchi* would also support each other through life's most expensive rites of passage, namely, weddings and funerals. Thus a funeral procession, for example, would be led by the household head (or successor) of the departed, carrying the mortuary tablet; next came members of the *kabu-uchi,* bearing rice, incense, and candles; and only then came the coffin, on a mounted carriage. In this way, members of the *kabu-uchi* played a symbolic role in lining the route between the worlds of the living and the dead—a role that was also spatially reflected by the close proximity of *kabu-uchi* household graves to each other. The practice of dividing land into *kabu-uchi* is thought to have ended sometime in the early Meiji period, by which time there were fifty-three such units.[15] But the social ties engendered by the *kabu-uchi* lasted well into the twentieth century—and indeed the funeral custom to a certain extent continues even today.

The significance of these ritual-social ties is illustrated by the Matsuya *kabu-uchi.* "Matsu-ya"—the pine tree was traditionally a symbol of good fortune in Japan—was the Edo period household name of the Matsumoto family. The Matsumoto household was one of the largest landowners on Iwaishima, and, along with the Ujimoto and the Tao households, it served as one of the hereditary lay priests of the Kōjin shrines. Moreover, the Matsumoto and Tao households, along with parish priest Moritomo, also hosted the Imi priests on the occasion of the weeklong *kanmai* festival. Matsumoto, in other words, was an elite household on Iwaishima, and the fact that the *kabu* name and the household name were the same indicates that it was also the principal landowner within the *kabu-uchi.* The junior members of the Matsuya *kabu-uchi* were the Matsubara, Matsuoka, Matsui, and Ebesu households. (It seems possible that the common root of the Meiji period surnames, with the exception of the final name, may reflect the Edo period membership that they all shared in the *kabu-uchi;* Matsumoto, which can mean "origin of the Matsu," would thus have referred to the principal household of the Matsuya *kabu.*)[16]

In March 1891, Matsumoto Bukichi and his wife Tsuru, then aged twenty-one and nineteen respectively, went to work in Hawai'i. Although their original contracts were only for three years, they ended up moving to San Francisco, where Bukichi became proprietor of the Sanyow Hotel.[17] In San Francisco he was apparently good friends with Matsubara Daikichi, the third son of the main Matsubara household, who in 1917 donated the two monuments under the Thousand-Year Pine. The fact that Matsubara, in California, could arrange for his Russo-Japanese memorial to include a bronze eagle donated by Matsuoka Jinta, in Busan, suggests that *kabu-uchi* ties survived even the separation of oceans.

By 1917, however, Matsumoto Bukichi had already returned to Iwaishima. In 1914 he bought up significant amounts of land in an area called Kitano, in the northwest of the island, and became a founder member of the Kitano Land Rationalization Union. To the tune of 25,575 yen, the fifty-nine members of the union invested in what was, to date, the most ambitious construction project in the history of Kaminoseki municipal village: a ten-year plan to construct a small reservoir so as to irrigate fifteen hectares of newly reclaimed rice paddies. (Other than the few fields in Miura, rice had never been grown on Iwaishima.) On the one hand, the scale of the project was indicative of the limitations of the *kabu-uchi* system: where five- or six-household units had been adequate for primitive clearing and land development in the Edo period, by the early twentieth century much bigger partnerships were necessary in order to exploit the potential of new national markets, new technology, and new opportunities to borrow money.[18] On the other hand, Bukichi was probably encouraged to invest his hard-earned American dollars in the scheme by one of the union's fund-raisers, Matsui Tasaburō, a fourth member of the Matsuya *kabu*. Such fund-raising exemplifies the ways in which *kabu-uchi* loyalties could still affect business transactions even when the original function of the *kabu-uchi* had itself been rendered obsolete.

To a certain extent, the *kabu-uchi* might be considered one example of horizontal relations within the village—bonds that transcended the Edo period stratifications of class and power.[19] Another example of such bonds was the practice of intermarriage. Until the immediate postwar years, the historical trend on Iwaishima had been toward "island marriages": thus, of the 202 marriages registered between 1945 and 1950—the period in which Ujimoto Kuichi was married—91 percent were endogamous partnerships in which both husband and wife came from Iwaishima.[20] Inevitably, on an island with a population of just over three thousand people, this led to a high degree of consanguinity. One medical report in the early 1950s estimated that perhaps as many as 30 percent of all children were born from "close relative" marriages (*kinshin kekkon*), leading to the potential for "geniuses or duds," as one elderly man told me with a smile, "but not much in between."[21]

The density of blood relations was heightened by the practice not only of women but also of men marrying into different households, leading to a highly confusing pattern of familial ties. For example, Matsumoto Bukichi, the former hotel proprietor, was an adopted son, having been born into the Tahara household. Bukichi's "new" father, Matsumoto Isuke, was also an adopted son, this time from the Yamato household, and Isuke married off his (much) younger sister, Yamato Tsuru, to Bukichi. That Bukichi married the woman who was effectively his adoptive aunt meant that the Matsumoto and Yamato households were joined by marriage across two generations. The Yamato household, meanwhile, had long ties to the Ujimoto household. Yamato Gosaku, the nephew of Matsumoto Isuke, was first cousins with Ujimoto Sōtarō; when Sōtarō and his wife Fusa were unable to conceive, it seemed natural for them to receive Yamato Gosaku's second son, Kuichi, as an adopted heir. (Kuichi's older brother, who succeeded as head of the Yamato household, married a daughter of the Yakushi household, one of the Miura Three.) Ujimoto Sōtarō's adopted son Kuichi was thus biologically his first cousin once removed, while Kuichi's new wife (who had been adopted into the Ujimoto household from one of the island's many Kogawa households) was the great-niece of Kuichi's adoptive mother, Fusa. Thus were the Ujimoto and Matsumoto households linked by the blood of the Yamato household as well as by the ritual duties they shared as lay priests of the Kōjin shrines.

In ritual terms, the Ujimoto household was further linked to the Shigemura household through membership of the same *kabu-uchi*. Ujimoto Kuichi and Shigemura Sadao (1922–2011) had also been classmates at elementary school, and, like Kuichi, Sadao was an adopted son. Sadao's "new" father, Shigemura Hatsukichi, was the first postmaster on Iwaishima. Many years previously, Shigemura had adopted and raised four of the grandchildren of his own (much) older sister Haru, who had married Yoshida Genkichi, owner of the most successful sardine-fishing company on Iwaishima (see below). The eldest of these four Yoshida/Shigemura children, Sadako, became the bride to Sadao, while Sadako's younger sister married into the Shinagawa household. Shigemura Sadao, for his part, had originally been born into the Izuta family as the youngest of eight children. His biological father, Izuta Magokichi (son of aforementioned Izuta Masakichi), was an adopted son from the Ishimaru household, and Magokichi's wife came from the Ebesu household. Their eldest son and Sadao's oldest brother, Izuta Masaji, married a woman from the Sugiyama household; in turn, one of her sisters married into the Kunihiro household (hosts of the *kanmai* priests in 1972, 1976, and 1980), while one of her brothers married the sister of Shimanaka Hiroshi, town councillor from the 1960s to the 1980s and head of a branch (*bunke*) of one of the Miura Three households. Meanwhile, Shigemura Sadao's second eldest brother, Takeji, became an adopted son for the Ebesu household, thus continuing for a second generation the ties between the Izuta and Ebesu households that had been started by his mother. The Ebesu household was a member of the original Matsuya *kabu-uchi*—and so we arrive back, exhausted, at the Matsumoto household.

To map out these bonds of marriage and land on a piece of paper, as I have tried to do on numerous occasions, produces a spider's web of migraine-inducing complexity. But that, perhaps, is the point of the exercise: there was a complex web of social relations that bound Iwaishima society together throughout the centuries, of which I have described only a tiny part. Yet even within that tiny part, a pattern emerges: the Matsumoto, Tahara, Yamato, Ujimoto, Shigemura, Yoshida, Shinagawa, Izuta, Ishimaru, Ebesu, and Sugiyama households—eleven of the fifteen names mentioned above—were all among the top 15 percent of contributors to the 1896 *kanmai* festival. If such donations indicate gradations of economic power, then these households constituted part of the economic elite of the island.[22] The *kabu-uchi* and the practice of intermarriage may have been horizontal ties that bound society together, but they nevertheless reinforced the ritual, social and economic connections between landowning households.[23] In this way, the spider's web ultimately strengthened the basic hierarchical structure—the vertical structure—of island life, where owning land gave one a much higher social, political, ritual, and even economic status than that of a landless fisherman.

Nowhere were such hierarchical realities as keenly felt as in the fishing industry itself—particularly in the sardine-nets business. In the Edo period, primary rights over sardine nets had been one of the "privileges" designated to certain coastal hamlets by the Chōshū domain in return for the provision of corvée labor by those hamlets. Murotsu and Kaminoseki ports were two such privileged communities (*tateura*), whereas Iwaishima was a nonprivileged port (*haura*) that had to pay the privileged village a premium in order to be allowed to practice net fishing.[24] By the 1910s, however, the system had been liberalized and sardines had become the single most important catch in Kaminoseki municipal village (including Iwaishima), in terms of both weight and income: although all fishing data are notoriously unreliable, villagers appear to have netted between 100,000 and 130,000 kilograms of sardines in both 1913 and 1914.[25]

Sardine fishing required large nets that were manipulated by several boats and by a crew of around twenty men.[26] Given the major investment necessary for such nets, there were generally two methods of finance in Kaminoseki: private finance, where an individual investor, the *amimoto,* bought the net with his own capital; or joint-stock finance, where up to twenty households combined to buy a net, in return for which they each became a shareholder (*kabunushi*) in what was effectively a limited stock company.[27] On Iwaishima, there were three such companies and three individually owned (*amimoto*) nets; on the island of Yashima, all nine nets were owned by five individual *amimoto* households.

Despite a 1901 Fishing Law stating that net rights belonged to the village cooperative, in practice the *amimoto* households wielded individual control over rights for sardine nets (which they themselves had often been the first to develop).[28] Consequently, any household that could not afford to invest in a joint-stock company but that nevertheless wanted to participate in the lucrative sardine business had no choice but to become an employee of the *amimoto* household. By so doing, it was guaranteed a proportion of each daily catch—but a much smaller proportion than the *amimoto* household itself. Thus, in prewar Yashima, a single *amimoto* took 50 percent of the catch and divided the other 50 percent among his twenty or so employees—the equivalent of a chief executive officer awarding himself a salary twenty times higher than his workers.[29] In postwar Iwaishima, the *amimoto* claimed 40 percent of the catch, meaning that he would still take home more than ten times the catch of his employees.

The consequence of this system on Iwaishima was a solidification of landowners' grip on the overall economy of the island. For example, one of the aforementioned elite landowning households, the Yoshida, was among the top 15 percent of donors to the 1896 *kanmai* (donors who paid 70 *sen* and above). The household thus appears to have had the means to invest in their own net as *amimoto* sometime in the early twentieth century, and, by 1948, Yoshida Genkichi, *amimoto* of the Yoshida family net, was the joint top taxpayer on Iwaishima—along with Ujimoto Sōtarō.[30] For his part, Ujimoto Sōtarō was a shareholder in the Daitōsha Company net, while the Matsumoto household owned two shares in the Amagusa Company net, thus doubling its allocated catch compared to regular shareholders—who themselves claimed a higher proportion of the catch than the nonshareholding laborers who were actually operating the nets. Given that dried sardines could be used as fertilizer in the fields so as to increase productivity, this was a win-win situation for farming households that owned land.

Sardine fishing thus reflected and also exacerbated the stratification of income and power in mid-twentieth-century Kaminoseki. The households that made the original investment in nets (either as *amimoto* or as shareholders) had to be prosperous in the first place, politically connected in order to protect their rights, comfortable with the leadership entailed in employing a score of men and the secondary laborers required to boil the sardines, and owners of sufficient land on which to lay out the fish to dry. Moreover, the profit structure of the industry served to solidify the position of *amimoto* as leaders in the political sphere. On Yashima, the district head (*kuchō*) between 1947 and 1955 was Ōshita Kameo, whose father had been *amimoto* to the Tsurui nets, while Ōshita's successor, Ishizaki Oji (1955–1982), was grandson of one of the original five *amimoto* on the island.[31] As a "boss" in employment terms, *amimoto* could call on favors and service at almost any time; as wielders of such power, it was not surprising to see them become "bosses" in the political world as well.[32]

An outside observer to Iwaishima's 1948 *kanmai* would doubtless have been impressed by the organization, the group ethic, and the sense of common purpose in the preparations. But beneath this apparently smooth surface, the hidden networks of hometown politics and economics were constantly at work: the men on the roof of the temporary shrine followed the directions of Kanata Fukuta, who was responsible for overseeing its construction, not just because he was a skilled engineer, but also because he was an *amimoto* and as such a man of great power. The shrine they were building, moreover, would serve as the stage for a ritual reenactment of the contributions of elite households to the historical development of island society.

The cyclical rituals of the *kanmai* and the *kabu-uchi* thus defined and simultaneously reinforced a basic division on Iwaishima between households that owned land and those that did not. The key point was less the size of the holding than the fact of owning it: to judge by a late Edo period list of names that survives on Iwaishima, landownership appears to have guaranteed if not a surname then at least the privilege of a household name (*yagō*)—a basic marker of identity that landless laborers were not accorded.[33] Indeed, in a limited physical space such as an island, many individually owned plots were actually very small, meaning that the Occupation-led land reforms (1946–1947) appear to have had very little impact on the overall structures of Iwaishima daily life—or, for that matter, on Nagashima life.[34]

As in the Kaminoseki port district, the sea connected Iwaishima to the outside world and was thus central to the development of a land-based agricultural community. But the story of that development was used to reinforce an insular, hierarchical conception of society in which vertical networks, as seen in the structure of sardine net ownership, effectively excluded fishermen from power. Throughout the postwar decades, Iwaishima would have the appearance of being half-farming, half-fishing (*han-nō, han-gyo*). But though this may have been approximately true in statistical terms (in 1975, there were 192 farmers and 174 fishermen on the island), the reality in terms of political influence was very different.[35] Just as there was a long tradition of individual households exerting an oligarchic control over village politics in Murotsu and Kaminoseki, so was there a long tradition in Iwaishima of landowning households exerting political power over nonlandowning households. Both traditions would play a role in the unfolding of the town's nuclear crisis in the 1980s.

PART III

Living with a Changing World

6

Overseas Migration at the Turn of the Twentieth Century

One of the most extraordinary aspects of Kaminoseki's modern history is also one of its least studied. From the late nineteenth century onward, hundreds of men and women left the town to earn money abroad, in Hawai'i, Korea, Taiwan, Canada, the South Seas islands, the mainland United States, Karafuto, Manchuria, China, Brazil, and Peru. Some stayed for many years or even their whole lives in their new host cultures; others worked overseas temporarily, for three or four years, in what seems to have been an international extension of the Edo period pattern of off-season out-migration. Today, however, only the vestiges of Kaminoseki's transnational era remain—objects such as Matsubara Daikichi's monument to his ancestors, erected in 1917 under Iwaishima's Thousand-Year Pine.

The record of the town's transnational era officially begins with a *Statement Concerning Emigration to the Kingdom of Hawai'i,* written on 1 November 1888 by the district head of Murotsu village, Yoshizaki Gisuke (no relation to the Yoshizaki household of Chapter 3). As Yoshizaki explained to the head of Kumage county, "Murotsu is by far the most impoverished village: there is [high] population relative to the amount of land, such that our economy could not survive without out-migration labor; we are in great hardship." Presently, "the authorities are recruiting for emigrants to the Kingdom of Hawai'i. Among our villagers, the number of applicants to the village office for such migration has reached approximately 150 men and women." But since the first information in 1884, he complains, there have been no subsequent announcements concerning recruitment; and moreover the rules and application procedures are unclear.[1]

Yoshizaki had good reason to be annoyed by the lack of progress in Kumage county, for in Ōshima county, a morning's sail to the northeast of the Kaminoseki straits, the situation was different. There, recruitment on the government-sponsored emigration program (*kan'yaku imin,* 1885–1894), under which 29,000 Japanese crossed to the (still independent) Kingdom of Hawai'i to work on three-year contracts, had been proceeding apace since the "information" in 1884. On the program's first official crossing, arriving in Honolulu on 8 February 1885, a third of the 944 laborers were residents of the islands of Ōshima county.[2] This established a trend that continued throughout the government-sponsored period: the vast majority of Hawaiian emigrants—some three-quarters in all—came from the western prefectures of Hiroshima and Yamaguchi, and more than 3,000 came from Ōshima alone.

Many of the emigrants' home villages were characterized by the kind of problems mentioned in Yoshizaki's *Statement,* in particular overpopulation and a historical reliance on seasonal out-migration labor. But these were hardly circumstances unique to Hiroshima or Yamaguchi. The fact that so many emigrants hailed from Yamaguchi in particular (10,424 out of 29,084 nationwide), suggests that other factors may have been at work. Many of the Chōshū domain's revolutionary generation of 1868, for example, were now highly placed in the new government—men such as Inoue Kaoru, who was foreign minister of Japan between 1879 and 1887, at the time that the new emigration program was established. Although Inoue himself is thought to have been cool to the idea of mass Japanese emigration,[3] he was nevertheless part of a network of politicians and businessmen who were enthusiastic promoters of the scheme.

The foreign minister was close friends, for example, with Robert Walker Irwin (1844–1925), an American businessman who had arranged for Inoue to visit the United States in 1876 and who later married a Japanese woman through Inoue's introduction.[4] Throughout 1884, Irwin lobbied Tokyo to accede to Hawaiian government demands that an emigration program be established to meet the kingdom's chronic labor shortage, and following his success he was employed as a special agent of the Hawaiian Bureau of Immigration. Irwin, in turn, was close friends with Masuda Takashi (1848–1938), who like Inoue Kaoru was a native of Chōshū. In 1876, Masuda founded the Mitsui Trading Company, which was one of the companies contracted to ferry the emigrants to Hawai'i from 1885 onward. Mitsui Trading further set up a separate company, Shōkyōsha, specifically to handle the recruitment and paperwork for emigration, and Masuda instructed his employees to recruit in the western prefectures of Yamaguchi, Hiroshima, Kumamoto, and Fukuoka in particular.[5] Masuda's weekly newspaper, the *Chūgai bukka shinpō,* advertised the benefits of Hawaiian migration in purple prose from late 1884 on, while in Yamaguchi prefecture the government-sponsored program was promoted in the *Bōchō shinbun* newspaper, which was founded in 1884 by Yoshitomi Kan'ichi, the first speaker of the prefectural assembly—and a childhood friend of Foreign Minister Inoue Kaoru.[6]

There was therefore an influential network of politicians, businessmen, and media proprietors whose interests and regional loyalties led them to focus the program's development on western Japan and on Ōshima county in particular. Indeed, Masuda Takashi claimed in his autobiography that he personally recommended to Irwin that workers be recruited in Ōshima, which in 1884 was the second most densely populated county in Yamaguchi.[7] Perhaps he had been made aware of Ōshima's economic plight by the prefectural governor, whom he met sometime in early December 1884: the governor explained that around four hundred islanders had already applied for the new program.

Kaminoseki was not entirely absent from national discussions during these planning stages: Masuda and the governor agreed at their meeting that successful applicants would sail to Yokohama on a chartered steamship leaving from Kaminoseki port. As it turned out, however, the ship left from the nearby—and bigger—port of Iwakuni.[8] Moreover, during the first four years of government-sponsored emigration, no applicants were accepted from either Murotsu or Kaminoseki villages, or indeed from Kumage county as a whole, despite its having the third-highest population density in the prefecture.[9] Hence the tone of frustration in Yoshizaki's 1888 *Statement*: the Murotsu applicants "cannot keep quiet," he wrote, "and have frequently made requests for [travel grants] to the village clerk. We ask that by means of some kind of special consideration, the wishes of the applicants be accepted. " Yoshizaki's appeal appears to have had an effect on the authorities. On the seventh official crossing of the program, which arrived in Honolulu on 26 December 1888, 73 applicants from Kumage county were accepted for the first time, including 38 from Murotsu village and 16 from Kaminoseki.

But who were these applicants lining up outside the village office? Why were they so "impoverished" that they wanted to leave? This chapter uses the rediscovered Murotsu documents to offer a more detailed analysis of some of the causes of Japan's overseas diaspora than has been previously attempted, in particular by linking the provenance of the overseas migrants to the Edo period administrative division of both Murotsu and Kaminoseki villages into "port" and "inland" areas. This longer perspective enables us to measure the economic decline of the straits communities in quantitative and qualitative terms, while Chapter 7 offers new evidence to highlight the equally understudied issue of the impact of the overseas communities on hometown life.

Okada Usuke (Inland Area to Hawai'i)

"I was born on March 20, 1888 in Murotsu-mura, Kumage-gun, Yamaguchi Prefecture, Japan. Koto Katsura was my mother, and Ukichi Okada was my father. I had two sisters—Ume, who was three years younger than I, and Mitsu, who was three years younger than Ume."

Thus begins the short unpublished autobiography of Okada Usuke, dictated in English to his daughter in Honolulu in the summer of 1967.[10] Okada left Japan in January 1908, having realized that he "could never be a success in Murotsu." In fact, he had a reasonable job in the years before he emigrated: from 1903 to 1905, he worked for Yoshida Shūzō, postmaster of the Murotsu village post office, for a salary of 8.25 yen a month. Compared to the wages of the "many people [who] were emigrating to Hawaii," however, the money must have seemed inadequate for a boy who wanted to become a "success."

Okada would have heard about such wages through an extensive network of family relations: his mother's cousin, for example, was already working in Honolulu in 1908 and lodged Usuke when he first arrived. These relatives sent home letters and news from across the Pacific—letters such as that written by Niikawa Ichisuke, son of a Kaminoseki shipbuilder, in May 1903.[11] After the opening formalities, Niikawa gives news of himself:

> As for me, I'm safely leading a pretty mundane existence, so please be at peace. These days, Hawai'i is also in a real slump, & monthly wages are falling. Until last year, men who worked in the hills [in the sugar fields] received 20 yen & women 12 or 13 yen, but from this year a man's 19 yen has become 18 & his 17 yen has become 16, & women get 9 yen. These are the wages for hill-work.
>
> But on the 13th of the new year, I myself entered the [sugar] mill. My wages in February were 19 yen, but now they've been raised to 23 yen. If I learn to speak English, they'll be raised again.
>
> The actual work isn't too tiring, but I'm in [the mill] from roughly six in the morning till five in the evening, so I do get tired of the place.
>
> I'm pretty sure that today is payday.[12]

Niikawa's letter helps explain the continued popularity of Hawaiian emigration on both sides of the Kaminoseki straits. He was writing at the height of the private emigration period (1894–1908), but the appeal of a contracted monthly wage—guaranteed even during a slump—held equally true two decades earlier.

At the beginning of the emigration program, a farmer in Ōshima county, for example, made an average wage of 3.2 yen per month (for a thirty-day month), although the poorest farmer laborers earned as little as 2.1 yen.[13] By contrast, a Hawaiian emigrant could earn about 17.7 yen a month (at 1885 exchange rates), with the additional security of a three-year contract and free accommodation.[14] Working conditions in Hawai'i were unremittingly harsh for the early emigrants, but as they began to send back wage remittances, rumors of Hawai'i as a place "to make money" spread throughout Ōshima—and presumably beyond, to neighboring islands and villages.[15] It was perhaps such rumors that emboldened at least three Murotsu men to break the rules and register as "temporary residents" of Ōshima, thus ensuring their passage to Hawai'i sometime before the first official Murotsu residents left in December 1888.[16] We do not know whether these three sent letters back home in the manner of Niikawa Ichisuke in 1903, but rumors, letters, and the hard evidence of wage remittances on neighboring Ōshima were probably as important in popularizing Hawaiian emigration in the Murotsu imagination as official reports and media campaigns.[17]

Such, in brief, were the "pull" factors. The "push" factors in the Inland Sea coastal communities of southeast Yamaguchi and southern Hiroshima prefectures included the collapse of the local bleached cotton industry owing to competition from cheaper Portuguese imports, the decline in salt production as a result of domain protection being removed after the Meiji Restoration, and, from the 1880s onward, the so-called Matsukata deflation. The latter referred to a range of monetary and fiscal policies introduced by then finance minister and Satsuma native Matsukata Masayoshi (1835–1924) in an attempt to deal with a crisis of confidence in the Japanese currency.

One consequence of the deflationary measures was a sharp decrease in the price of rice: whereas prices had risen by 100 percent during the period of rampant inflation, 1877–1881, they now fell more than 50 percent between 1881 and 1884; salt prices also halved during the period of the Matsukata deflation.[18] As impecunious farmers struggled to pay their land tax bills and other debts, and as their income from traditional by-employments also fell, the amount of tenant farmland increased by 12.8 percent nationwide between 1883 and 1907; the highest rates of increase were in northern Japan, whereas in Yamaguchi prefecture the average was 10.8 percent. Nevertheless, by 1897, half of all agricultural land in Kumage county was cultivated by tenant farmers, compared to a nationwide average of 45 percent.[19] Moreover, a survey of farming households in 1891 revealed that after Ōshima county, Kumage had the second-lowest average income per household in Yamaguchi prefecture: farmers earned just over 4.1 yen a month to split among a five-person household.[20] Although there are no figures from Murotsu or Kaminoseki to indicate the extent to which the accumulation of land by rich landowners increased in this period, we might guess that elite households such as the Yoshida, Yoshizaki, and Ogata bought up significant landholdings, while many other village households were rendered landless, debt-laden, and thus in urgent need of new sources of income.

For all these reasons, scholars of Hawaiian emigration have suggested that early emigrants were mainly poor, rural farmers.[21] But the emigrant data from Kumage county offer a more detailed insight into exactly who these "farmers" from Kaminoseki were. Between December 1888 and the last of the government-sponsored crossings in June 1894, just over 1,600 men and women from Kumage county went to work in Hawai'i. From within the county, the villages that sent the most emigrants were Murozumi (243), followed by Murotsu (223) and Kaminoseki (202).[22] In other words, three of the Chōshū domain's most prosperous Inland Sea ports in the 1840s were also responsible for sending Kumage's highest numbers of emigrants to Hawai'i at the turn of the 1890s. This suggests that the decline of domestic trade may have been the single most important push factor in explaining the popularity of Hawaiian emigration in Kumage county's port towns.

In fact, the story is more complicated than the initial statistics imply. Around half of the emigrants from Kaminoseki village came from the outlying islands of Iwaishima and Yashima, whose economies had been only marginally connected to the Edo period prosperity of Kaminoseki's port. So in order to establish a more definitive connection between port decline and Hawaiian emigration, we would need to know exactly where in a particular village the emigrants came from. We would expect, for example, to see a number of emigrants from the districts that in the Edo period had been known as the port area, but we would predict a higher proportion of emigrants from the inland area. This is because it was the inland area that had supported the influx of landless laborers from the mid-eighteenth century onward—people who had made a living by working in the ports and who thus had no property or alternative source of income to fall back on when trade through the ports collapsed.

In general, it is almost impossible to trace the precise provenance of each individual government-sponsored emigrant from Yamaguchi prefecture because their addresses were recorded using the old *yashiki-banchi* system. This was replaced by the current district (*ku*) and number (*banchi*) designation in the late 1890s, and the two systems appear at first sight to bear no relation to each other. But with the extraordinary richness of the Murotsu village archives and with extrapolation and educated guesswork based on contemporary maps and local land records (*tochi daichō*), it is possible to calculate the data in Table 6.1. Momentarily leaving aside the data on Korean emigration, Table 6.1 indicates that the majority of government-sponsored Hawaiian emigrants—over 60 percent—hailed from households located in the inland area of Murotsu hamlet. When we add the outlying (inland) hamlets of Ōtsu, Nerio, and Shida to the total, the proportion of inland area migrants from Murotsu village was closer to 80 percent.

Within Murotsu hamlet, the highest concentration of such emigrants was in Shirahama, a small community on the southern tip of the Murotsu peninsula, separated from the port area by a steep ridge—on top of which was the district of Yamaga, boasting the second-highest concentration of emigrants.[23] (Yamaga, literally "mountain house," was where Okada Usuke grew up; see Figure 2.2.) As long as the port's economy was growing, the majority of what were officially "farming" households in a district like Yamaga or Shirahama could survive without owning land: they could trek an hour up Mt. Ōza to till a small rented plot for their own needs and otherwise make do on their income from work in the port. But if the port no longer provided regular employment or by-employment, the picture changed. Thus, although Murotsu official Yoshizaki Gisuke identified the village's economic troubles in 1888 purely in terms of the "high population relative to the amount of land," perhaps he should have noted that such population density became a serious problem only after the *kitamae*-ships stopped docking and the port economy began to atrophy. As we have seen, this economic transformation was apparent by the turn of the 1880s, and, by the time Yoshizaki wrote his *Statement*, there was probably a strong connection between the decline of the port and the Hawaiian applicants who "cannot keep quiet."

The steady flow of emigrants to Hawai'i appears to have continued after the summer of 1894, when the government-sponsored program ended and the private emigration system was established. From this time until 1908, nearly five times as many Japanese crossed the Pacific as had during the decade of the government program—some 148,420 in total.[24] Calculating precise figures from

TABLE 6.1

Estimated provenance of Murotsu village emigrants by Edo period area

Modern District Name	Designation in 1842 (*Reports*)	Household Member to Hawai'i, 1888–1894		Household Member to Korea, up to 1910	
		Households	*% of subtotal*	*Households*	*% of subtotal*
Shirahama	[inland]	22	25.3	1	1.6
Shiraura	[inland]	8	9.2	4	6.3
Yamaga	inland	20	23.0	4	6.3
Maruyama	inland	4	4.6	4	6.3
Seto	port	0	0.0	10	15.6
Naka-machi	port	6	6.9	8	12.5
Hon-machi	port	11	12.6	11	17.2
Nishi-machi	port	0	0.0	3	4.7
Shin-machi	port	4	4.6	9	14.1
Address recorded but modern district unclear		12	13.8	10	15.6
Subtotal (Murotsu hamlet)		87	100	64	100
Outlying hamlets (Ōtsu, Nerio, Shita)		67	n/a	3	n/a
Address not recorded		0	n/a	88	n/a
Total households from Murotsu village		154	n/a	155	n/a

Source: Data from Oshima's Museum of Japanese Emigration to Hawai'i database; MYM 298, 772, 1076 (1 and 2), 1127; *BFC*, pp. 221–222.

Note: For ease of analysis, I have converted the total number of individual Hawaiian emigrants (223) to a figure based on the household unit: if two emigrants (e.g., two males) had as their address the same *banchi* number, I assumed that they were brothers and counted them as one household.

Murotsu and Kaminoseki is extremely difficult, as demonstrated by Table 6.2.[25] Nevertheless, it is clear that workers continued to leave Kaminoseki village during the first few years of the new system—at a lower overall rate than during the government-sponsored program, but with year-to-year increases. An 1897 list of emigrant applications in Murotsu village further reveals heavy recruiting in the

TABLE 6.2

Hawaiian emigrants from Murotsu and Kaminoseki villages, 1888–1898

Year	Murotsu Village	Kaminoseki Village		
		Nagashima	*Yashima*	*Iwaishima*
	GOVERNMENT-SPONSORED			
1888	38	11	5	0
1889	92	34	12	2
1890	18	4	0	9
1891	7	4	7	32
1892	0	0	0	0
1893	57		76*	
1894	11		6*	
	PRIVATE			
1894	?	5	0	0
1895	?	6	1	5
1896	?	14	13	2
1897	52	27	10	0
1898	?	42	0	0

Source: Data for the government-sponsored period: database of the Museum of Japanese Emigration to Hawai'i. For private emigration from Murotsu: MYM 412; from Kaminoseki: *Hawai-koku tokōshanin meibo, Kaminoseki-son* (private collection of the late Ueda Kichisuke, location now unknown).

*The government-sponsored emigrant address data for 1893 and 1894 do not include details of subdistricts within the Kaminoseki village municipality.

village by the emigration companies, chief among them Morioka Makoto.[26] As a result, in the two-week period between February 19 and March 4 alone, thirty-five applicants successfully completed the paperwork to emigrate.[27] The annual increases in emigrant numbers from Kaminoseki and the active presence of emigration company agents in both Murotsu and Nagashima therefore suggest that the local peak in emigrant numbers to Hawai'i may have occurred sometime between the end of the local records in 1898 and the US government's tightening of immigration restrictions in 1908. Indeed, according to ministry records there were at least fifty-seven emigrants from Kaminoseki in 1902 alone—the year before Niikawa Ichisuke's surviving letter to his father at home.[28]

The fact that Niikawa and Okada Usuke crossed to Hawai'i in this period indicates that a new type of Kaminoseki and Murotsu emigrant was emerging by the early twentieth century. Okada may have hailed from Yamaga, but his family was clearly not "impoverished": unusually, he completed not just his compulsory elementary school education, but also three years at "higher" elementary school (*kōtōka*), for which fees were payable. As for Niikawa, he was the son of a successful turn-of-the-century shipbuilder in Kaminoseki port, a man whose household tax payments in 1917 placed him in the top 15 percent of households in Kaminoseki municipal village (including Yashima and Iwaishima).[29] In other words, even fairly prosperous households began to send family members abroad to make money during the private emigration period. If the government-sponsored program had mostly been popular among landless "farmers" (however we define the term), then the private emigration system saw the increased participation of landowning and even semi-elite families.[30]

Such families did not only seek new opportunities in Hawai'i. As Okada recalled in his autobiography, "Actually, I had wanted to go to Korea, but I was advised not to go there by my parents for a number of reasons: mainly, there was little work there for men except in hard labor, as stevedores, etc. Further, my sister Uno [Ume?] had gone to Seoul, Korea at age 14 to work as a ho-oko [*hōkō,* servant]. But, ten months after her arrival in Korea, she died of rickets, due to the poor water there." If we assume that Ume went to Korea in 1905, then she was part of a surge of Japanese emigrants to the peninsula around the turn of the century—particularly between the Sino-Japanese (1894–1895) and Russo-Japanese (1904–1905) wars. In terms simply of human traffic, the number of Japanese who crossed to the Korean peninsula rose from just over 8,000 in 1890 to 41,000 in 1900; in terms of Japanese who were actually resident in Korea, there was a sevenfold increase, from just under 12,000 in 1896 to 78,000 in 1906. As with Hawaiian emigration, a significant proportion of those who went to Korea came from western Japan: 27 percent of the Japanese residents in Korea in 1896 came from Yamaguchi (second only to Nagasaki prefecture); Yamaguchi also accounted for 17 percent of the 1906 residents (the highest proportion nationwide, followed by Nagasaki and Fukuoka).[31]

But the work was not just "hard labor as stevedores." Usuke's fellow villager Kōno Takenosuke, for one, left for Korea in 1895 to try his luck in commerce—and within a decade, he had become as much of a "success" as any Murotsu boy could imagine.

Kōno Takenosuke and Awaya Torazuchi (Port Area to Korea)

Born in the last days of the Tokugawa shogunate, Kōno Takenosuke was the third son of Naozō, the proprietor of one of Murotsu's most successful shipping stores and most probably a port shipping agent in the Edo period. Through a series of family misfortunes, Takenosuke ended up as head of the household at the age of twenty, and, although he was among the top 1 percent of Murotsu household taxpayers in 1891 and owned at least eight houses, he appears to have made some kind of catastrophic business miscalculation a year or two later, which caused his household to lose many of its assets. According to a biographical dictionary entry in 1917, Kōno saw that he would be "unable to continue business in his hometown," and in March 1895 he left Murotsu, first for Busan and then for Incheon.[32]

By the time he arrived, the Sino-Japanese war had just ended, and Incheon was a boomtown, a magnet for petty capitalists who hoped to make a fast yen. With Japanese troops advancing north through 1894, there had been a ready market for Japanese imports that could be sold at extortionate prices—a market that small-time merchants and peddlers had exploited with gusto. As the flow of yen increased, quadrupling in Incheon between May 1894 and November 1895, there was more money to be reinvested in imports from the Japanese mainland, spurring an overall increase in trade from 3.8 million yen in 1895 to 20.4 million yen in 1904.[33] Even after Japanese troop numbers declined, there was the Korean market to develop: thus, in his first business transaction in June, Kōno bought up stock in Incheon and then received permission from the Japanese consulate to travel and sell in the Korean interior.

In April 1896, Kōno opened his first sundries store in Incheon. He was also a founding member of a group of armed merchants (the Busō Gyōshō Dantai), and later in 1896, he opened a shop in Pyongyang, which from then on became the main focus of his business. He would stock up on Japanese imports in Incheon and transport them (first by road, then by ship) to Pyongyang for the Korean market. In return, he bought up rice to sell to the Japanese domestic market, where increasing urbanization fueled growing demand. At the turn of the century, Kōno could buy 800 *koku* of Korean rice for 5.10 yen; by the time he had shipped it to Japan, he stood to make a profit of 2,000 yen.[34]

Fortunes could thus be made in Incheon, which caused the city's Japanese population almost to double (from 2,500 to 4,500) between 1894 and 1895 and then to surge again during the Russo-Japanese war of 1904–1905. But for each success story like Kōno's, there were also many tales of failure—of petty capitalists who made poor investments and left behind a trail of debt, of carpenters and stonemasons who were attracted by higher wages than in Japan but who did not anticipate the higher living costs, of merchants who lost everything in one of the conflagrations that seemed to be a regular feature of settler life in the city.[35] The Japanese population of port cities such as Incheon and Busan was thus characterized by high turnover, especially between the Sino-Japanese and Russo-Japanese wars. Those who came in this period were generally poor and economically displaced—the type of migrant that Ōkuma Shigenobu (1838–1922), who became prime minister in 1898, called "corrupt, coarse, arrogant, rough, violent, and bullying."[36] Those who succeeded were either aggressive to the point of illegality or brave pioneers, depending on one's point of view. Not surprisingly, Kōno's hagiographic biographer in 1917 preferred the latter interpretation, reminding readers of the daily risks undertaken by the early emigrants—risks such as traveling on poor roads and the danger of "bandits" on the Incheon-Pyongyang transit route. Doubtless these "bandits" (presumably Korean nationalists) provided the justification for merchants to carry weapons as they crossed the interior. But one also wonders whether there might not have been a connection between the armed Japanese merchants and the rice that Kōno purchased at such exceptionally low cost.

Japanese rule on the Korean peninsula was formalized with the annexation of 1910—a step that the more radical settlers had been urging for some years. At this point, Kōno's business network included several more branch and subbranch stores and a soy sauce factory. By 1914, he was also supervising the business operations of the late Matsumae Saisuke (a fellow Murotsu resident) in Busan and Mokpo; he was working as the Incheon agent for New Zealand Fire Insurance, Standard Oil, and various other Western companies; he had invested in a small landscaped park for the pleasure of his fellow Japanese residents; he was a key member of the local chamber of commerce and the Incheon-Yamaguchi Prefectural Association; and he had received a personal commendation from the governor of Yamaguchi for his donation, in 1911, of 300 yen to build a new assembly hall at Murotsu's elementary school.

The decision to build an assembly hall in Murotsu had been formally taken by the village council on 28 March 1910. By calling it the "Korean Hall," village authorities hoped to fund the entire construction project through donations from Murotsu residents currently living on the peninsula.[37] To this end, a fundraising committee of thirty eminent emigrants was formed (including Kōno himself) and the appeal launched in August. The list of potential donors who were contacted thus gives us a good idea of how many other Murotsu residents had emigrated to Korea by mid-1910. In total, 184 Murotsu emigrants were contacted, of whom 94 eventually made donations totaling 3,203 yen. While the average donation was thus 34 yen, just over half the donors made a payment of 10 yen or less. In other words, the fact that Kōno emigrated to Korea in the preannexation period was not of itself unusual, for many other Murotsu villagers emigrated too. What was unusual, rather, was the extent of his wealth and the speed with which he accumulated it.

If Kōno's meteoric career reveals some of the "pull" factors that drew other Murotsu men and women to the peninsula, then the fact that so many villagers crossed the Japan Sea at the turn of the century suggests that "push" factors were equally if not more important. As with Hawaiian emigration, these push factors can better be understood by examining the exact provenance of the Korean emigrants. The 1910 list reveals that 64 percent of those whose addresses are known came from the districts that had made up the port area in the 1840s (see Table 6.1)—an inverse of the pattern previously noted for government-sponsored Hawaiian emigrants. One possible explanation for such contrasting origins is that, compared to the late 1880s, when Murotsu villagers first started crossing to Hawai'i, the economy of the port by the mid-1890s had deteriorated further, leading to a new wave of emigration now centered on the historical port area itself.

Evidence of further economic decline in the port can be found in the merchants' petition to the Murotsu authorities in July 1894, in which they complained about the behavior of local fishermen in forcing "outside fishermen" to leave the port (see also Chapter 4). These were the very outside fishermen who "came to buy their daily food and drinks necessities at our shops and thus managed to help keep afloat our commercial industry. . . . Ah! Once more we lost the means to become happy, and the disadvantages to our merchants could be calculated in minute detail. They are declining ever more and becoming still more destitute, and there is nothing we can do!"[38] The language might have been somewhat hyperbolic, but the merchants' despair was apparently genuine: the tax records for 1894 contain more than twenty applications by small-scale merchants and fishermen to close their businesses, and at least one such shopkeeper would subsequently move to Incheon. Moreover, within a decade, one of the petition's cosignatories had himself emigrated to Korea: Suzuki Taneichi became the manager of Kōno Takenosuke's branch shop in Nampo and later donated 150 yen to the Korean Hall campaign.

The surviving records of Hawaiian and Korean emigration, though imperfect, thus allow us to measure the breadth of transnational connections in Murotsu at the turn of the twentieth century. By 1894, it seems that 29 percent of the village's total households could boast at least one household member who had either been to or was still in Hawai'i (154 households out of 536—see Table 6.1). Similarly, the 184 individuals contacted in Korea in 1910 appear to have come from 155 households—or 27 percent of the then village total. Given that the numbers of Hawaiian emigrants continued to increase after 1894, we can be certain that by the time of Korea's annexation at least half and perhaps as much as 60 percent of Murotsu's households had either a previous or ongoing transnational connection, even allowing for some overlap between Korean and Hawaiian emigrants (see Chapter 7). By any standard, that is an astonishingly high proportion, and it seems not improbable that some similarly high proportion occurred in Kaminoseki village too—testament to the economic difficulties that the Murotsu merchants so emotively articulated in the 1890s.

But the trouble with the Kōno case study is that personal misfortune appears to have been the main reason for his crossing to Korea: as such, Kōno's story does not directly connect the port prosperity in the 1840s to the popularity of emigration half a century later. Without such a link, the case for port decline being the major "push" factor in subsequent overseas migration remains circumstantial. However, the connection between former prosperity and emigration can in fact be suggested by returning to the Kaminoseki port area and to the Awa-ya household.

In 1936–1937, Awaya Torazuchi (1880–1952), head of the Awa-ya household since his adoption some thirty years previously, built a new house in the central Korean province of Gyeonggi. It was a farmhouse, and it cost 6,200 yen to construct, including 545 yen for the building materials to be shipped from Japan. With a floor space of 105 square meters (32 *tsubo*), it was slightly smaller than the ancestral home in Kaminoseki, but this was more than compensated by the farmland that surrounded it—some 45.6 hectares by March 1942, more than any one individual could ever imagine owning on Nagashima.[39] The house itself was destroyed in the Korean War (1950–1953) and remains only in a blurred photograph, ripped from a family album in the rush to escape Korean retribution after the Japanese surrender in 1945. But the construction of the farmhouse, the cultivation of the pear orchards and rice fields around it, and not least the fact that Torazuchi could afford a photographer to record it all for posterity suggest a second flowering of the Awaya household fortunes in the late 1930s. Thus, following the example of his ancestors, who along with a score of other Kaminoseki households had made a donation to the village's Kamado Hachimangū shrine in 1827 to celebrate their trade-related prosperity, Torazuchi offered 100 yen in 1937 to install electric lights on the stone staircase leading up to the shrine.[40]

Awaya had emigrated to Korea in May 1912 at the age of thirty-one. Exactly how much the Awaya fortunes had declined by the time that he left is unclear, but we can try to guess in two ways. First, after the dismantling of Chōshū's *koshini-gata* system and the end of the shipping agency business, the household turned to straightforward retail. By the mid-Meiji period, sometime after the compilation of the *Customer Register,* theirs was apparently the only shop in Kaminoseki to specialize in fishing equipment such as lines and wire hooks.[41] This meant that they were ideally placed to exploit the growth of the fishing industry in the straits communities from the 1870s onward, but it also suggests that they would have been hard hit by fishermen-merchant disputes such as those outlined above. Second, Awaya originally went to Korea in order to serve as "manager" of apple orchards owned by the Hagiwara household, also from Kaminoseki: the title could not disguise the fact that he was effectively a tenant, not a landowner.

When Awaya did eventually start to buy his own land, the pattern of his acquisitions in Korea also suggests that the household had rather limited means. Although his first purchase of land was in 1916, fifteen years passed between his arrival on the peninsula and his first sustained period of buying. Such purchasing inactivity is particularly surprising given Japanese government incentives to help farmer-settlers in Korea. A cadastral survey between 1906 and 1915, for example, had resulted in much crown and untitled Korean land being claimed by the imperial authorities and sold to land management companies such as the Oriental Development Company (founded in 1907), which provided low-interest loans to encourage first-time Japanese buyers. With the government fearing rural unrest in the home islands in the wake of the 1918 Rice Riots, the Program to Increase Rice Production in Korea (1920) also provided generous subsidies to help cover the cost of irrigation improvements for larger landowners (over 10 hectares) in Korea.[42] Although Awaya would later become a landowner of such scale, by 1927 he had bought only 0.8 hectares, or less than 2 percent of the total he would eventually own. Given the government incentives and given that nearly half his portfolio (22.3 hectares) was purchased in a ten-year spending spree between April 1932 and March 1942, we might assume that Awaya was not the sort of man to sit on his money if he had some to spare. That he made so few acquisitions during his first fifteen years in Korea therefore suggests that he left Kaminoseki with only limited capital in hand.

The changing fortunes of the Awaya in the century between the construction of their two-story house in Kaminoseki and their subsequent home in Korea thus reveal the extent to which the post-Meiji decline of the ports affected even once prosperous households. More important, the Awaya story helps us understand that the fear of decline at home—the fear that a young man in Kaminoseki "could never be a success," to borrow Okada Usuke's phrase—may have been as important a motivation for emigrating as the excitement of the foreign unknown. Like merchant Kōno Takenosuke in Incheon, farmer Awaya Torazuchi became sensationally rich in Korea. Yet perhaps it was not merely the new money and land that inspired him, but also a sense of duty to his ancestors—the sense that he too needed to live up to the standards they had set with their striking new white-walled house and their community donations in the 1820s. Awaya came from a stratum of society that had dominated Kaminoseki life at the beginning of the Meiji emperor's reign. But as he left Japan, just two months before the death of the emperor, perhaps he too experienced an anxiety similar to that articulated by the character Sensei in Natsume Sōseki's novel *Kokoro* (1914): "I felt as though the spirit of the Meiji era had begun with the Emperor and had ended with him. I was overcome with the feeling that I and the others, who had been brought up in that era, were now left behind to live as anachronisms."[43]

To emigrate from Kaminoseki, we might speculate, was not just to escape economic decline but to avoid becoming an anachronism of a past age.

7

The Transnational Hometown: Zenith and Decline

One sunny day sometime in 1939, some forty of Iwaishima's great and good assembled in the island's elementary school playground: among their ranks were the district head (*kuchō*), post office master, school principal, doctor, head of the Farming Cooperative, and priests from the temples and the main Miyato shrine. Almost all the men were dressed in emblazoned kimonos and doffed their homburg hats as they watched Matsuoka Jinta (in a three-piece morning suit) and his eldest son Yoshitetsu (in high school uniform) officially unveil a bronze statue of Kusunoki Masashige, a legendary medieval warrior. (See Fig. 7.1.)

The statue stood just to the east of the school's main entrance. To the west stood seven rectangular memorial stones, roughly one meter in height, that recorded the names of islanders who had made substantial donations toward the construction of the elementary school itself, completed in January 1934: six of the seven benefactions were sent by islanders residing overseas. By tracing the life histories of these six donors plus that of Matsuoka Jinta, we begin to grasp the myriad impacts of Kaminoseki's transnational connections on individual lives and on the prewar hometown communities in general. Indeed, as Table 7.1 shows, the legacy of the overseas communities in the hometown was highly significant in institutional terms, with schools, temples, shrines, and even war memorials being built (or rebuilt) throughout the 1910s, 1920s, and 1930s as a result of benefactions from emigrant villagers. This is important because the story of Japan's post-1868 modernization is often told in terms of national-international axes (the country's attempt to "catch up" with the West)

Figure 7.1. The unveiling of the Kusunoki Masashige statue, Iwaishima, 1939 (Courtesy of Mita Tsutomu)

or national-local axes (the center's attempted subsumption of the regions). But the financial dependence of Kaminoseki and Murotsu villages on their overseas communities indicates the extent to which the local, national, and international aspects of prewar society were constantly intertwined at a grassroots level: institutions of the nation state were constructed in the local village because of villagers whose lives traversed the so-called borders of the Japanese.[1]

But the significance of Kaminoseki's transnational era was not merely institutional: the demographic effects of emigration spread across two or sometimes three generations. Moreover, thanks to the "success" of their overseas compatriots and the pride engendered thereby, those villagers who stayed at home would also have been aware of the impact of the Japanese diaspora in the social and economic routines of their daily lives. The shrines and temples at which they gathered, the paving stones they walked over to reach those temples, the electric lights illuminating the steps to worship, the schools in which their children studied, the maps those children used in geography classes, the education broadcasts they heard on the new radio, the two-story houses around the town, the clothes some villagers wore, even the potato salad they ate: these and much more were the transnational legacies of the Kaminoseki

TABLE 7.1

Major prewar benefactions to Murotsu and Kaminoseki villages from overseas migrants

1895	Hawaiian emigrants from Yashima donate a ceremonial pillar to the island's Jōkei-ji temple.
1904	Hawaiian emigrant Katō Zensaku gathers donations in order to build the Taishi-dō (Temple to Kōbō Daishi) on Yashima.
1904–1905	Korean emigrant Matsuoka Toyozō funds the construction of the En-no-gyōja shrine on Iwaishima.
1911	Ninety-four Korean emigrants donate 3,203 yen to construct a new assembly hall (the "Korean Hall") at Murotsu elementary school.
1915	Hawaiian emigrants contribute to the retiling in copper of the roof of Kaminoseki's Kamado Hachimangū shrine.
1916	Twenty-eight Hawaiian and North American emigrants donate 1,976 yen to build the "America-Hawai'i Hall" at Murotsu elementary school.
1917	California emigrant Matsubara Daikichi funds the construction of the Russo-Japanese war memorial on Iwaishima plus a monument to his ancestors.
1918, July	California emigrant Nishida Mansaku donates 100 yen to pay for a new organ at Kaminoseki elementary school.
1918, August	Seven Murotsu residents in Korea contribute 700 yen toward the Mutual Prosperity Association to help subsidize rice during a period of high prices.
1926, January	Twenty-seven Hawaiian emigrants pay for new paving stones at Kaminoseki's Amida-ji temple.
1926, October	Thirty-one Hawaiian emigrants in Honolulu raise 850 yen for Kaminoseki elementary school to buy its first ever radio; memorial stone erected in 1927.
1929, October	Kaminoseki residents in Hawai'i, the United States, Korea, Taiwan, and Manchuria raise 1,022 yen toward the cost of a new elementary school assembly hall.
1931	Karafuto emigrants Fujinaga Yosaku and his wife Chiyo contribute 2,500 yen to the construction of a new elementary school on Iwaishima; there are also donations from Matsubara Daikichi (North America, 1930, 300 yen), Matsumura Rinzō (Hawai'i, 1930, 50 yen), and two other overseas residents.
1935	Hawaiian returnee Yano Banji donates 270 yen to the rebuilding—including a new tiled roof—of Yashima's Jōfuku-ji temple. Yoshimoto Fukuji (who runs a delivery business in Honolulu) also donates 100 yen.

1937 (?)	Korean emigrant Awaya Torazuchi donates 100 yen toward electric lighting on the path to Kaminoseki's Kamado Hachimangū shrine.
1937, November	Murotsu Village Emigrants' Association in Hawai'i donates 1,006 yen toward comfort packs for serving frontline soldiers (in China); there are further fund-raising efforts in 1938 and 1939.
1939	Korean emigrant Matsuoka Jinta (son of Toyozō, see 1904-1905) funds the construction of the bronze statue of Kusunoki Masashige on Iwaishima.

Source: Data from Hori, *Hawai ni watatta kaizoku-tachi,* pp. 109, 136–137, 175, 294; MYM 773; MYM, *Kifu-bo* (not catalogued); KYM, *Kaminoseki jinjō kōtō shōgakkō kōdō kenchiku ni kansuru ikken, Shōwa 3-nen 8-gatsu* (not catalogued); memorial stones around the two municipalities.

diaspora, and to study them is to understand an important and often ignored everyday aspect of Japan's modern transformations.

The Matsuoka Household

When Matsuoka Jinta and his son Yoshitetsu posed for a commemorative photo with Iwaishima's civil society leaders in 1939, the iconography of Kusunoki Masashige must have seemed perfect for the occasion. In school textbooks, in sculptures, and on banknotes, the Kusunoki of the early twentieth century was an icon of Japanese imperial rule, and the Matsuoka success story had itself been made possible through Japan's ongoing penetration of the Asian mainland.[2]

Jinta's father, Matsuoka Toyozō, first emigrated to Korea in 1900. Previously, he had worked as an independent shipper transporting salt throughout the Inland Sea.[3] Although the local salt industry had been devastated by competition following the opening of Japan's ports to international trade, the collapse of Korean production after a series of natural disasters in the early 1880s created a new opportunity for the Yamaguchi industry; thus, by the mid-1890s, more than three-quarters of Japan's salt exports were bound for the Korean peninsula.[4] This may have been one way in which Toyozō became familiar with the business opportunities on offer in Korea. Indeed, as Kimura Kenji's pioneering research has shown, independent shippers from the island of Umajima (just north of Iwaishima) had been active in trading between western Japan and Korea throughout the Edo period. These shippers developed new routes after the opening of Busan in 1876, and, when faced with competition from Japan's more established shipping companies in the early 1890s, they settled on the peninsula in large numbers and turned instead to trade and retail.[5]

Toyozō himself moved to Busan after the death of his wife in 1900.[6] He took his son Jinta and daughter Chiyo, aged seven and four respectively, and joined a tide of immigrants who caused the city's Japanese population to treble between 1898 and 1907.[7] Back in 1895, newly arrived merchant Kōno Takenosuke, from Murotsu, had found it hard to break into the Busan market and instead moved to Incheon, but Toyozō had an asset unavailable to most fellow emigrants—sake. Iwaishima had a long tradition of sending farmers to work in the sake-brewing industry during the agricultural off-season, the young men leaving the island after the fall festival (under the Thousand-Year Pine) and returning for an April spring festival in which they quaffed the product of their winter labors with elan. Sake brewing continued to be a growth industry in western Japan during the Meiji period, and Toyozō's great insight was to spot that increasing numbers of Japanese on the Korean peninsula would lead to a demand for sake that was brewed locally and that was therefore cheaper than alcohol imported from the homeland.[8] Toyozō duly set up shop in Busan, employed brewmasters from Iwaishima, and in February 1904—the month that Japan declared war on Russia with an audacious attack at Port Arthur—celebrated his success by paying for the construction of a brand new shrine high on the mountain above Iwaishima's port. This would be the first of several benefactions from the Matsuoka family over the next four decades.

One way in which the Matsuoka story indicates the impact of emigration on the hometown is by virtue of the fact that Jinta and his younger sister Chiyo were both children when they left Iwaishima and were thus both taken out of the local school system. Although no detailed school records survive from Iwaishima, the Murotsu village records allow us to reconstruct the cross-border movements of elementary school children during the 1910s in particular (see Table 7.2). We can calculate, for example, the total number of pupils who were due to complete their education between 1910 and 1921 (T1) and then compare that to the number of pupils who were resident abroad and thus receiving their education away from Murotsu, or who quit their studies halfway through in order to move abroad (presumably with their parents), or who were returnees from overseas. Across the decade, an average of 19 percent of students had some kind of overseas connection. Given that in almost all cases this "connection" involved living and attending school abroad, we can conclude that

TABLE 7.2

The impact of overseas migration on Murotsu elementary school, 1910–1921

	1910	1911	1912	1913	1914	1915	1916	1917	1918	1919	1920	1921	Total
Total number of students due to complete schooling (T1)	88	71	97	56	57	89	95	106	93	88	88	108	1036
School attendees in Hawai'i/United States	0	0	0	0	1	3	6	1	4	7	7	11	40
School attendees in Korea	0	0	0	0	0	1	7	2	10	12	10	14	56
School attendees in Taiwan/China	0	0	0	0	0	0	1	2	1	1	1	2	8
Students who left for Hawai'i/United States before completion	1	0	0	0	0	0	0	0	1	0	0	1	3
Students who left for Korea before completion	3	8	15	11	3	7	5	7	4	2	4	4	73
Students who left for Taiwan/China before completion	0	0	2	0	3	0	0	0	1	0	0	0	6
Number of returnees from Hawai'i/Japanese empire	0	2	2	0	0	0	0	1	1	1	1	3	11
Total number of students with overseas connection (T2)	4	10	19	11	7	11	19	13	22	23	23	35	197
Percentage of students with overseas connection (T2/T1)	4.5	14.1	19.6	19.6	12.3	12.4	20.0	12.3	23.7	26.1	26.1	32.4	19.0

Source: Data compiled from MYM 917–922, 932, 933.

the continued overseas flow of Murotsu residents had, by the early 1920s, caused a reduction in the school population of almost a fifth of all students.

For some households, this cross-generational trend was triggered by the presence of a government-sponsored emigrant in the family. Focusing still on Murotsu, seven of the village's fifty-two private applicants in 1897 had immediate family (fathers, brothers, husbands) who had left Murotsu between 1888 and 1894.[9] Moreover, at least a fifth of those households who sent away a government-sponsored emigrant still had one of their members—sometimes the original emigrant, sometimes a sibling or a child—still living in Hawai'i in 1915.[10] As with the Matsuoka household in Korea, anecdotal evidence from around the town reinforces the impression of long household engagements to Hawai'i and the United States across several generations. Iwaishima's Tachibana Fusakichi, for example, first emigrated to Hawai'i with his wife Hana on the nineteenth government-sponsored crossing in 1891. Although they returned to Iwaishima, their daughter Tami and adopted son-in-law Kojirō subsequently emigrated, first to Hawai'i and then to Los Angeles, whence they returned to Iwaishima in about 1955, when Kojirō was seventy years old. (Kojirō, who was a town councillor between 1962 and 1966, is credited with having introduced potato salad to the presumably grateful islanders.)[11]

Unlike the Matsuoka and Tachibana households, however, the cross-generational pattern of migration could also include a cross-diasporic element. The Murotsu archives reveal that at least nineteen households could boast prewar connections to both the United States (including Hawai'i) and Korea.[12] Eleven of these households had family members simultaneously resident in Asia and America. In the case of five other households, the fathers had been to Hawai'i as migrant laborers during the government-sponsored program; two decades later, they sent their children to Korea. The ages of these children (ranging from nine to twelve) and the fact that their school records make no reference to the fathers themselves being resident in Korea suggest that the children were also migrant laborers, perhaps going to work on the peninsula for two or three years as domestic servants or apprentices. (Okada Usuke's sister, for example, had crossed to Seoul at the age of fourteen to work as a domestic servant.)[13]

The first and most basic impact of Kaminoseki's prewar engagement with the outside world was thus the transformed working horizons of individual households—horizons that could lead to highly complex patterns of employment across generations. Of all the hamlets that make up today's municipality,

Iwaishima and Yashima in particular boasted a long history of seasonal out-migration, in the sake-brewing and whaling industries respectively. Unfortunately, a lack of data on how these migrant laborers in the Edo period felt about their off-season work means that it is almost impossible to compare Edo period practices of, say, sake brewing with the new practices opened up by transnational working opportunities (assuming that Edo period migrant households became Meiji period emigrants, which itself is unclear). But what does seem clear is that in addition to the demographic consequences of overseas migration on the population as a whole, the experience of working overseas left a much deeper economic and therefore social impression on individual emigrants and their families than did migration in the Edo period. Indeed, just as historians of modern Britain are increasingly using the concept of "transnational families" to erode scholarly borders between domestic and imperial historiography,[14] so the evidence suggests that we should consider the Matsuoka household and many others in Kaminoseki as "transnational households."

To understand more about the economic and social significance of these transnational households, we can turn to six of the seven donation stones that stood to the immediate west of the Kusunoki Masashige statue.

The Iwaishima Elementary School Donors

The late Mifuji Masako, who ran a mom-and-pop store with her husband on Iwaishima, once told me about her maternal uncle. Matsumura Rinzō, who donated 50 yen toward the construction of the Iwaishima elementary school, first went to Hawai'i on the eighteenth government-sponsored crossing in May 1891, following the course of his elder brother Chūzō, who had left Iwaishima the year before. Rinzō ended up training as a dentist and staying in Hawai'i the rest of his life, but Mrs. Mifuji remembered his returning to Iwaishima for summer holidays when she was a child before the Second World War. He would bring clothes as gifts for his relatives, and he was also the only man on the island to own an outboard motor. He would attach it to a fishing boat and speed his family off on fun excursions.[15]

Iwaishima's *kanmai* festival was held a few months after Rinzō left, in the summer of 1891. It was next held in 1896, when he is recorded as having donated 15 *sen* toward the festival costs and his brother Chūzō 45 *sen*. The fact that both men appear in the records suggests that they had returned to Iwaishima after completing their three-year contracts (Rinzō must therefore

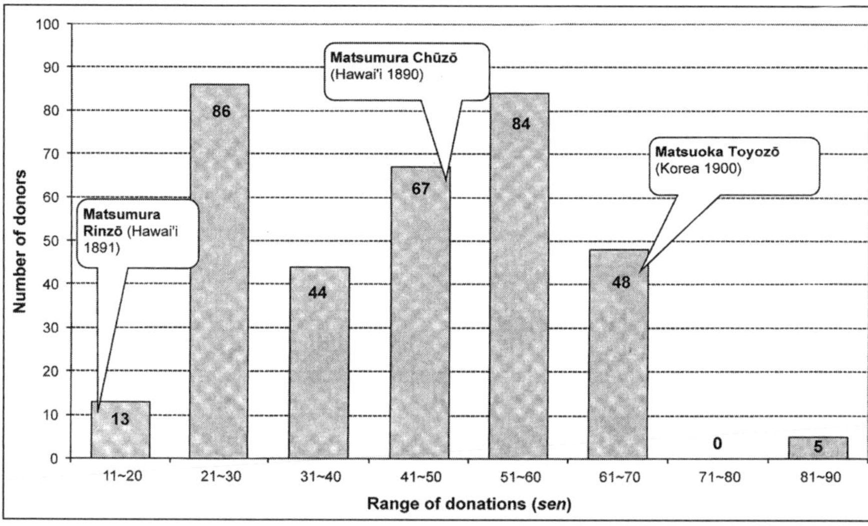

Figure 7.2. Donations to Iwaishima's *kanmai* festival, 1896 (Data from Kaminoseki-chō Kyōiku Iinkai, *Suō-Iwaishima no kanmai gyōji,* pp. 149–154)

have crossed once again to Hawai'i during the private emigration period). The festival list gives no indication of the economic status of the Matsumura household before the two brothers emigrated. But in the absence of tax data from Iwaishima, the festival donations can be used to indicate the relative status of individual households on the island during the main decade of Hawaiian emigration. Figure 7.2 reveals that Chūzō was apparently of middle-ranking wealth in 1896—perhaps because, as first son, he stood to inherit family land. By contrast, his younger brother, who may by this point (at age twenty-nine) have been forced to establish a branch household with very little or no land, appears to have been considerably poorer: his 15 *sen* placed him among the lowest 4 percent of donors on the island.

There is a striking contrast between Rinzō's apparent poverty in 1896 and the glamorous excursions that his niece recalls in the 1920s. Indeed, by 1930, Rinzō had become prosperous enough to make an individual donation to the construction of Iwaishima's new elementary school, for which he earned an engraved memorial stone next to the main school gate. Fifty yen was equivalent to just under one month's gross salary for a white-collar government official in Tokyo, indicating that Rinzō's success in Hawai'i had raised him to the level of urban, lower-middle-class Japan—a world far removed from Iwaishima.[16] This change in fortunes demonstrates the extent to which overseas migration could transform the lives of individual emigrants as well as the lives of their extended families. Many emigrants sent their relatives remittances, and by 1892—the year after Rinzō crossed to Hawai'i—remittances were the eighth leading source of overseas revenue for Japan. In Kumage county, emigrants remitted an average of 118.27 yen in 1903 alone, money that was used first to repay debts and thereafter to buy new land, bonds, fishing boats, and tools. Those who returned to the hometown often brought cash in hand, while particularly successful returnees built new houses such as the graceful two-story pine and zelkova structures that even today line the narrow street linking the "port" and "inland" areas of downtown Kaminoseki.[17]

But it is possible to place too much emphasis on the economic impact of emigration. The example of Murotsu's Tanaka Kamegorō, who got married three months before he departed (alone) for Hawai'i in 1893 and then divorced on his return in 1896, reminds us that the balance sheet for "impact" must include personal as well as economic costs.[18] For all Mrs. Mifuji's happy family memories, there is a need for more research, if the sources can be found, on the impact of male overseas migration both on marital relations and on the roles and status of the women who remained at home.

In November 1906, Fujinaga Yosaku (c. 1854–1937), who donated 1,500 yen to Iwaishima's elementary school, inherited a house on Iwaishima from Fujinaga Yūkichi.[19] Nobody knows whether Yūkichi was the father of Yosaku, but if he was (as seems likely), then it suggests that the Fujinaga household was not very prosperous: ten years previously, Yūkichi had given only 30 *sen* to the *kanmai,* placing him among the lowest third of contributors. Yosaku sold his house to another family member in January 1913—at which point he disappears temporarily from the historical record.

He reappears in the Japanese colony of Karafuto (the southern half of Sakhalin island) in the late 1920s. Nobody knows when he and his wife first moved to the colony, whose population numbered just over 300,000 by the mid-1930s, but like Awaya Torazuchi in central Korea, Fujinaga was probably attracted by the image of a hinterland where enterprising Japanese settlers could buy and develop great swathes of land.[20] And, like Matsuoka Toyozō in Busan, he was intent on using the brewing skills of his fellow islanders in order to build up a sake empire. At the time of his donation, he owned not only branch shops but also branch breweries in the cities of Sakaehama, Shisuka, and Esutoru, as well as the main shop and brewery in Karafuto's largest city, Toyohara. In later years, he additionally tried his hand at moneylending, advancing private loans to Japanese businessmen engaged in the Karafuto timber and coal industries and charging 45 percent annual interest.[21] His money-making success is demonstrated by the size of the combined contribution that he (1,500 yen) and his wife, Chiyo, (1,000 yen) made to the school.

In Karafuto, Fujinaga employed young islanders from Iwaishima to help with the business. One such worker was seventeen-year-old Okada Kōichi, who arrived at the grand Fujinaga residence in Toyohara in November 1936. Before going to Karafuto, Kōichi worked as a shop assistant in Kobe and attended evening school. (His employment history is a reminder that villagers also engaged in domestic migration to other cities in prewar Japan, although no statistical data survives on the number of such migrant workers from Kaminoseki.) Okada's salary in Kobe was 14 or 15 yen a month, whereas in the Fujinaga brewery and shop he earned 30 yen. This was somewhat higher than off-season sake brewers at factories on the mainland and considerably more stable: Kōichi worked in Karafuto not just in the winter months, but all year round, until he joined the army in December 1939.[22] In addition, he got to live rent-free with the Fujinaga family in their magnificent two-story house, its vast reception room replete with electric lights (see Figure 7.3). The brewery was next door, surrounded by several hectares of land to the north and south.

Kōichi lived with the Fujinagas because his boss Yosaku was a blood relative. This was true also of the many other households who sent children to work for the Fujinagas: the Isozaki and Ebisu boys, for example, were relatives of Yosaku's wife Chiyo (née Isozaki), as was the Nishiyama household's oldest daughter, who worked as the Fujinaga maid in the mid-1930s.[23] The manager of the Fujinaga empire, who oversaw business after Yosaku died in July 1937, came from the Koizumi household on Iwaishima and was married to Yosaku's younger sister. Thus, at any one time, the Fujinaga main and branch breweries in Karafuto probably employed fifteen or sixteen islanders; additional labor was drawn from Niigata, Iwate, and other prefectures in the Tōhoku region of northeastern Japan.[24]

The example of the Fujinagas demonstrates the wider point that the home community benefited not only from generous overseas benefactions, but also from the employment opportunities successful emigrants offered its young

Figure 7.3. The Fujinaga residence, Karafuto, 1935 (Courtesy of Isozaki Hisao)

men, women, and even children.[25] Numerous further examples from Murotsu village and the other islands of Kaminoseki reinforce the point that blood and kinship networks in the home community influenced business networks in the host culture, thus creating an active link between home and abroad.

After Fujinaga Yosaku and Chiyo, the second largest donation to the Iwaishima elementary school construction fund, with the value of 300 yen, was made from San Francisco by Matsubara Daikichi. Although very little is now known about Matsubara on Iwaishima itself, he was listed in the fourth edition of the *Yamaguchi Overseas Association Newsletter* (1922) as one of many "success stories" (*seikōsha*). His six-line biography notes that after arriving in the United States (probably in 1902), Daikichi opened a tailor's shop specializing in cleaning and dyeing, from which he made "an enormous profit." He then branched into miso production, in which he was also successful.[26]

The newsletter further lists Matsubara as an executive member of the San Francisco branch of the association. There were seventy-three members in the branch, and, by 1926, Matsubara had risen to the position of accounts auditor.

Three other members from Iwaishima were listed in 1922, including Morishige Yosaku and Tsuchitani Ryūji. This is significant because both Morishige and Tsuchitani also donated 100 yen and 50 yen respectively to the elementary school fund. Furthermore, the Matsubara, Morishige, and Tsuchitani households on Iwaishima were neighbors, as was the Matsumura household from which brothers Chūzō and Rinzō emigrated. In other words, not only kinship but also informal neighborhood ties appear to have been maintained among emigrant communities and then deployed in order to raise funds for the home community. In addition, Matsubara used his *kabu-uchi* ties (see Chapter 5) in order to fund the 1917 Russo-Japanese war memorial on Iwaishima with Matsuoka Jinta.

At the municipal level, neighborhood ties were formalized in groups such as the Honolulu-based Murotsu Village Emigrants' Association, whose members donated 1,006 yen in November 1937 toward a village campaign to send comfort packs to soldiers serving on the front line in the China War; the association made further fund-raising efforts in 1938 and 1939. In Korea, there was apparently no official village organization, but emigrants made regular donations to a number of different Murotsu campaigns. In August 1918, for example, during a period of high rice prices that led to rioting across many areas of Japan, fifty-four eminent Murotsu residents raised a total of 1,632 yen for the village Mutual Prosperity Association (Murotsu-son Kyōei-kai), of which 700 yen was sent from seven villagers living in Korea. This money was used by the association to regulate and subsidize rice prices for the next four months.[27]

At such times of distress in the Edo period, the wealthiest landowners of the village—the upper stratum of rural society referred to by historians as *gōnō*—would be expected to distribute rice and food from their own private storehouses. In addition to being landlords, *gōnō* such as the heads of Murotsu's Yoshida, Yoshizaki, and Ogata households were also village officials and local employers engaged in commerce, small-scale manufacturing, moneylending, and local philanthropy.[28] The early days of Hawaiian emigration tended to reinforce the status divisions between such elite society and migrant shopkeepers, artisans, and tenant farmers. In 1888, Murotsu official Yoshizaki Gisuke and the landed elites who made up the village bureaucracy were the spokesmen of the "impoverished" villagers who were so desperate to apply for the government-sponsored program. In the private emigration period, they were the guarantors of prospective applicants, and, in 1918, when the Bōchō (Yamaguchi) Overseas Association was established to promote further emigration, founding members included Yoshizaki Eisuke, mayor of Murotsu between 1913 and 1925, and

Sakuraya Seihachirō, mayor of Kaminoseki between 1919 and 1927—both descendents of Edo period shipping agents.[29] Such local officials and village headmen were often employed as agents of the emigration companies along with former samurai: as traditional "men of status," it was easier for them to sign up farmers and other applicants.[30]

Within seventy years of the end of the Edo period, however, it was not only the old elites but also successful emigrants who engaged in providing employment, building local institutions, and offering alleviation in times of distress. Based on the donations listed in Figure 7.2, we can be fairly sure that Matsumura Chūzō and Rinzō were not born into a *gōnō* household. As for the Fujinaga and Matsubara households, whose ancestors cannot be traced with absolute certainty back to 1896, we might expect that if they were former *gōnō* their names would appear among the first lists of Kaminoseki village councillors from the late 1880s; the fact that they did not suggests that neither was considered to be an elite household on the island. Yet by the early 1930s their donations to the new school made the Fujinaga (2,500 yen), Matsubara (300 yen), Morishige (100 yen), Matsumura (50 yen), and Tsuchitani (50 yen) households highly regarded on Iwaishima. Their names were engraved for posterity on memorial stones at the school gate; for Fujinaga Yosaku and his wife Chiyo, who gave by far the biggest benefaction, there were especially tall stones. Greater height for greater philanthropy was thus indicative of another way in which transnational connections affected the prewar home community: success overseas could potentially lead to a dramatic rise in social status, to be expressed in new two-story houses, generous gifts, or the simple pleasure of owning the fastest boat in town.

Unlike the members of the above households, some emigrants returned to the hometown in the prewar years and used what we might call the "social capital" of their enhanced status to play a more prominent role in village life. In Chapter 5, we encountered Iwaishima's Matsumoto Bukichi, who used some of the capital he had earned as a hotel proprietor in San Francisco to invest heavily in new rice fields on the island. In Kaminoseki, men like Iwaki Kisaku, who worked in Hawai'i between 1898 and 1902, or Ueda Shinkichi, who went to Hawai'i on two occasions and was principal donor to the Kamado Hachimangū shrine in 1915, returned and eventually became village councillors; in the case of Iwaki, he even became a prefectural assemblyman in 1927.[31] Yet the problem with these examples is that the Matsumoto, Iwaki, and Ueda household heads were relatively wealthy landowners even before their sons went abroad. Given that village politics was becoming relatively more pluralistic by the 1920s and that Iwaki Kisaku's own father had been a village councillor in the 1890s, it seems rash to attribute his election in 1917 purely to the fact that he had been an emigrant.[32]

Nevertheless, emigrant experience did sometimes have an impact on the politics of the village. Kaminoseki's Nishida Mansaku, for example, first emigrated to Anaheim, California, in around 1915 and started work as a potato and orange farmer.[33] By 1918, he had made enough money to purchase a new pipe organ for the Kaminoseki elementary school, and one of his surviving savings books shows that he had saved nearly $4,000 by 1924. Thus, when he returned to Kaminoseki in 1926 with his wife and four children, he was rich enough to finance the endless rounds of drinking that were an accepted part of election campaigns. After he was elected a village councillor in 1933, he used more of his American savings to build a twelve-mat room at the back of his house where he could engage in political meetings and council-related socializing away from the prying eyes of the main street. For Nishida, there was a clear connection between overseas success and a subsequent political career.

These stories underline the extent to which the economic and social lives of individual households, and through them the hometown as a whole, were transformed as a result of the overseas diaspora. Indeed, the evidence suggests that there was a mutual need that bound the home and diaspora communities to each other in Kaminoseki—a pattern that was repeated in many other emigrant-sending communities throughout East Asia. On the one hand, the hometown benefited from the injection of monetary capital from overseas emigrants; on the other hand, the emigrants used such donations in order to impress on their compatriots their increased social capital as a result of success abroad.[34] The extent to which Kaminoseki's prewar shrines, temples, and schools were rebuilt as a result of overseas donations suggests that emigration should be analyzed at the local level not just as one response to the late-nineteenth-century economic decline of the town, but also in terms of the benefits that the hometown community and its residents derived.

For a few short years after 1939, the Kusunoki Masashige statue served as a backdrop to the photographs for which Iwaishima's young men posed before their conscription into the Imperial Army or Navy. The statue thus represented not only the "success" of one transnational household, but also the seemingly inexorable spread of the Japanese empire in a time of international conflict. But sometime after 1943, the statue was dismantled so that its bronze could be recast for the war effort.

Kaminoseki's transnational connections were similarly dismantled by the upheaval of 1945. Surviving members of the Matsuoka, Fujinaga, and Awaya households—and hundreds of other Murotsu and Kaminoseki families besides them—were forced to flee the empire. Matsuoka Jinta ended up in Kyushu and Fujinaga Chiyo moved to Hokkaido, while Awaya Torazuchi decided to return to his ancestral home in Kaminoseki's port area. Indeed, by 1956, repatriates accounted for just under 10 percent of the town's total households.[35] As for first- and second-generation villagers residing in the United States, the homeland had for nearly four years been the enemy, with communication to family members all but impossible. Even when those ties were restored, the SCAP-inspired Land Reform of 1946–1947 defined emigrants who still maintained links to their home village through landownership as "absentee landlords": for the most part, they were forced to sell their deeds, thus breaking another transnational connection.[36] Although a handful of overseas and returnee donations continued until the late 1960s, the last major group benefaction from Hawai'i was toward the rebuilding of the Murotsu junior high school following a devastating typhoon in October 1951—the same storm that blew down Iwaishima's Thousand-Year Pine.[37]

In this sense, the cost of defeat was arguably greater for the people of Kaminoseki than the cost of war itself. For the most part, the war was a site of suffering located away from the hometown. In the final months of the conflict, the sights and sounds of everyday wartime life for the townspeople included the passing of battleships through town waters, the training exercises of a new submarine corps (the Kaiten) based in nearby Hirao and Ōtsushima, the drone of American B-29s passing up the Bungo Suidō channel overhead, and the arrival of young soldiers to enjoy the fleeting pleasures of Kaminoseki's and Murotsu's brothels. At the same time, townspeople continued the mundane tasks of digging air-raid shelters on the school grounds, tending vegetable plots ever higher up the mountain slopes (as food rationing intensified), or undertaking absurd bamboo-spear training with the women of the hamlet.[38] The presence of at least a handful of Korean laborer households in the town—an aspect of transnational hometown life that, unsurprisingly, people were less able to recall and about which there is hardly any documentation—was another reminder of the consequences of a conflict that occurred mainly beyond the borders of the hometown.[39] The odd occasion when fighting did come to Kaminoseki, as when an oil tanker ran aground in Iwaishima's Miura Bay and was strafed by American fighter pilots, may perhaps be considered the exception that proved the rule.[40]

All this changed in the last two weeks of the war. Iwaishima islanders had watched as Tokuyama and Iwakuni, two industrial cities on the Inland Sea coast of Yamaguchi prefecture, were bombed by the Americans as early as March 1945. But the strange cloud rising high into the sky over Hiroshima on the morning of 6 August—a cloud that could be seen clearly from Iwaishima, if not from the straits communities—was an unsettling indication that the site of conflict was edging closer to home. Townspeople were not to know it on that summer morning, but several of their fellow villagers had been killed in the first atomic bomb attack, including the father of the Iwaishima household in which I stayed during fieldwork in 2004–2005.

Then, at lunchtime on 14 August 1945, islanders watched as squadrons of B-29s attacked the naval arsenal in nearby Hikari city. For some months, the older elementary school boys of the town had been conscripted to work in the arsenal, along with young female civilian workers (mainly students from local high schools). As the fires burned into the night of August 14—a night of high tension far away in Tokyo, where Iwaishima farmer Matsumoto Takeji was in a corps of bodyguards protecting the emperor at the Imperial Palace—some Iwaishima children took their futons up into the west graveyard to watch the arsenal glowing brightly on the horizon.[41] Thus, while the iconic image of the following day is of stunned subjects kneeling to hear the emperor's declaration of surrender over the radio, in Kaminoseki, August 15 saw frantic mothers from all parts of the town sailing to Hikari to search for survivors, the injured, the charred corpses of their children.[42] Among the 738 people killed in the attack numbered 45 of the town's youth, including 20 boys and girls from Iwaishima alone.[43]

For the people of Kaminoseki, the first days of the "postwar" were therefore marked by the worst traumas of war itself: the identification of bodies, the funerals and cremations, the grieving. The immediate postwar months and years also brought new pressures on the hometown community, in particular the return of soldiers and repatriated colonists to already overcrowded lands. In the midst of such living pressures, a new generation of young men and women became active in the Kaminoseki Combined Youth Association, which organized social events, speech contests, shrine-related festivals, and sports days in Nagashima, Yashima, and Iwaishima. In the pages of the association's monthly journal, *Village Culture* (*Mura no bunka*), they pondered the meaning of defeat and the future of their country. In 1949, for example, after a village sports festival had been held successfully on Yashima for the first time, Ujimoto Kuichi, the chair of the association, commented, "We have written one page of a history of which the young people of Kaminoseki may be proud" (*hokori aru rekishi*).[44]

Such sentiments give us an insight into how townspeople "embraced defeat," in the words of John Dower.[45] A public speaking contest at the village agricultural festival, in December 1948, was another opportunity to come to terms with the realities of defeat. There, Shimanaka Hiroshi, who (like Ujimoto) would later become a town councillor for Iwaishima district, gave a speech titled "The Convictions of Young People and the Democratization of Japan." Shimanaka's underlying argument was that the abolition of feudalism in Japan and the release of human dignity and freedom after the war offered the Japanese people an opportunity. "We must beautifully display the dignity and freedom of a Japanese race that will know no further defeat and that has given up arms; we must create a great history [*idai na rekishi*]," he proclaimed in his opening sentences. Such a vision must begin at the village level, and "moreover, the people who stand at the head of this reform must be us young people. . . . It is especially us young people who will save the country."[46] Of thirteen speakers, Shimanaka was runner-up in the contest: first prize went to a young woman and fellow islander, Isobe Chikako, who spoke on "The Personal Appearance of Women." But the theme of youth and a new Japan was one to which Shimanaka would return. A few months later, he wrote an essay titled "The Road to Rebuilding the Motherland," in which he concluded: "Our future prospects are tough and complicated. But believing in our own youth alone, we should plunge forward with the fortitude to overcome. In this way, the dazzling Japan of tomorrow [*kagayakashii asu no Nihon*] is promised to us."[47]

Yet the villagers of Iwaishima, and indeed of Kaminoseki and Murotsu, would find it more difficult to experience the dazzling future than they imagined. As the next chapters show, there was indeed a bright future in postwar Japan, but for the most part it remained beyond the grasp of everyday lives in the hometown. And as for the town's "youth," their roads toward the "Japan of tomorrow" increasingly led away from Kaminoseki.

PART IV

Living with the Bright Life

8

Bridging the Postwar Divide

The billing was enthusiastic, if perhaps somewhat over the top: in April 1969, the residents of Kaminoseki town were invited to an event designated "The achievement of the century, the realization of our dreams: the celebrations to mark the completion of the Kaminoseki Great Bridge."[1]

To bridge the hundred-meter-wide straits between Nagashima and the mainland had indeed been a dream of town planners for many years. The earliest mention of it in the *Kaminoseki Town News* (*Kaminoseki kōhō*), published by the town office and distributed to all households in the municipality, came as early as August 1959, just eighteen months after Kaminoseki and Murotsu villages had merged to form Kaminoseki town. The merger had been a highly contentious affair, spread out over two years. Kaminoseki residents, noting the island identity of their village (Nagashima, Yashima, and Iwaishima), were reported to be cool on joining administrations with mainland Murotsu. Murotsu villagers were reported to be more enthusiastic, although their mayor warned against being "subsumed" into Kaminoseki. At one point Murotsu village councillors even voted to leave Kaminoseki high and dry by merging instead with Yanai, before common sense eventually prevailed.[2] The subsequent 1959 election campaign for the mayoralty of the new municipality featured—for the first and last time in the new municipality's history—three candidates, with Nagashima's Kanō Shin eventually beating his rivals from Murotsu and Iwaishima. Thus, at one level, the completion of the bridge may have been perceived as a symbolic act in the healing of intratown divisions.

But the energized rhetoric of town officials in 1969 suggests that there were deeper expectations at play. In the months leading up to the bridge's opening, on June 21, it was variously described as "epoch-making," "long awaited," "the fervent wish of isolated islands," and "the bridge of our dreams."[3] A competition was launched to compose a new song and folk dance routine that would be performed on the day and recorded as a professionally produced LP—the producers and dance teachers invited to Kaminoseki all the way from Tokyo. As the ceremonies approached, the editors of the *Town News*—officials who worked in the town office—noted: "Together with our rejoicing at the completion of the Great Bridge, the fact that our place of abode has become a poem, a song, a dance and a record moves us deeply—a joy that we can never forget. Please send the record, poem, and song to natives of the town who have moved away so that they might remember this beautiful hometown [*kono utsukushii kokyō*]." In reporting the colorful opening ceremonies, the editors returned to a familiar theme: "The realization of this bridge, directly connecting Nagashima to the mainland, is both a historical achievement and something that will surely play a great role in advancing the economy and culture of every district in the town."[4]

Here, then, was the true expectation of the bridge's future potential. But, as this chapter will argue, the official emphasis on "advancing" (*zenshin*) the town's economy and culture grew out of a shared sense, by 1969, that Kaminoseki was in fact lagging behind the rest of the country. The precise nature of this lag changed across the 1950s and 1960s, as can be seen by analyzing first economic data, then discourses of "culture" as debated in the town media, and finally population statistics. Such analysis shows that the late-1950s rhetoric of a "bright life" (*akarui seikatsu*), implying "modern," middle-class living and the ownership of "divine" electrical goods, was beyond the reach of most Kaminoseki residents, especially if they remained in the hometown.[5] Although standards of living did improve during the 1960s, along with the general infrastructure of the town, the hyperbole of *Town News* editors in 1969 could not hide the basic fact that between the Kaminoseki and national economies there remained a divide that even "the realization of our dreams" could not bridge.

Welfare Households, Cultural "Lag"

The Shōwa Thirties, as the decade 1955 to 1964 is known, have in recent years become a new object of popular nostalgia in Japan. From 2001, the city of Bungo Takada, in northern Kyushu, started to restore its downtown area as a living museum to be known as Shōwa Town. "The Shōwa Thirties," reads the front page of the promotional website, "when every day we played till the sun went down, when we'd be scolded for spilling the rice or for diving in the bath: [when] we were innocent and spontaneous and full of life."[6] This image of the late 1950s was further popularized for a younger mass audience through the 2005 film *Always—Sunset on Third Street* (*Always—sanchōme no yūhi*), whose depiction of 1958 street corner life in Tokyo swept the 2006 Japan Academy awards.[7] Capitalizing on the commercial success of *Always*, an exhibition titled Those Were the Days: Nearby and Nostalgic Shōwa toured western Japan in 2007 and 2008. In the summer of 2007, it came to Yamaguchi city, where young women could be seen poring over cartoon characters or confectionary first marketed at least two decades before they were born and murmuring, "It's all so nostalgic."

From the perspective of Japan's economically troubled start to the twenty-first century, there was an obvious attractiveness in packaging a ten-year period that began with the country's emergence from the post-Korean War recession and ended with its triumphant staging of the 1964 Tokyo Olympics.[8] This was a decade, it seemed, when the economy could do no wrong, with each cycle wrapped in the sacred language of Shinto mythology. Thus the years 1955–1958 were known as the "Jinmu boom" (annual GNP growth of 7 percent) after the nation's first purported emperor; this was followed by the "Iwato boom" (1959–1964, annual growth of 12 percent), a reference to the ancient legend that the Sun Goddess had returned to bring light to the world after temporarily retreating into a cave; and the later 1960s would also witness the "Izanagi boom" after the founding patriarch of Shinto mythology.[9] Each appellation implied that the "end of the postwar" (as an Economic White Paper famously announced in 1956) and the beginning of a new era was an achievement comparable to the founding of the nation. The Shinto theme continued with the popular designation of key consumer goods in the late 1950s as the "three divine treasures" (*sanshu no jingi*)—referring not to the sacred mirror, sword, and jewel passed down to each new emperor upon accession, but rather to the electric refrigerator, the electric washing machine, and the black-and-white television.[10] Even the most cutting-edge scientific technology was discussed in language that harked back to mythical beginnings: following Japan's first successful attempt to split the atom in August 1957, the government's nascent nuclear power program was described as being "in the age of the gods" (*kamiyo jidai*).[11]

Early-twenty-first-century visitors to the Those Were the Days exhibition or viewers of *Always* were thus invited to gaze at 1950s and 1960s life through a double prism of nostalgia: the Shōwa Thirties both as a mythical new beginning, following the war and poverty of the Shōwa Tens and Twenties (1935–1954), and also as a time of vitality and innocence compared to the Japan of today. The fact that there was little popular understanding until the late 1960s of the worst excesses of the Shōwa Thirties—such as the mercury-poisoning scandal that blighted lives in the southern Kyushu city of Minamata—meant that discussion of the socioeconomic costs of the Jinmu and Iwato booms could be avoided in exhibitions and films.[12] And although there was general acknowledgment that the late 1950s were still a period of "poverty" and "inconvenience," the visual emphasis was less on this underside of daily life than on the "bright life" promised by gleaming fridges or fourteen-inch Mitsubishi televisions.[13]

In fact, in Kaminoseki, the very first mention of the three divine treasures in the pages of the *Town News* was made with reference to rats. From 1 December 1960 until 31 January 1961, it was announced, anyone who caught a rat in the town should take its tail to the town office, where they could exchange it for a raffle ticket (one tail per ticket), which would then be entered into a special drawing—the prizes for which included a television and a fridge.[14] Unfortunately, the competition was open to "three prefectures in the Chūgoku region," so the chances of winning were fairly remote; but nevertheless the townspeople responded enthusiastically, delivering 684 rats' tails over the two-month period.[15] The significance of the *Town News* announcement was its juxtaposition of modern consumer goods with antivermin campaigns: for all the sanitized images of the Shōwa Thirties appearing half a century later, in reality the 1950s was a decade in which warnings about diphtheria, dysentery, polio, and other diseases were published on an almost monthly basis in communities such as Kaminoseki. This continued official concern about public health—even at the height of the Iwato boom—was one indication of the "poverty" that popular exhibitions such as Those Were the Days acknowledged but did not analyze.

A remarkable record of everyday poverty was in fact compiled by prefectural researchers in the early months of 1957. *The Living Conditions of Residents in the Districts of Murotsu and Kaminoseki* is not an entirely unproblematic document. As with the village *Reports* compiled by the Chōshū domain in 1842, it is unclear how much we should read at face value data supplied to government officials concerning income—although the attractions of downplaying one's income and thus qualifying for central government welfare support were probably counterbalanced by the local stigma attached to that status. There is also more than a hint of modernist bias from the authors: Kaminoseki's economic structure is dismissed as "precapitalist" at one point and "unmodern" at another—a lens that is particularly problematic when it comes to analysis of data from the late Edo period.[16] But these reservations notwithstanding, the report enables us both to measure in nonnostalgic terms the complex realities of the Shōwa Thirties for one rural town and also to understand the longer-term causes of the depopulation crisis in the 1970s—a crisis that eventually led to the consideration of nuclear power in Kaminoseki itself.

In March 1957, the area soon to become known as Kaminoseki town was judged to have the highest poverty rate in the whole of Yamaguchi prefecture, as defined by the proportion of households that qualified for assistance under the Daily Life Security Law (1946, revised 1950).[17] Officially, 6 percent of households received government aid, although when "borderline" households were also figured into the equation, as much as a third of the town could be considered to be suffering from severe poverty.[18] According to the authors of the *Living Conditions* report, the cause of such poverty was overpopulation relative to the strength of the local economy. Demographically, Kaminoseki's 1955 population density of 351 people per square kilometer was high compared to 264 for Yamaguchi prefecture and 241 for the country as a whole. Pressure on the land had been exacerbated by the number of returning soldiers at the end of the war and by the number of repatriates from the empire.[19] The baby boom of the immediate postwar years added further pressure by creating a bottom-heavy population (see Figure 8.1), such that the town's dependency ratio (the number of nonworkers to each hundred people of working age) rose to 82 in 1955, compared to a nationwide average of 63.[20]

Despite the increased pressure on natural resources, the land itself had very little left to give: the age-old problems of lack of water and the low ratio of rice fields to dry fields remained a hindrance to agricultural development. Although just under half of the town's population was still engaged in farming in 1950, it was on a subsistence scale, with only tangerine (*mikan*) cultivation turning in any profits. Land plots were tiny and spread high across the hills with almost 80 percent of Kaminoseki's farmers owning less than half a hectare (1.24 acres) of land, compared to 46 percent in Yamaguchi and 41 percent nationwide.[21] As in the Edo period, farmers were thus highly dependent on by-employment and off-season work in order to supplement their income.

The effect of these structural problems on daily life is illustrated by income and spending patterns. In 1956, the average monthly income for a working

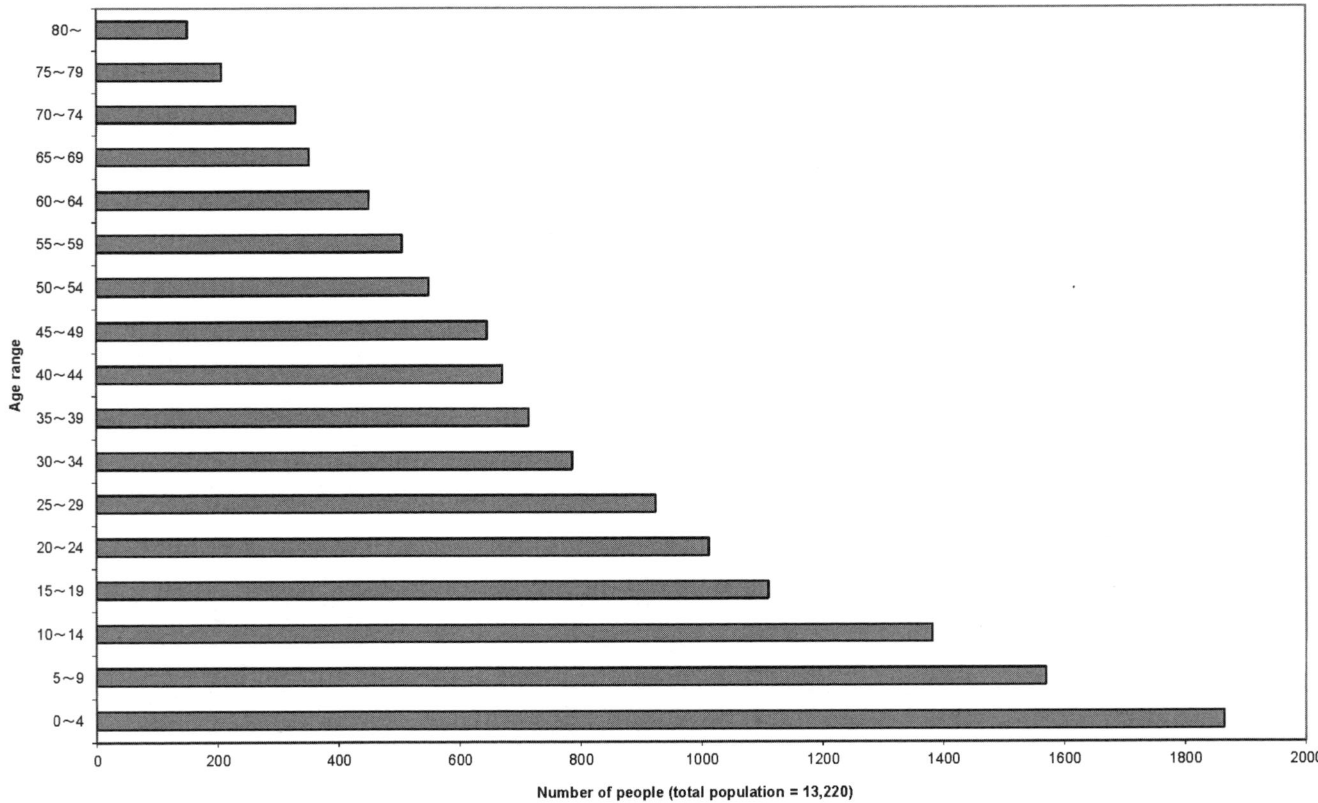

Figure 8.1. The population of Kaminoseki and Murotsu villages (combined) by age, 1950 (Data from Kaminoseki Town Office)

household in the cities was just over 30,000 yen, or 6,800 yen per person. In Murotsu and Kaminoseki, by contrast, people living in welfare-receiving households (6 percent of the total) had an average income of less than 2,000 yen per person, while the income of fully 84 percent of all households in the town was lower than that of the average city household.[22] (To put these figures in context, a Sharp television in 1957 cost 84,500 yen.)[23] As a consequence, Murotsu and Kaminoseki residents were forced to spend a far higher percentage of their income on basic necessities: 52 percent on food, for example—a figure that rose to 64 percent for welfare-receiving households—compared to a nationwide average of 43 percent.[24] Even so, the higher food expenditure of town residents in relative terms did not translate in absolute terms: welfare-receiving households generally spent only 36 yen on food per person per day, compared to 59 yen for "normal" households. Both figures were well below the nationwide average of 73 yen, and a breakdown of that expenditure further suggested that town residents were particularly missing out on fruit and protein consumption (red meat, eggs, milk) by comparison to the average Japanese person—although purchases of sake were proportionally higher than the nationwide average.[25]

With their higher disposable income, households in the cities were able to spend more money on "wholesome and cultured" expenses—a phrase that deliberately echoed Article 25 of the 1947 Constitution ("All people shall have the right to maintain the minimum standards of wholesome and cultured living"). Such expenses included medical treatment and educational costs, both of which were significantly higher for isolated islands such as Nagashima, and particularly for Iwaishima and Yashima. Until July 1957, for example, there was no health clinic on Yashima (or any regular electricity supply), meaning that the sick had to pay for the ferry ride nine kilometers across the sea to Dr. Takeuchi's surgery in Kaminoseki. There were also no high schools in the municipality, meaning that students wishing to continue their education beyond junior high school had to pay considerable transport and dormitory expenses as well as normal tuition fees.

The report continued, in excruciating detail, for twenty-nine pages, with another thirty pages of tables and charts outlining the plight of the town. But the conclusion was as clear as could be: other than practicing better birth control,[26] the authors recommended that people seeking work would do best to leave the overpopulated town.

As we might expect, the response of local administrators to the poverty revealed in the 1957 report was somewhat more nuanced. In January 1961, Kaminoseki mayor Kanō Shin addressed his New Year's message to the people of the town under the heading "A Bright and Rich Town-Making."[27] The year 1960, he began, had been "the worst year," with severe typhoon damage and an outbreak of polio in the town; but three years after the merger of Murotsu and Kaminoseki, he claimed, the new administration was at last beginning to realize a new town-making plan that would result in an expansion of land for agriculture and urgent improvement of the ports.

Although the actual language of town-making (*machi-zukuri*) was new, Kanō's message marked the continuation of an older discourse in Kaminoseki.[28] Until 1961, articles in the *Town News* regularly referred to "the construction of a bright town" (*akarui machi no kensetsu*) or, in the premerger period, "the construction of a bright village"—both phrases that echoed Prime Minister Katayama Tetsu's famous call, in 1947, for the "construction of a democratic nation of peace, a nation of culture" (*heiwa kokka, bunka kokka no kensetsu*).[29] In the immediate postwar years, the discourse of "construction" was thus both figurative and literal: a vision both of a better state and of a bomb-scarred landscape built anew. For communities such as Kaminoseki and Murotsu that had been spared physical destruction during the war, "construction" appears to have referred to building one's way out of poverty. In the early 1950s, this had meant road repairs to improve transportation, reclamation of the sea, and the erection of seawalls for protection from typhoons. By the turn of the 1960s, the plans were grander: new fields for farmers, a major redesign of Kaminoseki's historical port and those of smaller communities such as Iwaishima (completed 1961–1965), a plush, three-storied welfare center on the Kaminoseki seafront (1968), the Great Bridge (1969), a new junior high school on Nagashima (1971), a community center on Iwaishima (1971), and eventually the new municipal center in Murotsu, on the former site of the Higo-ya residence (1974).

But as with the construction of a new state at a national level, town-making in Kaminoseki was not merely limited to physical rebuilding. The discourse of construction throughout the 1950s was also linked to a more profound debate about what kind of Japan might emerge from the rubble of defeat and what role village communities might play in the molding of a "democratic nation of peace, a nation of culture." Indeed, a phrase that appeared in Kaminoseki and Murotsu publications throughout the 1950s almost as regularly as "village/town-making" was “cultural improvement” (*bunka no kōjō*). In his New Year’s message of 1954, for example, the mayor of Murotsu listed a number of ways in which village finances could be made “rich,” before concluding, “It goes without saying that based on [ongoing] village development and *cultural improvement,* we shall have bright village-making.” Two years earlier, another author had written an article titled “New Village-Making of the Future,” in which he argued, “At the earliest opportunity, farmers must with their own hands build a rich, bright, and *culturally new* village. For that they must rationalize agricultural management, both in terms of modernization of measurements and of organization.” And in the first edition of the *Kaminoseki Town News,* published a week after the 1958 merger, the caretaker mayor of the new town wrote, “The future of this town lies in promotion of industry, *cultural improvement,* and welfare progress.”[30]

This emphasis on development, modernization, industry, and welfare indicates that the discourse of culture was, at one level, a frame through which to address practical issues of daily life in the town. Such was the view of one contributor to the magazine *Village Culture* (*Mura no bunka*), published by the Kaminoseki Village Combined Youth Association between 1948 and 1949: “Culture is not something that should be distinguished from politics and economics. Rather, we should think of culture as an organic whole [comprising] multiple philosophical and practical aspects, which include *food, clothing, and shelter,* and also everything other than politics and economics. Above all, the most important thing is to show that culture permeates and guides the organization of the life of the masses and functions as a life-forming power that serves to raise everyday life to an ever richer and higher level.”[31]

The link between cultural development and daily life was also recognized by the authors of the 1957 *Living Conditions* report, who noted that the poorer residents of the town devoted considerably less money to “wholesome and cultural” expenditure than their city counterparts precisely because such a high proportion of their income was spent on food, clothing, and shelter. As an example, the report discovered that the diffusion rate of radio sets in the two villages was considerably lower than the prefectural average: 49.5 percent in Kaminoseki and 68.4 percent in Murotsu, compared to 73.4 percent in Yamaguchi as a whole. Consequently, the authors concluded, “many residents suffer a cultural lag [*bunka no okure*], where they are unable to access positive [solutions] to the problems of everyday life.”[32] When town leaders spoke of “cultural improvement,” therefore, they were partly addressing some of the local problems of everyday life revealed by the report.

But radios also helped the people of Kaminoseki join the airwaves of the nation. That is, "cultural improvement" referred not only to raising the daily life of the town to a higher economic level, but also to enabling townspeople to understand better what it meant to be Japanese.[33] This was considered to be particularly important considering the high number of young people in the town—girls and boys who had been born into poverty and many of whom had suffered at a formative age the intense shock of defeat. In February 1947, Ishimaru Hirohito, the recently retired wartime mayor of Kaminoseki village and native of Iwaishima, wrote a message to the island's youth association bemoaning the fact that, two years after the end of the war, "our country is heading down the road to extinction." Given that the Japanese had been "stunned" (*bōzen jishitsu*) at a defeat their country had never experienced in two thousand years of history, it was understandable that young people were increasingly turning to pop music, he wrote. But we must "wake up": "Even in defeat, the strength of Japan is recognized by the whole world. Rather than feeling shame at our defeat, we should be shamed by our behavior after defeat. Let us drink manfully [*isagiyoku*] from the bitter cup of defeat and step forward undaunted on the straight and narrow. . . . Based on openness and kindness, with immediate haste we must once again make Iwaishima—at the very least Iwaishima alone—a bright hometown community [*meirō naru kyōdo*]: this is the great responsibility given to the young people of Iwaishima."[34]

For the former mayor, the project of rebuilding the hometown was thus inseparable from the wider project of constructing a new nation; indeed, this was a point regularly made throughout the 1950s in village and town newsletters.[35] A further way in which the hometown might hope to access the culture of the nation was through the institution of the community center (*kōminkan*). Within the area that would become Kaminoseki town, the first such center was established in Murotsu in August 1954; it came to be known as "the cultural improvement base" (*bunka kōjō no kichi*), and one of the first exhibitions to be held there was a touring photograph display on the peaceful uses of atomic technology.[36] The year following the exhibition, village mayor Nakamori Shōji ended his New Year's greetings by writing, "We are standing at the start of an era in which the peaceful uses of nuclear power are internationally studied and acknowledged; for the sake of peaceful nation-making and village-making, I believe that the whole village must become one and step forward."[37]

The discourse of culture in 1950s Kaminoseki and Murotsu thus bridged both the particular needs of the village (especially poverty alleviation) and the

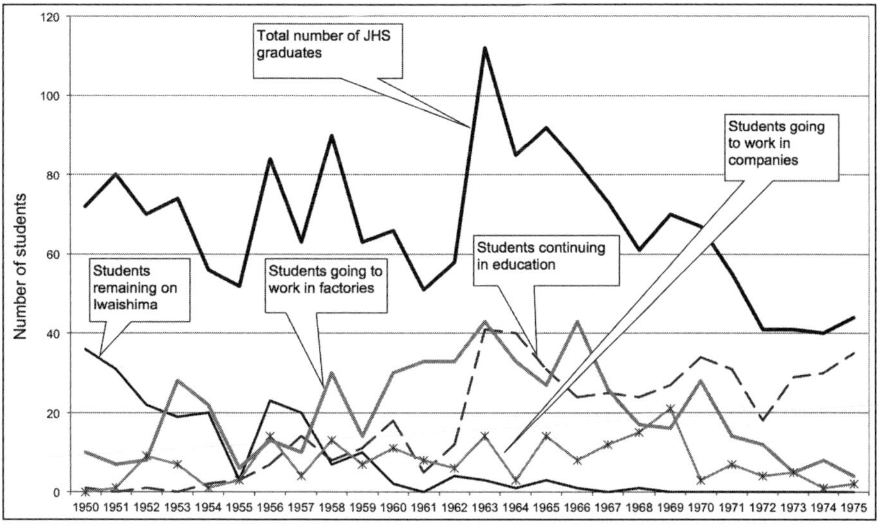

Figure 8.2. Graduation patterns from Iwaishima's junior high school, 1950–1975. Not included in the breakdown of school leavers are "other" or "unknown." (Data courtesy of Iwaishima Junior High School, July 2004)

more general goal of constructing a new postwar nation. Yet there was an inherent tension within these different discourses: the young people whom former Kaminoseki mayor Ishimaru charged with rebuilding the hometown community and hence aiding Japan to overcome bitter defeat were the same young people whom the authors of the 1957 *Living Conditions* report urged to leave the town in order to reduce the problems of overpopulation and poverty. As Figure 8.2 shows, for a few years at the beginning of the 1950s, boys and girls graduating from the junior high school on Ishimaru's native Iwaishima were split between those who left the island for immediate employment or to continue their education and those who stayed mainly to work in fishing, farming, or a family business.[38] By the class of 1960, however, only 2 graduates stayed on the island, while 50 (out of 66) found direct employment in the factories of the rapidly industrializing Inland Sea cities. Iwaishima teachers even started an "Island Newsletter" (*shima dayori*) in order to keep in touch with former students and help them overcome their loneliness.[39] These boys and girls were helping to build a revived nation by providing the cheap labor of the Jinmu and Iwato booms, but their efforts were at a cost to Iwaishima society, which by the late 1960s was waving good-bye to all its junior high school graduates.

Moreover, whereas the discourse of the late 1940s and 1950s had emphasized the "cultural improvement" of the community as a whole, by the early 1960s the *Kaminoseki Town News* made reference to Article 25 of the Constitution in terms of individual rights. The previous year, it noted, only 47 percent of school leavers continued to high school, compared to an average of 72 percent in the prefecture. The main problem was the distance from Nagashima and the outlying islands to high schools—something that made commuting to school and living in dormitories "as expensive as university." Nevertheless, it argued, to give up continuing one's studies for this reason is "pitiful for the children." Despite the attractions of sending one's children straight into employment, another article counseled parents, "what's more important than anything else is to make a decision based not on starting salary but rather on [the child's] future."[40]

Such educational advice implies that "wholesome and cultured living" was more within the reach of some families in Kaminoseki by the early 1960s compared to even a few years earlier—an indication that Japan's astonishing economic growth had led to an improved standard of living even in rural communities.[41] Nevertheless, there was a price to such development: by the early 1960s, the cultural rights of the individual—to secure a meaningful education—were increasingly drawing young people away from Kaminoseki. Although this undoubtedly helped the baby boom generation further reduce the cultural "lag" that had been a concern of the *Living Conditions* authors, it would be clear by the turn of 1970 that the cost was to the community as a whole.

Disappearing Households

In his New Year's message of January 1969, with the completion of the bridge in sight, Mayor Nakamori looked back across the span of modern Japanese history: "Taking last year as an ending—the centenary of the Meiji Restoration and of Japan's becoming a fully fledged modern state—we welcome this new year as the first step forward toward a new era; and, as for our own Kaminoseki, we pray that it is a dazzling [*kagayakashii*] year for the development of the town."[42]

In three different ways, a new era was indeed beginning in town history. In purely demographic terms, Kaminoseki's history from the late eighteenth century until the 1960s had been characterized by population growth. To some extent, new town industries filled some of the gap left by the collapse of domestic trading routes in the late nineteenth century and thus supported the growing population: the fishing industry provided an important source of income to some landless households; the marine transportation industry was another important outlet (see Chapter 9); and the existence of licensed quarters in Kaminoseki and Murotsu ports—at least until their outlawing in 1957–1958—served to attract ships passing through the straits. New agricultural land was cultivated in Iwaishima in the 1910s and 1920s, and the opportunity to work abroad, even for only two or three years, helped support otherwise "impoverished" households.

But from a peak of 13,200 people in 1950 (up from 9,900 in 1944, owing to the repatriate community and especially to the postwar baby boom), the town's population began to fall with alarming speed. Between 1955 and 1960 alone, the population decreased by 1,566 people, or 12 percent; between 1960 and 1975, it fell by another third.[43] Monthly statistics from the *Kaminoseki News* show that this exodus was particularly concentrated around the beginning of the new employment year in April. In the Edo and Meiji periods, March and April had traditionally been the months in which off-season workers, such as those employed in the sake-brewing industry, returned to the town in order to prepare for the summer harvest. But throughout the early 1960s, the proportion of people leaving in March, April, and May accounted for around half of the total number moving away each year. Newspaper photographs from March 1964, kept in the albums of the Iwaishima junior high school, show one such leaving ceremony held at the port. Seven young graduates—mere girls and boys, their uniforms hidden by garlands of origami flowers hung about their necks—stand stiff and unsmiling as hundreds of women and children wave them off.[44] The photographs imply the departure of a whole generation from the town, an impression partly confirmed by official statistics. Figure 8.3 shows a particularly gaping hole in the subsection of the population aged between fifteen and thirty-nine in 1995: compared to the triangular pattern seen in 1950 (see Fig. 8.1), the transformed demographic structure of the town within the time frame of one generation was startling.

Thus the 1960s witnessed a major shift in the employment patterns of townspeople: the days when out-labor might be seasonal and combined with agricultural work were gone, to be replaced instead by year-round work away from Kaminoseki. Those who were leaving were primarily young men and women

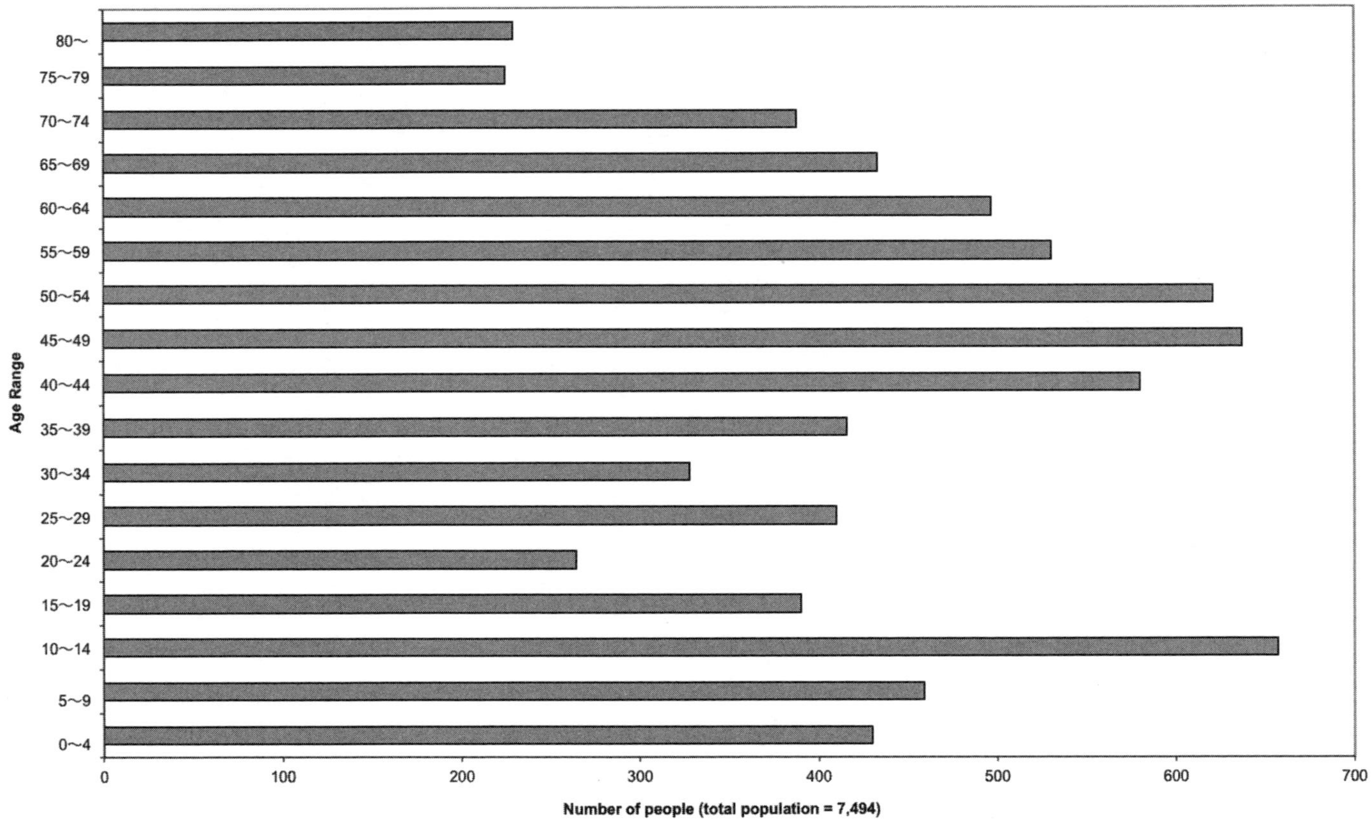

Figure 8.3. The population of Kaminoseki town by age, 1975

born in the immediate postwar years—the generation attending school in 1957, when the *Living Conditions* authors identified a strain on town resources. If those young workers then married after several years away from Kaminoseki—particularly if they married someone from outside the town—there was a high possibility that they would establish a new household permanently away from the hometown, a phenomenon that had not been so common even in the era of transnational migration.[45] As if to acknowledge this concern, in his New Year's message of January 1970, Mayor Nakamori used for the first time in reference to Kaminoseki the phrase "depopulation countermeasures" (*kaso taisaku*). Moreover, in August 1970, the town became one of twenty-four municipalities in Yamaguchi to be targeted under the new nationwide Law on Emergency Measures for Depopulated Areas. Within less than fifteen years, demographic discourse within Kaminoseki had turned 180 degrees from the language of "overpopulation" (blamed for the poverty of the 1950s) to that of "depopulation." It was not the bridge that marked a new era in Kaminoseki history, but rather the depopulation problem.

Of course, the bridge exacerbated the depopulation problem, as town councillors would later realize. But even as early as 1971, it was clear that its completion was not necessarily an unalloyed blessing. In that year, a professor at Yamaguchi University published a report titled *Prospects for the Development of Kaminoseki Town* (*Kaminoseki-chō kaihatsu shindan*). After listing a familiar litany of demographic and employment problems in the town, he turned to the emerging tourist industry. Despite fluctuations in particular years, the overall number of tourists coming to Kaminoseki had increased substantially, to over 100,000 visitors annually in the mid-1960s, he noted. But although he predicted that the completion of the bridge would see this trend continue, most visitors were henceforth likely to be day-trippers: there was thus a fear that the consumption of local services by tourists would not necessarily increase in line with the number of tourists per se.[46] In other words, the great bridge, far from "advancing the economy and culture" of the town, threatened instead to nullify the potential benefits that increased numbers of tourists might bring.

Indeed, the report's concern highlighted a second, more abstract way in which 1969 marked a new era in Kaminoseki's history. Those who lauded the bridge as a "historical achievement" and as a "step forward" in the development of the town made no mention of the fact that its construction actually flew in the face of the town's previous historical identity. In the past, it had been the sea that connected Kaminoseki to the nation, the sea that helped develop the economy and culture of Kaminoseki's communities. Now, however, the sea rendered the town "isolated": the sea must be bridged. Henceforth, outsiders who came to Kaminoseki would do so by car or bus, not by ship, and if they were mainly day-trippers, the place of inns in the local economy—inns that had been so important in the development of the town in the eighteenth and nineteenth centuries—would all but disappear.

In a third and final way, the bridge epitomized a new trend in the economy and culture of the town, albeit a trend that had started in the immediate postwar years. Up until the 1930s, major infrastructure projects in the municipality, such as the construction of schools, roads, new farmland, and communications, were partly supported by the personal benefactions of political elites in the town or by individual and particularly group donations from successful overseas emigrants. In the postwar period, however, the greater scale of infrastructural "improvements"—a new fishing port, a bridge, the deepening of the straits channel to accommodate bigger shipping—effectively precluded such individual philanthropy. In one sense, this was part and parcel of what Shimanaka Hiroshi called, in December 1948, the "democratization of Japan": to become a village official, or even an elected village councillor, a young man no longer needed to display the ability to finance projects for the public welfare of the community. (Electoral success did still partly depend on the candidate's ability to fund private networks of supporters, as we shall see.)

One consequence of this withdrawal of individual donors from major public works projects and of the much greater scale of such projects in the postwar period was that the municipal administration became concomitantly more dependent on the economic intervention of central government in daily life. At the same time, members of the newly expanded electorate expected their local administrators to be able to access those pots of money. This, indeed, was a trend that concerned the author of *Prospects for the Development of Kaminoseki Town* in 1971: "It has become gradually more difficult to live in farming and fishing villages," he wrote, "and life has become harder [*seikatsu ga kurushiku nattekimashita*]. However, compared to the past, life in farming and fishing villages has somehow become better. If people look around their daily lives, the number of electrical devices has increased, and meals have become better. At the very least, compared to the prewar period, the standard of living has improved. But this sense that 'somehow things have gotten better' is a problem: it leads to a sense that 'if things stay like this, then somehow, something [good] will also happen.'"[47]

Yet, as the author knew and as town officials began to fear in 1969–1970, very little good was likely to occur for Kaminoseki if the exodus of young people continued. Therefore, as the ability and willingness of individual philanthropists to support local development projects decreased, so municipal leaders increasingly looked toward Tokyo and toward corporate investment to provide some means of employment. In this way, they hoped to realize the still distant dreams of a bright tomorrow.

9

Furusato Boom, Kaminoseki Bust

> *Let us preserve nature: let us reconsider the cultural assets in our midst!*
>
> Cultural assets are said to be the *furusato* of our heart. Such cultural assets in the natural world—the various assets that over time have been nurtured in our midst—are now gradually being lost owing to pollution and the transformation of the social environment. We must therefore look anew at those precious assets, in the present environment, that have been passed down from old: we must become intimate with them, treat them with care, and preserve them as inheritances that will truly give pleasure to the next generation.

Thus began a front-page article in the *Town News* edition of 20 November 1971, some six months after the election of the new mayor, Kanō Shin. In part, the article is of interest because of the language of "cultural assets" (*bunkazai*): whereas in the mid-1950s, cultural discourse in Kaminoseki had been tied to the desired "improvement" of everyday living conditions and to the construction of a "culturally new" municipality, by the early 1970s, it instead looked back to the "old" (*furui*) times of the past. But exactly what should be preserved from that past and in what form it should be passed on to the next generation became the subject of increasingly heated debates in the late 1970s and 1980s.

The significance of those debates was heightened by the discourse of *furusato,* appearing in the pages of the *Town News* for the first time. Literally meaning "old village," *furusato*—which can also be transliterated as *kokyō*—has been translated by scholars as "native place," "home village," and "my old country home," but to my mind "hometown" best captures the sense of roots, tradition, and nostalgic community harmony implied by the word. Before the 1970s, there had been two major waves of *furusato/kokyō* popular discourse in Japan, in the 1880s and in the 1920s—both periods that coincided with intense urbanization and that thus found young urban newcomers pining for the supposedly simpler, better community life that they had left behind.[1] But the third, postwar wave, known as the "*furusato* boom," was different: whereas the city dwellers who had yearned for their hometowns in previous periods were likely to be first-generation migrants who had specific memories of a particular village and who maintained ties to that village through older relatives, their counterparts in the 1970s were generally two or three generations removed from the countryside. As numerous scholars have argued, this meant that city dwellers idealized rural Japan to an extent even greater than in previous waves, as they projected their desire for an unpolluted and "natural" environment onto supposedly unspoiled hometowns—the real travails of which they were ignorant.[2]

The *Town News* article suggests that local administrators in communities such as Kaminoseki attempted to voice similar concerns over nature, pollution, and the social environment from the early 1970s onward. But as this and subsequent chapters reveal, the discourses of hometown life at the local level would develop in very different ways from those crafted by consumers of the *furusato* boom in the cities. Indeed, to study the *furusato* boom of the 1970s is more to study the experiences of people who left the hometown than of those who stayed behind. What, we might ask, did people *in* the hometown feel about their *furusato*?

The postwar history of Kaminoseki offers us one answer to that question not only because we can reconstruct the reality of everyday life in significant detail, but also because Kaminoseki became the particular object of idealized *furusato* representations in the mid-1970s. In April 1974, the Japan Broadcasting Corporation (Nippon Hōsō Kyōkai) began to screen a new "morning drama"—a genre of television soap opera that regularly drew more than 20 million viewers right through the 1960s and 1970s.[3] *Hatoko's Sea* (*Hatoko no umi*) told the fictional story of a young girl, orphaned by the Hiroshima atomic bomb, who grew up in Kaminoseki, moved to Tokyo at the age of twenty, and then eventually returned to her hometown in the drama's final episodes, set and screened in March 1975. By juxtaposing the fictional story of Hatoko with the concerns and expectations of Kaminoseki town councillors, this chapter highlights the extent to which another postwar divide, between urban representations and rural realities of hometown preservation, had emerged in Japan by the mid-1970s.

But *Hatoko's Sea* was also important for a second reason: the drama was made, and screened, at a particular time in Japanese history, when the aftermath of the first Oil Shock (October 1973) threatened to undermine the very foundations of the postwar economic model, thereby bringing the "bright life" to a premature end. A significant subplot in the drama is thus the importance of atomic energy as a substitute for Japan's overdependence on Middle Eastern oil. Although the author of *Hatoko's Sea* could not know it, this was a story line that resonated in Kaminoseki itself—not because of the nuclear power plant plan, which was still more than five years away, but because the livelihoods of hundreds of Kaminoseki households were tied to the evolution of Japan's mid-twentieth-century energy policy. To understand the concerns and expectations of Kaminoseki's town councillors at the time that *Hatoko's Sea* was screened, we therefore need to understand those leaders' experience of Japan's postwar energy transformation—a story that will take us back, for the moment, to the early Meiji period.

The Kase and Katayama Households

On the northwest side of Nagashima island stands the village of Shiraida, a settlement whose 148 households, in the early 1840s, ascended steeply from a small port. In the Edo period, Shiraida "farmers," like their counterparts in other neighboring settlements, engaged in by-employments: while young laborers from Iwaishima went to sake breweries and those from Yashima served as crew on whaling ships, Shiraida's men went to work in the salt fields of Mitajiri, in central Chōshū. Early modern salt manufacturing entailed boiling concentrated sea brine to produce salt crystals. For this purpose, coal was transported to the Inland Sea from the rich seams of northern Kyushu; by the late nineteenth century, half of all the coal mined from northern Kyushu was used for salt production.[4] The coal was carried in small, thirty- to forty-ton cargo ships, and, starting in the 1870s, Shiraida villagers began to join these ships as an alternative source of by-employment—one that was less back-breaking than working in the salt fields.

The wooden ships sailed not only between northern Kyushu and central Yamaguchi prefecture (as Chōshū had become), but also to the salt fields of Okayama and, on the northern coast of Shikoku, Ehime and Kagawa.[5] Thus the straits communities once again found themselves on a key shipping route through the western Inland Sea. As small harbors with a history of welcoming *kitamae*-ships, they were ideally placed to service the overnight needs of the coal transporters, which were themselves of an ideal size to navigate the narrow channels of the Inland Sea.

Similar to their Edo period predecessors, the small ships sailing through the straits at the turn of the twentieth century were generally operated by independent owners rather than franchised by large corporations such as Mitsubishi or Mitsui. As the demand for coal rose in newly industrializing Japan and as steel also began to be transported eastward from the huge new factory at Yawata in northern Kyushu (opened 1901), there were new employment opportunities for anyone who could afford to buy a ship. If there happened to be shipbuilders in the village (such as Kaminoseki's Niikawa household, whose son went to Hawai'i), construction costs could be kept local and thus somewhat reduced. If the aspirant ship owner was bound into a complex network of household and kinship ties (similar to the pattern on Iwaishima), then he effectively belonged to a mutual assistance association that could lend him money and thus keep debts within the community. And if there was a surplus of young workers who owned no land and who had no steady income stream, then there were many potential crew members who could be cheaply employed, helping to reduce operational costs and thus enabling the ship owner to repay his debts faster.[6] Such was how the marine transportation industry (*kaiungyō*) began to develop in Shiraida, where the number of ships owned by hamlet residents increased from 31 to 50 between 1906 and 1913, and ship tonnage also increased by as much as eightfold, to more than 300 tons per vessel in the mid-1930s.[7]

For an enterprising young man such as Kase Mihosuke (c. 1877–1932), the development of the marine transportation industry offered an opportunity to restore battered household fortunes. Mihosuke was the third son of Kase Chūnoshin, a former sword smith who had worked in the mid-1860s under the professional name Seiryūken Moritsugu. The *tsugu* of his given name, meaning "next," indicates that he was probably the chosen successor to Seiryūken Moritoshi II, a master sword smith who worked for Lord Kikkawa, daimyo of the Chōshū subdomain of Iwakuni.[8] The Seiryūken swords were not particularly famous outside of Iwakuni, nor are they rated very highly by experts today, but to be a sword smith in the direct employ of a daimyo at least guaranteed one a steady income from the domain. Moritsugu/Chūnoshin, who was probably born in the mid-1840s and whose workshop was in the Kaminoseki port area, may have believed he had a promising career ahead of him—especially given that Japanese sword smithery had revived in the first half of the nineteenth century, following the perception of a new threat from the West.[9]

Unfortunately for Chūnoshin, it was not to be. In 1871, the new Meiji government not only abolished the Edo period domain governments, but also, in an effort to be seen as "modern" by the Western powers, forbade the carrying of swords. Having effectively been made redundant, Chūnoshin was asked by the Shinto priest of Shiraida to use his metalwork skills to make agricultural tools for local farmers.[10] Relative to farmers, rural blacksmiths could earn a decent income in mid-Meiji Japan: in nearby Ōshima county, their average monthly income was 4.7 yen in 1885 (5.7 yen for the most successful practitioners), while that of the average farmer was 3.2 yen—although both incomes were much smaller than those earned by Hawaiian emigrants in the same period.[11] Three of Chūnoshin's seven sons, including Mihosuke, also trained as blacksmiths, and, at some point between Chūnoshin's death (in 1892) and 1905, Mihosuke established a branch household and a workshop specializing in the manufacture and repair of spades, scythes, knives, scissors, harpoons, and other agricultural and fishing tools.[12]

As he looked across the straits from his Kaminoseki workshop to the sail-powered coal transporters passing by, Kase Mihosuke realized that the village's "culture" could no longer rely on the production of knives, scythes, and the like. In the mid-1910s, he began to hear about a new type of internal combustion engine that had been developed in the West and was now being manufactured in one or two Inland Sea shipyards. Known in Japanese as *yakidama,* the hot-bulb engine was safer, more efficient, and easier to operate than its steam counterpart. Thus Mihosuke decided to send his brother-in-law and apprentice, Nishiyama Yōichi (born 1892), to study the design of hot-bulb engines at the Nakatani Engineworks in Okayama prefecture.[13] When Nishiyama returned, the Kase workshop began to manufacture engines for local ship owners. As demand picked up—with the Kase engines becoming known as far afield as Hiroshima, Ōita, Kōchi, and even Shanghai—Mihosuke also sent his eldest son, Kiyotoshi (born c. 1907), to study hot-bulb engines at technical high school in Hiroshima; he had chosen the *toshi* character for his son in memory of Seiryūken Moritoshi II, the given name of his father's sword smith master.

From swords to ploughshares and now to engines: in just two generations, the Kase household had reinvented itself as a manufacturer not of traditional weaponry but of modern technology. In so doing, it entered a period of remarkable prosperity: in 1914, Mihosuke paid the median rate of household tax in Kaminoseki, but by 1948 his son Kiyotoshi was the joint-highest taxpayer in the village municipality, with former apprentice Nishiyama Yōichi also ranked in the top 5 percent of taxpaying households.[14] Nishiyama, for his part, bought a prime plot of land next to the Kase Engineworks in 1931 and constructed his own two-story house there five years later; his "unprecedented" success apparently caused him to be seen as a "hero" on Iwaishima, whence he originally came.[15] At its zenith, the Kase workshop employed up to thirty local workers and apprentices, some of whom went on to establish their own engineworks on Iwaishima or in the outlying hamlets of Nagashima.

One of the Kase Engineworks' first local customers would have been Katayama Shimazō, from the village of Shiraida. Although Shimazō was the son of a master shipbuilder, he decided to construct his own ship and then to make a living as a ship operator, not as a carpenter.[16] As coal production continued to expand through the 1920s and the 1930s, reaching a peak of nearly 57 million tons in 1940,[17] perhaps his decision reflected the greater profit a ship owner could potentially make: more coal meant more money for men like Shimazō. Although records from 1931 indicate that the Katayama household paid only the average rate of household tax relative to others in Shiraida, five years earlier, Shimazō had been one of the first men in the village to attach a hot-bulb engine to his ship.[18] In so doing, he turned a sailboat (*hansen*) into a hybrid engine-sail boat (*kihansen*) and thus was at the forefront of a dramatic increase in such hybrid boats throughout the Inland Sea region.[19] In Shiraida itself, of the 76 ships registered to the hamlet in 1939 (a ratio of more than one ship to every three households), 42 were hybrid engine-sail ships, while only 34 were traditional sailboats.[20]

With new power, Shimazō was also able to travel farther afield: in the 1930s, he regularly carried a cargo of timber from Mokpo in Korea to Osaka, at the same time initiating his first son, Hideyuki (born 1931), into the ways of the sea. From the outbreak of the Pacific War onward, Shimazō worked as a captain on an oil tanker, transporting that precious commodity from Southeast Asia back to the Japanese mainland. But as the United States tightened its submarine blockade of the archipelago in 1944–1945, the merchant navy was particularly vulnerable to attack. Shimazō's tanker was sunk by a bomb late in November 1944: the captain lost both legs in the blast and died soon afterward in Taiwan.[21]

Katayama Hideyuki was just thirteen when his father died, and instead of entering high school, as he had planned, he joined one of Shiraida's hybrid engine-sail ships as a junior crew member so as to support his widowed mother.

From 1947, coal production in western Japan began to recover from the devastation of war, and Hideyuki's ship transported coal from the Ube mines, in central-southern Yamaguchi, to the generating plants of Kansai Electric Company in Amagaseki, near Kobe. The years 1947–1952 were a period of "easy money" for shippers,[22] and Hideyuki, who had become a captain in around 1950, began to save money in order to buy his own engine-sail boat—a dream that he achieved five years later, when he bought a 100-ton secondhand ship from a friend in Shiraida. The cost of the boat was 1,000,000 yen: a mutual association fund raised one-third of the money, relatives lent another third, and the final 300,000 yen was given by his wife's relatives to mark the occasion of Hideyuki's marriage. Hideyuki now became one of Shiraida's sixty-five hybrid ship owners—a ratio of one boat to every four households—and in a pattern repeated throughout the Inland Sea, his wife joined his ship as a crew member. The engine-sail boats were family businesses in every sense of the word.[23]

The first three months of 1957 thus saw Katayama Hideyuki continuing to make money at sea and Kase Kiyotoshi (Mihosuke's son) entering the third and final year of his term as head (*kuchō*) of Kaminoseki district—a reflection of the ongoing political and economic status of the Kase Engineworks within the village. One of Kase's duties in these months would have been to assist researchers from Yamaguchi prefecture as they gathered data on every aspect of economic life in the municipality. Their subsequent report, *The Living Conditions of Residents in the Districts of Murotsu and Kaminoseki,* highlighted the importance of the marine transportation industry to the town's wider economy. In general terms, marine transportation accounted for 41 percent of the total income generated by town industries in 1955—equivalent to that generated by fishing and farming combined. The particular dependence of the local economy on the engine-sail ships could be gauged in three other ways. First, nearly a third of the town's 160 manufacturing laborers were employed in engineworks such as that owned by Kase Kiyotoshi. These workshops, each staffed by no more than fifteen people in the 1950s, were the biggest single manufacturing employers in the municipality.[24] Second, 95 percent of the 113 ship-owning households in the town employed between two and nine workers (the standard crew for an engine-sail ship was four or five people). Since the vast majority of these employees were locals, more than four hundred townspeople—around 8 percent of the total workforce—earned their living as crewmembers in the hybrid ships. Third, 94 percent of the ships that docked at either Kaminoseki or Murotsu ports in 1955 and on which shopkeepers, inn owners, and brothel proprietors were dependent, weighed below 500 tons—the majority of them hybrid boats from other regions of the Inland Sea.

In other words, the economies of several hundred ship-owning, engine-building, and crew-providing households in Kaminoseki plus several hundred more shop-proprietor households were either directly or indirectly dependent on the proliferation of engine-sail boats in the mid-twentieth-century Inland Sea. As long as coal remained the primary source of fuel for the Japanese economy, these households were assured some kind of livelihood—even if, as the report revealed, the standard of living in Kaminoseki was lower than anywhere else in Yamaguchi prefecture.

All this changed with the first energy revolution—a shift from domestic coal to the cheap imported oil that underpinned the so-called Jinmu boom (1955–1958) and thus coincided with the emergence of the "bright life" rhetoric in postwar Japan.[25] As oil replaced coal, steel tankers came to be necessary: this meant a decline in business for Kaminoseki's shipbuilders, who generally specialized in wooden construction. As steel tankers replaced wooden ships, stronger engines came to be necessary: this meant that traditional engine-works, such as the Kase/Nishiyama workshop, increasingly dealt not with hot-bulb but with diesel engines, which were too complex for them to manufacture on site and which also cost more. As the costs of tankers and engines increased, new forms of capital were necessary: for would-be ship owners in a small community with an already high poverty rate, this meant applying for bank loans, which were more difficult to acquire than mutual association arrangements between local friends. And as the size and navigational capabilities of ships improved, small harbors such as Kaminoseki and Murotsu became less convenient places to dock—especially once the licensed quarters had been outlawed in 1957–1958.

The 1960s thus witnessed a dramatic decline in the number of hybrid engine-sail boats not only in Kaminoseki, but also nationwide. Overall, the number of wooden cargo boats in the Inland Sea peaked at 25,600 in 1963 but declined to 6,600 in 1974. In the same period, the number of steel cargo ships (under 500 tons) increased fivefold, to 5,600, and the number of steel oil tankers (under 500 tons) increased almost threefold, to 2,200.[26] No statistics survive for the Nagashima hamlet of Shiraida, but if the rate of decline in wooden engine-sail ships reflected the nationwide figures, then perhaps fewer than twenty households remained as wooden ship owners by the early 1970s. The nationwide shift from coal to oil, and its consequences for Kaminoseki's marine transportation industry, was surely one explanation for the exodus of young people from the town between 1955 and 1975.

As with the economic transformations of Kaminoseki and Murotsu in the late nineteenth century, not everyone was a loser. In the Japanese idiom, ship owners in the late 1950s and early 1960s could become "fat" by selling their secondhand ships to others and upgrading to newer, bigger ships whose greater tonnage brought greater profits.[27] One such success story was Katayama Hideyuki himself: in around 1960, he became one of the first and only men in Shiraida to make the transition from wooden engine-sail ship to steel oil tanker—a 300-ton vessel that he bought with the help of a substantial loan from a local bank. Over the next decade, he kept upgrading to ships with a bigger tonnage, each time selling his older vessel cheaply to a neighboring ship-owning household.

By 1970, Katayama's company, Matsuyama Kisen, operated five oil tankers, each of which employed several local crewmembers. In this way, he created a web of social and financial dependencies that would serve him well when, in 1970, he was apparently prevailed upon to become a town councillor. Aged thirty-nine, Katayama was the youngest of all successful candidates that year. In the following 1974 election he polled more votes than any other councillor in the town, and in 1978 he became speaker of the council assembly.[28] His was a meteoric political rise in a town facing economic and population decline.

Hatoko's Hometown, 1974–1975

Born in 1931, Katayama Hideyuki was, at most, nine years older than the fictional Hatoko; like her, he had lost his father in the war. But as the opening episodes of *Hatoko's Sea* made clear, Hatoko lost everything in the war, including her name.

The opening scene of the first episode, broadcast on 1 April 1974, features Hatoko in her mid-thirties, strolling along an unidentified sandy beach—actually a beach in Murotsu—and gazing out to sea. As the camera zooms in, she turns to face us directly, and her tender features dissolve into a dark, featureless screen labeled "Shōwa 20 [1945], August." We see the mushroom cloud over Hiroshima and hear a child crying. A new scene opens: a scorching day, and a little girl limps along the side of a railway track, disheveled and in tears. As a passenger train trundles by, overflowing with refugees fleeing a destroyed city, a woman falls off and begs for water, her hands bearing the unmistakable scars of the bomb. The girl has nothing to give and must watch the woman die in agony.[29]

Eventually, the girl is picked up from the side of the railway track by a friendly soldier, a deserter on the run. She is taken to his hometown, a place called Yanai, and then on to a village called Murotsu. Cast ashore from Murotsu to drift in a rowboat across the straits, her journey ends in Kaminoseki: there she is adopted by the local people and given—in reference to the Old Testament symbol of peace—the name Hatoko, "dove child." She will be raised by a kindly family and attend school in the village until eventually she decides to strike off on her own for a new life in Tokyo. The year is 1959, and Hatoko is about to turn twenty: Japan is entering the Iwato boom as Hatoko enters adulthood.

As with many other NHK morning dramas broadcast since the genre's inception in 1961, *Hatoko's Sea* served as a lens on the social fabric of postwar Japan. At its most basic level, the story of an ordinary woman overcoming family hardships—a common theme in such dramas—was a metaphor for the recovery of Japan from the depths of war.[30] Thus Hatoko's memory loss, triggered (as the drama reveals) by witnessing at close hand the atomic bomb, stood for the collective trauma of 1945, while her growth to adulthood, according to a newspaper retrospective thirty years after the first broadcast, "traced the path of the postwar Japanese people."[31] In these ways, the protagonist was similar to that of another NHK morning drama in the 1980s, *Oshin,* in which grandmother Oshin is "Japan itself, and her life therefore takes the viewer on a guided tour of the landmarks of twentieth-century history."[32] (Along with *Oshin, Hatoko's Sea* was one of the most popular series NHK has ever made, with an average rating of 47.2 percent of all television viewers across the twelve-month period of its transmission.)[33]

At a second level, *Hatoko's Sea* was a story of a young woman's search for her own identity—an identity effaced by the bomb but eventually rediscovered at the end of the drama. In this way, Hatoko's life journey spoke to one of the central themes of the *furusato* boom, namely, the search for individual identity through domestic travel. The opening image of the drama, for example, echoed the iconic images of the 1970–1978 "Discover Japan" campaign, designed for Japan National Railways by the advertising giant Dentsu. Just as Hatoko was depicted walking alone on a deserted beach, so "Discover Japan" featured images of young women strolling pensively through beautiful but unidentified Japanese landscapes—crossing paths with a Buddhist monk on an ancient forest path bathed in sunlight, for example, or meeting a wrinkled old farmer near a quiet mountain shrine.[34]

The account executive of the campaign was Fujioka Wakao, a Dentsu employee who, like Hatoko, had been evacuated from Tokyo to western Japan during the war (in his case to Iwakuni, roughly halfway between Kaminoseki and Hiroshima). Fujioka later recalled that "Discover Japan" stood not only for the anticipated discovery that young women would make of a physical landscape, but also for the discovery of themselves: they sought "a stage on which they might play out their own journey."[35] Just as rural locations reached by train could be "stages" for these women, so Kaminoseki was merely a backdrop for Hatoko's journey of discovery. By watching the drama each morning, a viewer might learn plenty about the character of the protagonist but very little about Kaminoseki itself—about the depopulation crisis that was beginning, for example, in exactly the period she was depicted as leaving the hometown. In this way, both the drama and "Discover Japan" epitomized what one contemporary scholar called "the apparition of *furusato*," in which metropolitan viewers and travelers expressed an interest in generalized hometowns that were themselves stripped of any individuality and referenced instead by idealized images of mountains, rivers, forests, and (in the case of *Hatoko's Sea*) beaches.[36]

Hatoko may have discovered her own identity, but by the end of the drama's screening, Kaminoseki's leaders faced the loss of the town's, especially in the wake of the hybrid shipping industry's decline. In this regard, a third theme of *Hatoko's Sea* was important, at least in hindsight. After Hatoko arrives in Tokyo, she is courted by a young man called Kiyohisa, a nuclear physicist who works for Japan Atomic Power Company on the development of the country's first ever atomic reactor, located in the village of Tōkaimura, northeast of Tokyo. In a crucial scene, Kiyohisa attempts to convince Hatoko of the value of his research. "No matter how things ended up for you because of the atomic bomb," he pleads, having heard the story of how she was brought to Kaminoseki in August 1945, "I don't want you to mix that up with the research I'm now doing into the peaceful uses of the atom. Atomic power in itself is not evil; rather, it's the humans dealing with atomic power who have the problem."[37]

Kiyohisa's arguments spoke to the particular aftermath of the first Oil Shock, when the market price for a single barrel of oil jumped from around $3 in early 1973 to nearly $12 by January 1974.[38] With 62 percent of Japanese electricity generation dependent on oil,[39] Tokyo bureaucrats had long been aware of the economy's overdependence on imported oil: hence the construction of an atomic reactor at Tōkaimura in the early 1960s, a project on which the fictional Kiyohisa was working as he attempted to convince Hatoko to marry him. Indeed, a young politician and future prime minister called Nakasone Yasuhiro (born 1918) had been petitioning the US occupation authorities to permit Japanese nuclear research as early as 1951. Although Nakasone successfully requested a budget for such research from the Lower House of the Diet in March 1954, the attempts of the pronuclear lobby to make a distinction in the popular mind between nuclear destruction and "atoms for peace" were undermined by the *Lucky Dragon* incident in the same month, when Japanese fishermen were fatally exposed to radioactive fallout from US nuclear weapons tests on the Bikini Atoll.[40]

This so-called nuclear allergy, from which Hatoko and millions of other Japanese suffered, was one reason that a direct transition from coal-generated electricity to nuclear-generated electricity was never realized; the cheapness of Middle East oil and various technological difficulties were also factors in the shift first from coal to oil.[41] But the Oil Shock underlined the need for a second energy revolution, from oil to the atom, to be accelerated in the early 1970s. Apart from anything else, this was necessary for the maintenance of a standard of living by which millions of Japanese took it for granted that they could sit down and watch a fifteen-minute television drama each morning, on what was now in most cases a color television. The heroine of *Hatoko's Sea* thus found herself drawn into a wider debate, through Kiyohisa, about the nature of Japan's energy future. This was a fictional story line, depicted as occurring in the early 1960s, that nevertheless reflected a real debate that was taking place in Japan in 1974–1975, at the time of the drama's broadcast.

In Kaminoseki, the convergence of post–Oil Shock energy policy, the landscape of *Hatoko's Sea,* and the preservation of the *furusato* first occurred in November 1976, when Mitsubishi Corporation proposed the construction of a major storage depot for Liquified Petroleum Gas (LPG) in the municipality.[42] The promotion of LPG was one aspect of the Japanese government's response to the Oil Shock: no electricity had been generated by LPG in 1965, but by 1975 it accounted for 2 percent of nationwide generation, rising to 3 percent in 1985.[43] The overall strategic importance of weaning Japan off its dependence on imported crude oil was thus the first point made by Kaminoseki officials as they attempted to explain the benefits of the LPG plan to town residents.[44]

The national picture notwithstanding, municipal leaders were privately more focused on the local benefits of the proposal. Thus, in a confidential report prepared by senior town councillor Suzuki Ryōichi, we can sense the disappointment that some town leaders felt at the downturn in town fortunes since the heady days of June 1969: "Ten years ago, Kaminoseki bridge was completed and, at that time, great prosperity was expected for Nagashima and for the whole municipality. But looking at the trends of the last ten years, the ironic result is that depopulation has progressed and that the bridge has instead actually spurred the outflow of people [from the town]."[45] Indeed, statistics revealed to town leaders that as large numbers of workers left the town each year, tax revenues declined: local taxation (*chihōzei*) had accounted for 16 percent of the municipality's total income in 1960 but fell to half that figure in 1975. Conversely, Kaminoseki's dependence on central government subsidies (*chihō kōfuzei*) rose from 38 percent to 47 percent in the same period.[46] Thus Suzuki summarized "what we can expect" from the LPG plan: between 80 and 100 new workers in the town, leading to an increase of between 100 and 150 children in the future and thus a "halt" (*hadome*) to the ongoing exodus, with positive knock-on effects also for the town's farmers, fishermen, shopkeepers, and the local construction industry.

The planned site for the depot was a bay called Nakanoura, four kilometers west of the town center near Hetsu, a hamlet on the northern shore of Nagashima. Faced with the prospect of major land reclamation and the leveling of several hills around the site, landowners in Hetsu led a determined fight against Mitsubishi, and in 1980 the plan was quietly shelved—much to the bitter disappointment of pro-LPG lobbyists. Nevertheless, one significance of the proposal was that it indicated the extent to which town leaders were open to any and all proposals that might fulfill their avowed aim of "attracting business" (*kigyō yūchi*) to Kaminoseki—even if it meant ripping up the very beaches and seascape that made the town seem so idyllic to viewers of *Hatoko's Sea*.

This, therefore, was the dilemma posed by the discourse of *furusato* at a local level in mid-1970s Japan. On the one hand, the "cultural assets" of Kaminoseki were intimately tied to the preservation of the town's beautiful "nature": these were what attracted tourists and television producers alike to the town. On the other hand, the exodus of young people and the decline of the local economy threatened the "culture" of the hometown in terms of an older discourse of everyday life and standard of living. The *Town News* article of November 1971 claimed that the preservation of cultural assets "will truly give pleasure to the next generation." But councillor Suzuki, presumably echoing the concerns of many town administrators in his 1979 report, begged to differ. In explaining his wholehearted support for the Mitsubishi LPG plan, he wrote: "Our ancestors are important, but at the same time our children and grandchildren are also important. For the sake of those who will follow us, the preservation of Kaminoseki's fundamental elements, which have been entrusted to us, can be considered to be the true work of the town councillors."

Indeed, with Katayama Hideyuki as the speaker of the town assembly in the period 1978–1982, the "true work" of the town councillors was about to begin.

10

Nuclear Decision

In the early 1980s, a new player emerged in the life of the Kaminoseki hometown. With time, the presence of Chugoku Electric Power Company would seep into the everyday consciousness of townspeople. The company's branch offices on the main road into Murotsu; the bright green, three-storied Museum of the Future (Mirai-kan), adjacent to the former site of the Chōshū domain's administrative offices (*bansho*); the published tide schedules that fishermen consulted morning and night; the sponsorship signs on the Bōchō buses; the monthly newsletters delivered to every household; the small apartment complex for company employees just down from Jōyama Hill: by the early 2000s, these were the everyday markers of a thriving partnership between the municipality and Chugoku Electric.

It was less clear how that partnership had begun. As told by the company itself, the time line of events started in June 1982, when a Kaminoseki town councillor asked the mayor, Kanō Shin, about the possible construction of an atomic power station in the municipality. "If the townspeople are in agreement," the mayor responded, "then we may seek this development." Subsequently, a subcommittee of the council was established in order to consider initiatives that might attract investment to the town, and, in October 1984, the council formally requested that Chugoku Electric carry out a preliminary investigation (*jizen chōsa*) for a power plant. In response to this request, the company established a site office, and, in May 1985, it reported that the western tip of Nagashima island was "an eligible candidate site for a nuclear power station." During this period, the number of voices in Kaminoseki advocating the development of a nuclear power station increased, and in June 1985 eighteen different pronuclear civil society groups submitted a petition to the town council demanding that an official approach be made to Chugoku Electric—something that the council did in September 1985. Finally, in September 1988, the town mayor (now Katayama Hideyuki) made an application to the company formally requesting that it build a nuclear power station in the municipality.[1]

Two other sources, the regional *Chūgoku shinbun* newspaper and the *Kaminoseki Town History,* also begin their time line of Chugoku Electric's entry into town politics with reference to the summer of 1982. But, as this chapter will argue—partly using evidence from both those sources, complemented by interviews—there was a far more complex back story to the nuclear power station plan than first appears on paper. To tell this story is important for two reasons. First, it adds to our understanding of how and why contentious Japanese infrastructure projects have been sited in the postwar period: although scholars have analyzed the role of private utility companies and the central government in so-called site fights, there is still little understanding of the role that local people played in such controversies.[2]

Perhaps more important, the nuclear story enables us to understand the extent to which Meiji period hometown structures endured into the late twentieth century. Although the dispute over nuclear power in many ways ripped apart the social fabric of Kaminoseki, thus giving a different intensity to the crisis of the 1980s from those that the hometown had faced in previous decades (see Chapter 11), the ways in which the subject of nuclear power was first broached in Kaminoseki nevertheless underlined the survival of older forms of political and social interaction. In particular, power was concentrated—as it had been in the nineteenth century—in the hands of a few key men, including some from the oldest known households in the town. Just as their political predecessors appear to have used their social and economic status to influence the outcome of village elections in the 1890s, so Kaminoseki's politicians in the early 1980s practiced "status seduction" in an attempt to accelerate the nuclear proposal—something that depended on the survival of older forms of vertical, hierarchical relations in hometown life.

As in analyses of hometown life in the late nineteenth century, identifying underlying structures in the 1980s is one thing, but it is quite another to work out the individual motivations of the key players. In general terms, however, it is clear that the assumptions of many town leaders in 1981–1982 were framed by their experience of the early postwar decades. In this sense, nuclear power, which in national terms came to have added significance after the 1973 Oil Shock, was seen in local terms as simply one more proposal to attain the elusive "bright life" in Kaminoseki—the latest perceived solution in a long history of responses to economic decline in the hometown.

The Kanō Household

In the heart of old Kaminoseki, a few doors west of the warehouse in which the Murotsu and Kaminoseki village archives were rediscovered, stands one of the largest residences of the Edo period, the Kanō household (Kaga-ya). Like the Awa-ya household, the Kaga-ya was a shipping agent (*ton'ya*) in the mid-nineteenth century, specializing in the storage and sale of timber from the Hyūga region of eastern Kyushu (present-day Miyazaki prefecture). In those days, the main entrance to the two-story residence faced directly onto the straits: a stone lantern in front of the house, on what is now reclaimed land, would be lit every evening to guide the *kitamae*-ships into the port.

The fourth-generation head of the household in the mid-Meiji period was Kanō Sauemon, who was first elected to the village council in 1891 (see Table 4.1). Sauemon also served as the village's first postmaster between 1901 and 1905, and he or his son (also called Sauemon) was ranked in the top 1 percent of the village's 1,400 taxpaying households in 1914.[3] Kanō, in other words, was still very much an elite household in early-twentieth-century Kaminoseki, and it was into this elite setting that Kanō Shin was born, also in 1914. Although Shin was a second son, he eventually became the sixth-generation head of the Kanō household, and, in 1959, he continued the family line in politics by becoming the first postmerger mayor of the new Kaminoseki town.

In fact, Kanō's rise to political prominence was not as smooth as the above synopsis might suggest: following the premature death of the household head (Shin's father) in 1918, the family had nearly gone bankrupt and was forced to sell much of its former lumberyard land. Kanō himself had been a prisoner of war in Siberia until 1946 and then sold yet more land on his return to Kaminoseki.[4] Even his political career was not always successful: from head of the fishing cooperative in the 1950s to mayor in 1959, he then lost his reelection bid in 1963 to a candidate from Murotsu. Only in 1971 was he once again elected mayor, a position that he served, unopposed, for three terms until 1983.

By the late 1970s, one of the late mayor's many relatives told me, Kanō realized that Kaminoseki's "fire had gone out" (*hi ga kieta*).[5] For this reason, he was apparently an enthusiastic supporter of the LPG proposal, first made by Mitsubishi Corporation in November 1976.[6] When that plan failed, both the mayor and the then speaker of the town council, Katayama Hideyuki, used their annual greetings in the *Town News* to express their fears and frustrations. Both noted their concern over Kaminoseki's depopulation problem in 1979, for example, with Katayama warning that "we must devise a decisive policy that takes advantage of this town's land [resources]."[7] A year later, Kanō wrote of needing to attract business to the town (*kigyō yūchi*) as part of depopulation countermeasures, while Katayama, foreshadowing the pronuclear rhetoric of future years, prayed that the 1980s would be "an era full of vitality [*katsuryoku*] and profit [*uruoi*]" for the municipality.[8]

Shared concern over the future of the hometown thus made two very different men receptive to new ideas at the turn of the 1980s. Kanō Shin came from one of the oldest and most established households in the port area: in many ways he represented what we might call "old money." Yet just as financial success for the Edo period elites had always brought with it social responsibilities to the hometown, perhaps Kanō, who was by all accounts rather a patrician figure by the early 1980s, considered it his particular duty to generate new streams of income for the town in the same way that his ancestors had in the mid-1800s. Katayama Hideyuki, by contrast, was a self-made man—someone who had built up his business from scratch and, through his success, established a formidable political base in Shiraida. His particular household history, moreover, served almost to mirror the wider economic shifts that mid-twentieth-century Kaminoseki had undergone. It was the story of a father who had pioneered new shipping technology in the form of the hot-bulb engine in the 1920s and a son who had early on spotted the significance for his shipping business of Japan's postwar energy shift from coal to oil. Thus as Kaminoseki—and indeed Japan as a whole—grappled with the need to shift from oil to the atom in the early 1980s, Katayama may have considered himself the ideal man to lead that transformation at a local level.

So much for the outlooks of two of Kaminoseki's leading officials. But in order to understand why a power plant plan was forthcoming in 1981, we need to step back to the dark days of the winter of 1973–1974, when the first Oil Shock momentarily led to the dimming of the bright neon life in Tokyo.

In policy terms, one important consequence of the shock was that the Japanese government became far more interventionist and creative in its handling of the so-called nuclear allergy. Until the early 1970s, central civil servants had largely allowed the private market for commercial atomic energy to rule, with only occasional public assists—such as the Ministry of International Trade and Industry's (MITI) detailed surveys of hundreds of coastal areas, starting in 1960, which were intended to provide advance topographical and geological knowledge of potential host communities to the electricity companies.[9] In 1974, however, the Three Power Source Development Laws (Three Laws) were enacted. These allowed for the tax revenues paid by electricity users to be funneled back into power station host communities so as to fund major infrastructure projects (roads, schools, port development, and so on) over an initial five-year period. Although the money was made available to communities hosting hydroelectric and fossil-fuel plants, the largest subsidies were to be made to those municipalities with nuclear power plants in their midst.[10]

The Three Laws were one example of new incentives that central bureaucrats designed so as to appeal to specific local constituencies, such as farmers, fishermen, government officials, and women, that had the potential power to derail the whole nuclear siting process. Yet despite these targeted campaigns and the development of other incentive-driven policies, and despite opinion polls in the mid-1970s showing that close to 70 percent of respondents supported Japan's continued nuclear program,[11] the "lead times" for nuclear power plants increased from 90 months in 1975 to 160 months by 1980.[12] In other words, by 1980, the time between the initial planning application and a power plant coming on line was more than thirteen years.

One reason for this apparent paradox—that greater state intervention in the siting process coexisted with greater lead times in planned host communities—may have been the increased mobilization and cross-organizational cooperation of antinuclear groups in the 1970s. In October 1977, twenty-three antinuclear organizations, including the Japan Consumers' Union, housewives' organizations, and the Japan Congress against Atomic and Hydrogen Bombs (Gensuikin), gathered for the first time in Tokyo to campaign against nuclear power. Significantly, their activities that day included a "postnuclear seminar," to which victims of the atomic bombs were invited—a reminder of the uniquely Japanese frame of nuclear power discourse in postwar Japan. But antinuclear campaigners could also draw on international events, in particular the Three Mile Island accident, on 28 March 1979, to bolster their case: by November 1980, opinion polls indicated that only 30 percent of citizens were now supportive of Japan's nuclear plant–building program, down from 50 percent in the month before the accident.[13] These low figures occurred despite the second Oil Shock of 1979, following the revolution in Iran.

Such was the backdrop to Chugoku Electric Power Company's increasingly desperate attempts, by the turn of 1980, to find a municipality willing to host the construction of a new nuclear plant. Of all the nine Japanese regional power companies that used nuclear generation, Chugoku Electric faced a particular problem in that its headquarters were located in Hiroshima: as a government official commented in 1985, any attempt to locate a plant within the vicinity of the city would be "committing corporate suicide."[14] This left the company especially dependent on the cooperation of the other four prefectures within the Chūgoku region—Tottori and Shimane on the Japan Sea coast, and Yamaguchi and Okayama respectively to the west and east of Hiroshima. Although Chugoku Electric had been one of the first companies nationwide to open a nuclear plant (in northern Shimane prefecture in 1974), it had failed to gain prefectural support for new development in Hinase town, Okayama, in 1973: one major obstacle was the fact that the planned site was located within the Seto Inland Sea National Park.[15] The following year, MITI estimated that if no new plants opened in the company's jurisdiction by 1979, it would face a serious electricity shortfall of some 850 megawatts (almost twice the output of the Shimane reactor).[16]

In June 1977, Chugoku Electric made an official application to Hōhoku town, in the northwest of Yamaguchi prefecture, to start a preliminary investigation, the first step toward the eventual construction of a nuclear power station. As the regional newspaper reported in early July, the company had already reached its "time limit" in terms of rising electricity demand. There would thus be no time for the preliminary sounding-out phase of negotiations within the municipality; instead, the company would simply try, in a public campaign, to persuade local residents to allow construction.[17] To this end, it had the full support of the Yamaguchi prefectural bureaucracy, including Governor Hirai Tōru (served 1976–1996). The Liberal Democratic (LDP) government also played its part by using its new incentive-based tools to designate Hōhoku as an Important Electricity Resource Site—thus making the town eligible for greater central government subsidies.[18]

Hōhoku had been the object of a MITI coastal survey in 1969. This gave local residents, especially fishermen, an awareness of the issue that was crucial to enabling the quick mobilization of an antinuclear campaign eight years later.[19] To the surprise and concern of town officials, some 1,500 fishermen and residents (out of a total population of 18,400) protested against the nuclear plan in July 1977. By February 1978, pressure had built on the town mayor to the extent that he finally announced he would not accept the company's application—to the "shock" of the prefecture. Two months later, a barely quorate town council also voted to oppose the application, and, in mid-May (following the resignation of the previous mayor), a new antinuclear mayor was elected by a two-to-one landslide.

Following the election, a front-page article in the *Chūgoku shinbun* newspaper argued that a combination of the company's public relations campaign, the overwhelming pressure exerted by the prefecture, and the hastiness (*seikyū*) of the LDP government had provoked local residents into opposition.[20] The Hōhoku failure thus suggested that the government's new incentive-based tools, created in the immediate post–Oil Shock years, were in themselves of only limited effect. What would be needed to produce a more positive outcome for Chugoku Electric would be a combination of more subtle "behind-the-scenes" maneuvering by the company and "soft social control" tools by the government.

But the question was, where would the company next attempt to apply such maneuvering?

Sometime in the summer of 1981, Mayor Kanō was allegedly contacted by the speaker of the Yamaguchi prefectural assembly. Yoshinaga Shigeru, who served as speaker from May 1981 to April 1983, was the former mayor of Kaminoseki's municipal neighbor, Hirao town, and one-time secretary to former LDP prime minister (and Kumage county native) Satō Eisaku.[21] Not only did Yoshinaga's term as Hirao mayor (1955–1962) overlap with Kanō's first term in Kaminoseki, but he and Kanō were apparently classmates and friends from Yanai junior high school, which they had attended together.[22] The two men were thus part of a remarkable network of Yanai graduates that spread throughout the southeast of Yamaguchi and reached even to the highest echelons of prefectural politics: the then LDP governor of Yamaguchi, Hirai Tōru, was also a graduate of the school. Yoshinaga apparently suggested to Kanō that in light of the Mitsubishi LPG failure in Kaminoseki, the municipality should think about offering to host a nuclear power plant.

At more or less the same time, Katayama Hideyuki was also allegedly contacted by Matsunaga Tsuneichi, vice-governor of the prefecture. The vice-governor simultaneously served as chair of the Yamaguchi Prefecture Atomic Energy Policy Council, and he was an outspoken critic of the Hōhoku town administration as the Chugoku Electric plan collapsed acrimoniously in 1978–1979.[23] For his part, Speaker Katayama was known to have been a leading supporter of the Mitsubishi LPG plan in Kaminoseki, and he appears to have been very receptive to working with Chugoku Electric as the company secretly investigated a number of potential sites in the town (including Miura Bay, the original site of Iwaishima's *kanmai* celebrations). Such investigations were necessary because Kaminoseki, unlike Hōhoku town, had never been the object of one of the MITI topographical surveys. Company employees thus began to visit the town office regularly and to ask for maps, land data, and so on. These visits provided an opportunity for the employees to establish friendly relations with local bureaucrats and to explain that "there were things to talk about" (*o-hanashi ga atta to*). In this way, town officials became aware that a plan was afoot, but also that it was under wraps and taboo (*kinku*) for wider discussion.[24]

Despite such secrecy, by the end of September 1981, antinuclear politicians in the prefectural assembly had caught wind of the new developments. "I have heard that there is a movement to attract a nuclear power plant to Kaminoseki town, Kumage county, in the Inland Sea," a Socialist Party member stated in a debate. "Has the prefecture received any request for cooperation?" Prefectural officials demurred, saying they had "no information" about Kaminoseki. For his part, Mayor Kanō commented, "There has been absolutely no sounding out from Chugoku Electric. There's been a rumor that last summer [1981], Chugoku Electric employees conducted an 'investigation' while engaged in fishing, but the town has not considered either seeking [nuclear power] or opposing it."[25]

In fact, Kanō did allegedly know about the "fishing trips" and indeed had provided carbon-copy maps to help the company in its topographical investigations.[26] At the same time, in addition to accompanying Chugoku Electric representatives on their surveying activities, speaker Katayama allegedly began canvassing other town councillors for "bottom up" support.[27] The only councillor he excluded from these discussions was a known Communist Party member, Koyanagi Akira, who at the December 1981 session of the council asked Mayor Kanō what was going on. "I have heard that Chugoku Electric are carrying out an investigation of Kaminoseki as one of their current plans," the mayor merely replied.[28]

Such vagueness may be explained partly by the electoral cycle. One reason why Chugoku Electric and its local supporters were so keen to keep the plan secret, we might assume, was the company's recent experience of having seen an antinuclear mayor and an antinuclear majority on the town council elected in Hōhoku town. Indeed, the experience of the Ashihama dispute in Mie prefecture in the mid-1960s—the first time in Japan that a proposed nuclear power station was successfully rejected by local residents—had taught all nine electricity companies the dangers of allowing a situation to develop in which antinuclear campaigners could gain access to political power.[29] By delaying any official announcement until after the town council elections in February 1982 and by cultivating behind-the-scenes support in the meantime, the company may have considered that it had bought itself four additional years before the issue would have to go to the electorate—and by that time, the plans might be irrevocably advanced. If this indeed was the company's thinking, then the only remaining major hurdle would be to ensure that the scheduled 1983 mayoral election ended with a favorable result. To this end, by the winter of 1981–1982, Katayama Hideyuki had apparently already decided that he would be the proinvestment mayoral candidate twelve months hence—a fact that may explain why he did not stand for the town council elections in February 1982, despite being at the height of his political powers in the town.

The town council elections were consequently held in February 1982 without the impending nuclear project arising as an issue to be debated. Only in a June council session did councillor Koyanagi Akira first put on record his suspicion that "since around March [1982], Chugoku Electric company employees have been moving around the town, and members of the Chamber of Commerce and the women's division [of the chamber] have been going one after another to observe the nuclear power plant at Ikata [in Shikoku]." Mayor Kanō once again replied, "As a town administration, we have not touched on [this issue], although I have heard rumors. Until we hear anything officially from Chugoku Electric . . . But this is not something that I can decide alone."[30]

By extraordinary coincidence, something was indeed heard from Chugoku Electric on this very day: the company's president announced for the first time that Kaminoseki town was one candidate site—among several in the prefecture—for its long-planned second nuclear power plant. After months of secret maneuvering, the nuclear issue was at last out in the open.

"Good Times"

According to the political scientist Daniel P. Aldrich, state agencies around the world attempt, wherever possible, to avoid local resistance to the siting of controversial facilities such as nuclear power plants. In order to gauge whether or not they will encounter such opposition, bureaucrats attempt to measure the strength of civil society in a given locality by looking at membership of so-called horizontal associations: farming and fishing cooperatives, trade unions, parent-teacher associations (PTAs), chambers of commerce, voluntary associations, and so on. Because such associations are usually autonomous from the state, they can be indicative of the relative strength of civil society: the more horizontal associations and the higher the membership of those associations, the stronger civil society will tend to be—and thus the more groups there will be who, through their opposition, could potentially derail a controversial siting plan. As Aldrich has shown, the state will therefore actively avoid proposing controversial sites in localities "with stronger horizontal associations and deeper civic ties."[31]

Quite clearly, neither the central government, the prefectural government, nor Chugoku Electric itself had done its civil society homework in Hōhoku town. Indeed, as far as can be known, one of the company's mistakes in Hōhoku had been to focus only on the highest level of municipal administration—what the *Asahi shinbun* newspaper termed the "boss" level.[32] In Kaminoseki, by contrast, company strategy would be to focus on the community, especially on the smallest units of political control in Japan, the *jichitai* (literally "self-government body").

What was the process by which an outside company could reach down to this level of local society? As a hypothetical exercise, I asked one man who knew about Chugoku Electric's earliest strategy in Kaminoseki to describe for me whom a major corporation might contact if they wished to approach a small municipality. They would start of course with the mayor, he said, and then with the speaker and various other councillors, and then perhaps the district head (*kuchō*—the elected head of the *jichitai*), followed by the *hanchō* (group heads within each district). Then there would be the heads of the farming and fishing cooperatives, and they would certainly have already contacted the chair of the Chamber of Commerce.[33]

If Chugoku Electric's strategy in 1981–1982 did indeed follow something of this pattern, then the company would have been helped by the particular structure of Kaminoseki's civil society. The chair of the Chamber of Commerce in 1981, for example, was Tanaka Masami, who was Katayama Hideyuki's predecessor as speaker of the Kaminoseki town assembly (1970–1978). Tanaka was also the head (*kumiaichō*) for the Tenjin 2 subdistrict (*kumi*) of Kaminoseki district, meaning that he was responsible for ensuring that every household in his subdistrict paid their taxes on time and for helping to organize community cleaning and other such events.[34] Thus he was simultaneously active at both the highest and lowest echelons of community life in Kaminoseki. Similarly, the head of Kaminoseki district (*kuchō*) in 1981 was also a former town councillor, an anti-crime activist, and the chair of the Considering the Kaminoseki of Tomorrow Association, a pro-Mitsubishi lobby group that was officially independent of the town administration. In Murotsu district, Councillor Nishimoto Masao was deputy speaker of the town council during the term of Tanaka Masami (1970–1978) and was also active in community initiatives such as the anticrime volunteer group.[35] On Iwaishima, long-serving councillor Shimanaka Hiroshi—who called for a "dazzling" new Japan in the aftermath of the war—was the former head of the Iwaishima junior high school PTA (1970–1974), while his colleague, councillor Ujimoto Kuichi, was also head of the island's farming cooperative and hereditary elder (*sōdai*) of the Miyato Hachimangū shrine (see Chapter 5). After the February 1982 council elections, Ujimoto's successor as councillor was simultaneously the head of the Iwaishima fishing cooperative.

The list could go on: the point is that many leading politicians in early 1980s Kaminoseki were also highly active in civil society. Thus one characteristic of the hometown was that, because of the multiple roles that some of the municipality's most influential men performed, many of the so-called horizontal associations within civil society's sphere were only nominally autonomous from local government and thus, by extension, from the state itself. Moreover, the concentration of political and civil society influence in the hands of a few men suggests that there was an ongoing oligarchy of power in early 1980s Kaminoseki. With the exception of the Kanō household, the membership of this oligarchy was generally different from that of the late-nineteenth-century hometown, but the basic structures and patterns of power appear to have survived the transformations of the twentieth century: a small group of men—one might even call them "bosses"—made the key political decisions in the town.

By targeting these men in the earliest stages of its approach to Kaminoseki, a company such as Chugoku Electric would then have had multiple opportunities to penetrate town society one level below the "bosses." In practical terms, one way in which such penetration allegedly occurred in Kaminoseki was through secret drinking parties. Such gatherings are standard business practice in Japan: they are called *nemawashi,* which literally means "binding the roots" but which might be more appropriately translated as "laying the groundwork." *Nemawashi* has been described as "frequent chats over lunches, dinners, drinks, and during social events," which serve "as a congenial, informal context for discussion of proposals, possible courses of action, decision-making, and potential negotiating table strategies."[36] As a junior member of an association such as the Chamber of Commerce, for example, one might be invited by someone higher up in the organization to meet a company official at a local hotel. Over freshly diced sashimi and copious bottles of beer—which, it would be explained, were on the house—one might discuss the future prospects of Kaminoseki with that official and then, when the subject of a nuclear power station was broached, agree that there was really no other alternative to save the town. Repeated over a number of months from 1981 onward, perhaps with slightly different members each time, but all sworn to secrecy, one might begin to feel that the company had the best interests of the town at heart, that one's own small business might benefit—and that in any case, gathering regularly for free beer was a pretty good time.

One might even begin to feel in an "invitation mood" with regard to Chugoku Electric. This, indeed, was a key phrase by the fall of 1982. As the company reflected (*hansei*) on its previous mistakes in Hōhoku town, it let the regional media know that it would "wait" and respond only to an "invitation mood" (*yūchi mūdo*) in Kaminoseki.[37] Such a stance was significant in two ways.

First, it enabled the pronuclear lobby within the town administration to set the rhetorical frame of the debate in positive terms while simultaneously maintaining a position of official neutrality. On the one hand, Mayor Kanō emphasized the importance of atomic energy to Japan as a whole. Thus at a town council session in September 1982, he said, "When we consider the future energy [policy] of the country, we cannot ignore nuclear power generation."[38] Such an argument may have reflected his own genuine beliefs: after all, a photo exhibition on the peaceful uses of the atom had traveled to Murotsu village as early as February 1955 and had made a profound impression on Kanō's predecessor as town mayor, Nakamori Shōji, and the exhibition may also have been seen by Kaminoseki villagers.[39]

On the other hand, Chugoku Electric's official stance also enabled Kanō to make a general case for "halting depopulation" (*kaso wo kuitomeru*).[40] How this might specifically be achieved was an argument that could be left to individual councillors such as Suzuki Ryōichi (chair of the council subcommittee that had recommended the Mitsubishi plan), who in September 1982 urged an immediate "invitation" to Chugoku Electric. Equally, such arguments could be left to Tanaka Masami, chair of the Chamber of Commerce, who spoke directly of economic "development" in Kaminoseki.[41] Both men would have had in mind the subsidies provided by the aforementioned Three Laws, which in 1982 were estimated to be worth a total of 7 billion yen to Kaminoseki.

Considering also the annual tax income to be levied on the power station plus one-off "cooperation payments"—such as the 840 million yen reported to have been paid by Chugoku Electric to the host community of its nuclear plant in Shimane prefecture—it is easy to see why Kanō, Katayama, and so many other town leaders were enthusiastic about the plan.[42] As for fishermen, they would have been made aware of generous individual payments from the company—payments that were officially called "compensation" (for anticipated loss of fishing income) but that were equally effective in garnering cooperation. Once again, as with overseas remittances and donations, the townspeople appeared to have stumbled upon a lucrative source of outside money.

Officially, however, Chugoku Electric's decision to wait for an "invitation mood" enabled Kanō and his elected colleagues to maintain a fiction of neutrality. The company had merely announced Kaminoseki as a "candidate site." As long as there was no formal approach, the period had not yet come for open debate; rather, this was a time to "study." "For the time being," said Kanō in September 1982, "I will gauge the movements and intentions of the townspeople, and I myself will study." Again in October: "I am [now] studying nuclear power stations." And in November, when antinuclear protesters mobilized for the first time in order to hand over a 976-name petition to the town office, they were met by Assistant Mayor Arakawa Kan, who told them, "Since we've not had any formal application from Chugoku Electric, this is no time for approving or disapproving [the construction of a nuclear power plant]. The town is also in the process of studying [the issue]. I want you to understand this [*rikai shite hoshii*]."[43] The last point was particularly important. If the town was officially "studying"—a stance that it maintained until 1984—then conversely those people who had already jumped to a hasty conclusion in voicing opposition to the nuclear plan had, by implication, not adequately studied: they lacked proper "understanding." As the dispute escalated, the conviction on the part of pronuclear campaigners that the antinuclear lobby simply didn't "understand" the issue was to become a recurring theme of the debate—and one that could be found in nuclear disputes wherever they occurred in postwar Japan.[44]

By examining the precise content of that study, we see the second significance of Chugoku Electric's early strategy in Kaminoseki: it enabled both the company and central government to promote nuclear power in ways that actively stimulated the "invitation mood" even as, officially, they appeared passively to be "awaiting" the decision of the townspeople. Thus, in addition to alleged secret drinking parties, "study" referred to trips to other communities in Japan that already hosted nuclear power stations. As councillor Koyanagi put on record in June 1982, one location was Ikata town in western Shikoku—a nuclear facility, opened in 1977, that is just visible from Kaminoseki bridge on a clear day. Other destinations included Chugoku Electric's own nuclear power station on the northern coast of Shimane prefecture, Kyushu Electric's plant in Genkai (Saga prefecture), and Kansai Electric's facility in Mihama (Fukui prefecture).[45]

Officially categorized as "classes on electricity" (*denki kyōshitsu*), the trips aimed to demonstrate the "safety" of atomic generation—and it appears that many participants were convinced by what they saw. "I touched with my own fingers the sea into which coolant water is discharged," one man said of Shimane, waving the digits in question for dramatic effect; "I saw with my own eyes fish in the sea," another told me of Ikata.[46] When eighty antinuclear protesters from Iwaishima tried to land at Shidai port, in southwestern Nagashima, in December 1982, they were met by a pronuclear group of around sixty local residents. As insults were hurled both ways, pronuclear campaigners were reported to have yelled: "Have you been to observe nuclear power stations yourselves? How do you know if they're good or bad when you haven't been?"[47]

Such trips have been described as an example of "soft social control," whereby government agencies helped familiarize local citizens with existing nuclear sites as a way of convincing them of the "normalcy" of life near potentially dangerous facilities.[48] This is one important framework by which to understand the trips—one that can also be seen in the French nuclear industry's public relations campaigns during the postwar period. Residents living near the proposed nuclear waste processing plant in La Hague, for example, were flown in the early 1960s to the nuclear complex at Marcoule in order to help dispel rumors of seven-kilometer exclusion zones, deformed children, and so on.[49]

However, the French trips highlight a more mundane but equally important framework by which to understand the nature of "study" in Kaminoseki. In the words of one Marcoule visitor, "We flew down there and had a pretty good time, actually. . . . In the afternoon we saw over the plant. . . . Next day we were shown round the co-operative wine cellars. . . . We spent the evening in Marseille eating their special fish soup, then caught the train home via Saclay. Oh, we had a good time, all right, and there were those who took advantage."[50]

As for the residents of La Hague, for the residents of Kaminoseki the study visits in 1982 seem to have been a "good time," with the townspeople imbibing as much alcohol as hard facts. Many visits included an overnight stay at a local inn: photos from one trip, in September 1982, show fourteen men dressed in white bath-time *yukata* relaxing around a long, rectangular dinner table on which stand at least two dozen half-liter bottles of Kirin beer. On the occasions that wives and children were invited—as when members of Kaminoseki's Children's Association (Kodomo no Kai) were sponsored to don yellow hardhats and judge with their own eyes safety and "normalcy" issues—a side trip might be arranged, such as to the famous Uzumasa film studios in Kyoto.[51] Thus, by the autumn of 1982, about one thousand townspeople, or around one-sixth of the total population, had taken free "classes on electricity"—although this figure may include some who were so enthusiastic about their "studies" that they went on four or five separate trips.[52]

The widespread perception in Kaminoseki was that Chugoku Electric paid for the trips. This was important because if participants made an emotional connection between the company on the one hand and enjoyable free outings on the other, there was a good chance that they might see the company in an increasingly positive light.[53] The study visits thus enabled townspeople to become familiar both with the "normalcy" of life near potentially dangerous facilities and with the company itself. But the significance of Chugoku Electric's *nemawashi* activities—both the study trips and the alleged local hospitality—was not only that they created a direct social connection between certain chosen townspeople and company officials. Such activities strengthened a social bond that already connected ordinary townspeople to their political and civil societal "bosses." If, for example, one was invited to wine and dine with company officials in a local hotel, one might feel a sense of obligation both to the company and (perhaps more importantly) to the host of the evening or the acquaintance who had been kind enough to make the invitation in the first place. If one had enjoyed a free "study visit," especially under the auspices of a neighborhood club or association, the sense of social reciprocation when it came to a decision about nuclear power might be considerable—a process that Jeffrey Broadbent calls "status seduction."[54]

In other words, within a small community such as Kaminoseki, the essentially vertical structure of civil society and the company's subtle manipulation of that structure over time meant that an ordinary citizen's pronuclear decision was as likely to be based on social, political, and even historical obligations as it was on a clear grasp of atomic energy issues. While financial incentives from the central government no doubt had some impact on local residents, the nature of those residents' social bonds to town elites and to the wider community may have been most critical in determining their mood toward the proposed nuclear power plant.

For a brief period at the turn of 1987, it seemed as if Kaminoseki's inexorable population decline had indeed miraculously been halted. As Figure 10.1 shows, the town's population actually rose in a dramatic fashion—by 155 people between November 1986 and January 1987.

Unfortunately for the pronuclear lobby, closer inspection revealed that the population "increase" could in fact be explained as the fraudulent registration of nontown residents in advance of the April 1987 mayoral election. Moreover, key members of the pronuclear lobby were themselves engaged in this illegal behavior. A police investigation eventually discovered irregularities with the applications of 151 new "residents," and in March 1988 the police indicted 118 people—including 116 confirmed pronuclear supporters—for breaking the Public Office Election Law. Of these 118 defendants, 111 were summarily prosecuted and fined by the authorities in Yanai. That number included six employees of Chugoku Electric (which repeatedly denied having coordinated any wrongdoing), the deputy speaker of the town council, and the second son of Mayor Katayama Hideyuki.[55]

The election in question, on 26 April 1987, saw Katayama stand for reelection as mayor, having successfully fulfilled his ambition to be elected for the first time in 1983. By chance, the mayoral election also coincided with the first anniversary of the Chernobyl disaster in Ukraine, which is commonly seen as one reason that popular perceptions of atomic energy generation in Japan became more negative in the late 1980s.[56] Thus, for example, an antinuclear demonstration in Kaminoseki on 26 October 1986—a day known as Nuclear Power Day in the Japanese calendar—drew an attendance of between 800 and 1,200 protesters, the highest number to date.[57]

For Kaminoseki's pronuclear lobbyists, there must have been a real fear that their carefully nurtured plans would be blown off course by the sharp downturn in Japanese public opinion—a fear that can only have been heightened by the bad luck of having the election fall on the anniversary of Chernobyl. Hence, it appears, the special edition of the *Kaminoseki Town News* that appeared two months before the election, featuring a seven-page spread on a "Local Advancement Vision" (*chiiki shinkō bijon*) to be facilitated by nuclear power;[58] hence, we might assume, the concerted and extraordinary campaign

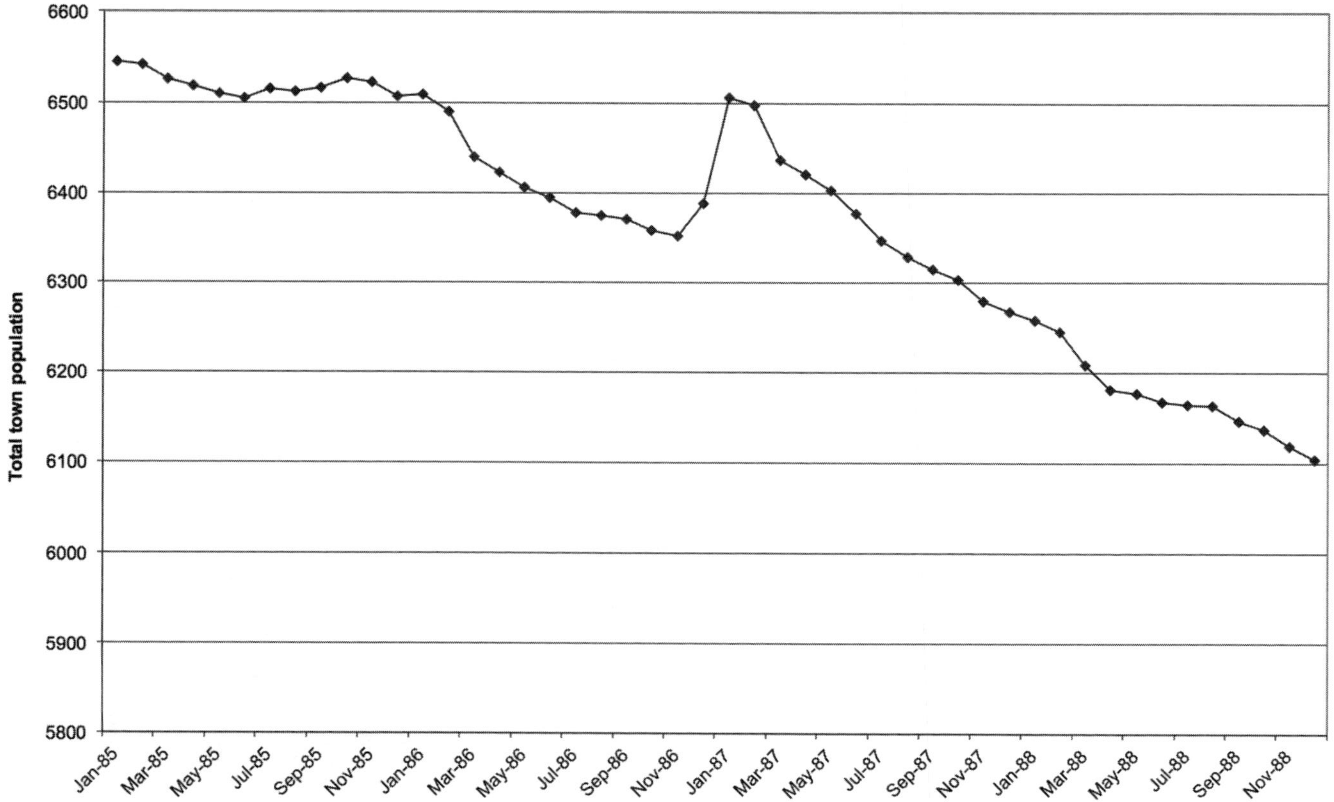

Figure 10.1. Kaminoseki town population, January 1985 to December 1988 (Data from *Kaminoseki kōhō*)

to break electoral law so as to return Mayor Katayama to office. In the event, the various strategies, legal and illegal, were successful: Katayama defeated his rival, Murotsu councillor Kawamoto Hiromasa, by 2,835 votes to 2,116 on a turnout of 96.46 percent, the highest of any local election in Japan that year.[59]

The 1987 mayoral election indicates the kinds of pressures placed on Kaminoseki's pronuclear lobby and on the company by external events. Of more serious concern, however, was what was happening internally in the town. On the surface of things, the nuclear plan appeared to be progressing smoothly: in June 1984, the town council took its first vote on the issue, deciding by a margin of sixteen to one (the only opposition being Koyanagi Akira, the self-declared communist) to request that Chugoku Electric carry out a preliminary investigation (*jizen chōsa*) in Shidai. For a municipality to urge an electricity company to carry out a survey rather than the other way round was, the print media noted, "exceptional" (*irei*); it was also a reversal of the Hōhoku strategy, in which the first official move had come from Chugoku Electric. But even as the company established for the first time a permanent office in Kaminoseki, with a staff of thirty-eight by May 1985, the pronuclear lobby continued to emphasize that the survey had nothing to do with whether the town should be pro- or antinuclear. "If we debate [the rights and wrongs of nuclear power] without awaiting the conclusion of the preliminary investigation, it will be an unproductive debate," claimed one councillor in an apparent variation on the original wait-and-study strategy.[60] Finally, in a landmark vote on 27 September 1985, the council agreed officially to invite Chugoku Electric's nuclear investment in the town. "Three years of hard effort have borne fruit," said Tanaka Masami, chair of the Association for Considering the Development of Kaminoseki.[61] A few months later, Mayor Katayama added his own rhetorical flourish, punning the nuclear image: "We are currently formulating a future vision of the town with the atomic power station as its nucleus [*kaku*]."[62]

But nobody seated in the second-floor chamber of the town office, observing the councillors' deliberations in the flesh, could have failed to notice the cacophonous demonstrations that coincided with each scheduled council session.[63] The tranquil everyday sounds of the straits—the chugging engine of a passing tanker, the fishing boats leaving port, the cry of the seagulls, metal being pounded at the Nishiyama engineworks, a passing car—were regularly drowned out by the massed chants of hundreds of antinuclear protesters, their "no nuclear power!" slogans broadcast from up to ten loudspeaker trucks. These trucks themselves competed for airspace with another ten black-painted buses mobilized by extreme-right-wing thugs, who would blast militaristic march tunes across the straits from Murotsu, their access to the bridge blocked by three hundred riot police bussed in from Yamaguchi. This, presumably, was not the sort of "invitation mood" that the pronuclear lobby had in mind: on one side, the serried ranks of the Japan Teachers Union (Nikkyōso), the Japan Senior High School Teachers Union (Nikkōkyō), the General Council of Prefectural Labor Unions (Kenryōhō), and the Japan Prefectural and Municipal Workers Union (Jichirō); and, on the other, right-wing groups such as the Dai-Nippon Shinseikai, three of whose members were arrested for assaulting antinuclear campaigners in October 1984.[64] After the early appearance of the teaching unions in a February 1983 demonstration (and their active support by a handful of teachers in Kaminoseki itself, much to the consternation of the relevant Boards of Education),[65] the chair of the Association for Considering the Development of Kaminoseki erected billboards in ten locations throughout the town declaring, "Let's develop the town under our own steam!"[66] Despite Chugoku Electric's own outsider position within the community, there was apparently no sense of irony in the appeal.

Yet what could not be ignored was that more than half of the sometimes seven-hundred-strong antinuclear crowds that gathered in the streets around the council chamber were themselves from "the town." Indeed, as the next chapter details, the arguments over how to "develop" Kaminoseki unfolded less between right-wingers and left-wingers, or Liberal Democratic Party supporters and Socialist or Communist Party supporters, than between and within different districts of the municipality. It may be that mayors Kanō and Katayama and the pronuclear lobby in the town bureaucracy saw Chugoku Electric's proposal as an opportunity to relight Kaminoseki's fire, with themselves standing forth as the beacons to guide nuclear riches into port, but instead they lit, along with the leaders of the antinuclear movement, a conflagration that licked through the community. As arguments passionate and at times petty raged, these were not, by any stretch of the imagination, good times in the hometown.

PART V

Dying for Survival

11

Atomic Power, Community Fission

One of the best views of Tanoura Bay, the site of the proposed nuclear power station, is from the stone steps leading up to Iwaishima's Miyato Hachimangū shrine. On a still day, the bay can feel almost in touching distance from the low, densely clustered houses that form Iwaishima village. Contrary to the residents of Nagashima island, for whom Tanoura may be considered out of sight and out of mind, the residents of Iwaishima thus see the nuclear site as they go about their everyday lives. If the pronuclear lobby in Nagashima can be characterized as Definitely In My Back Yard, then Iwaishima's opposition to Chugoku Electric is perhaps best explained as Not In My Front Yard.

Iwaishima's frontal position, four kilometers across the water from Tanoura, accounts for the particular emphasis that antinuclear campaigners placed—and continue to place—on the "dangers" of atomic energy. On 17 November 1982, five months after Chugoku Electric officially announced Kaminoseki's candidacy, the Loving Our Hometown Association (Aikyo Isshin Kai) was established on the island under the leadership of Kanata Toshio. A boat parade was held at sea, a 976-name antinuclear petition was handed over to the town office, and that evening Kanata addressed six hundred islanders outside the Iwaishima fishing cooperative, reiterating his position that "we shall absolutely oppose the construction of a dangerous nuclear power station."[1] This insistence on potential danger would become a central tenet of the antinuclear campaign, bolstered by the critical testimonies of a small number of islanders who had personal experience working in the Japanese nuclear industry.[2]

At its most basic level, the discourse of danger can be interpreted as an expression of collective fear. During her fieldwork in small communities located in the shadow of France's main nuclear waste processing plant at La Hague, Françoise Zonabend identified the "selective blindness" of residents:

> It is as if in these hamlets dotted over the plateau, the only inhabited points from which the reprocessing plant is visible, people have decided not to see it, using a fold in the ground, the way a garden faces, or the position of a housefront to eclipse this untidy, deeply disturbing section of the landscape from view.... So one way of defending yourself against the invasion of the reprocessing plant with its ever more numerous buildings (and no doubt against the fear that they inspire) is to decide not to see them. In some places this is not hard to do. In others, the landscape needs a little rearranging, but the mechanism is the same, namely denying the existence of the danger by refusing to see its architectural embodiment.[3]

If, in La Hague, the decision "not to see" constituted a denial of danger, then in Iwaishima a similar mechanism worked in the reverse: the daily unavoidability of seeing the planned site served to exacerbate the sense of danger—the fear that, if there were to be an accident, the islanders would become "refugees" from their own homes.[4]

But fear was not the only emotion at play. Gazing east toward Tanoura, antinuclear residents could also be forgiven for feeling a sense of powerlessness at the events of the early 1980s. Before the 1958 merger of Kaminoseki and Murotsu municipalities, Iwaishima men had at times played a leading role in the Kaminoseki village bureaucracy: Ishimaru Hirohito, the head priest of Kōmyōji temple, had been village mayor from 1942 to 1946, for example, and Ujimoto Kuichi was elected head of the Kaminoseki Village Combined Youth Association in 1949. Such prominence reflected Iwaishima's demographic vitality. According to unofficial statistics, the island population in 1947 was 3,342, out of a municipal total of just under 10,000, making Iwaishima equal with Kaminoseki district as the dominant constituency in the village.[5] Once Murotsu and Kaminoseki merged, however, the population center of the new town became concentrated in the ports communities, thus marginalizing Iwaishima in municipal affairs. The priest of the Miyato Hachimangū shrine, Morimoto Hiromitsu, stood as an Iwaishima candidate in the mayoral election of 1959 but was defeated, and an islander has never since become mayor. Such marginalization was exacerbated by the speed of postwar population decline, which was faster in Iwaishima, Yashima, Shidai, Kamai, and Shiraida—the hamlets farthest away from the ports—than elsewhere.[6] When it came to the 1985 invitation vote, therefore, many islanders felt disenfranchised from a decision that would disproportionately affect their daily lives.

For all their sense of fear and powerlessness, however, Iwaishima islanders were not above a little selective blindness of their own. As late as 2004, a map produced and circulated by the Island Rejuvenation Committee (Shima-okoshi Iinkai) was notable for a key omission. The map apparently showed every aspect of island life: where the bream, yellowtail, halfbeak, sillaginoid, and octopus could be fished, or the sea urchin gathered; where the tangerine and loquat groves were located, high on every slope of the island's 350-meter mountains; the site of the Heike warriors' graves and other memorials commemorating Iwaishima's legends; the roads, the three Buddhist temples, the elementary and junior high schools, and even the post office. But the Miyato Hachimangū shrine itself was missing.

This airbrushing was just one indication that the nuclear dispute on Iwaishima was more complex than it first appeared. The sense of fear concerning atomic energy, the desire to preserve rich fishing grounds, and a revulsion at the behind-the-scenes tactics of the pronuclear lobby were heartfelt emotions for some islanders, just as the desire to preserve the hometown community through nuclear power was a genuine motivation for some pronuclear lobbyists in Murotsu and Nagashima. As this chapter will argue, however, the antinuclear campaign also became a struggle about the nature of power and status in the 1980s hometown: hence the exclusion of the (pronuclear) shrine from the map. In particular, the tactics of leading antinuclear campaigners on Iwaishima exposed the social and political structures of everyday life and the extent to which islanders still observed the complex networks of loyalty and ritual described in Chapter 5. As such, the story of Iwaishima in the first decade of the dispute, and of the rearranging of historical and everyday landscapes in Kaminoseki more generally, helps us understand some of the continuities of hometown life from the mid-nineteenth to the late twentieth century—and the ways in which those continuities were broken in the ferocity of emotions provoked by nuclear power.

Divided Households

At the time of its formation in November 1982, the Loving Our Hometown Association claimed to have received the support of 93 percent of Iwaishima's population.[7] Yet the composition of the other 7 percent, the pronuclear minority, suggests that the opposition movement was driven by more than simply the perceived dangers of nuclear power: there was also a desire to seek redress against some of the most influential households in the community.

One problem, from the perspective of ordinary islanders, was that, in the period 1982–1986, Iwaishima's representatives on the town council—Shimanaka Hiroshi, Kishita Yoshitada, and Hashimoto Tadao—consistently voted in favor of nuclear power: it was therefore not just the postmerger balance of population within the municipality that disenfranchised islanders, but their own elected leaders. Where they could, disgruntled islanders expressed their anger within established institutional frameworks. Thus, in January 1983, the 129 members of the Iwaishima Fishing Cooperative voted by a margin of two to one to recall the cooperative's head, who happened to be Hashimoto Tadao (another example of the conflation of state and civil society interests in late-twentieth-century Kaminoseki).[8] But with the most recent council elections having taken place only in February 1982, the antinuclear majority on Iwaishima faced the prospect of at least three more years of powerlessness while crucial votes were being cast in the town council. Moreover, the pronuclear minority included not just elected councillors but men who stood at the hub of social, economic, and ritual networks on the island. Ujimoto Kuichi, the biggest landowner on the island and Hashimoto's predecessor as town councillor, was also perceived to be in favor of the Chugoku Electric plan, as was Moritomo Hiromitsu, the priest of the Miyato Hachimangū shrine and himself a former head of the fishing cooperative. As many islanders saw it, to participate in the ritual life of the village—where "participation" always included small votive donations (*saisen*)—was thus tantamount to supporting the pronuclear stance of the shrine priest (Ujimoto was also a shrine elder in the 1980s).

A sense of electoral powerlessness and a feeling that everyday life had been infected by nuclear politics help explain the antinuclear lobby's engagement in direct action. Under Kanata's leadership, members of the Loving Our Hometown Association were encouraged to believe that pronuclear households must be ostracized from the community. The phrase for "ostracism," in this case, is *mura hachibu* (literally "village eight parts"), which customarily entailed the breaking off of social intercourse with the targeted household, its exclusion from sharing common land or tools, and its being denied help at harvest time; the only two "parts" for which the village might offer help were to fight fires and to attend funerals.[9] On Iwaishima, therefore, pronuclear individuals were cold-shouldered on the streets,[10] they were denied access to the circulating bulletin board through which the town office communicates with townspeople, they were "purged" from civil society groups such as the elementary school PTA, and shops considered to be run by pronuclear households were boycotted—"the anti group has completely stopped shopping here since March," complained one proprietor in September 1983, "so my sales have declined to a quarter of what they were."[11] A pronuclear inn was removed from the telephone directory listed at the bottom of the island-published calendar, and, in an extension of the customary eight-part ostracism, some antinuclear activists also refused to attend the funerals of pronuclear households, occasionally even disrupting those services by banging pots and pans.

Moreover, on Monday evenings starting in the autumn of 1983, weekly antinuclear demonstrations were held on the island during which protesters would camp outside pronuclear households until late at night, chanting, yelling, occasionally throwing eggs, and in the most extreme cases lobbing empty beer bottles.[12] Because of the perceived pronuclear stance of priest Moritomo, donations to Iwaishima's Miyato Hachimangū shrine dried up, the entrance gate and other parts of the shrine grounds became overgrown from neglect, and, as we have seen, the shrine itself was erased from a tourist map published by the antinuclear group. When the year of the *kanmai* came round in 1984 and again in 1988, it was agreed that this was "no time for a festival": thus a pillar of island tradition that had apparently been celebrated more or less continuously for at least eight hundred years was canceled—a clear rebuke to the landowning elites, for whom it had served as a foundational narrative.

By October 1984, tensions had escalated to such an extent that an angry crowd of up to four hundred islanders surrounded councillor Shimanaka on the Iwaishima pier and prevented him walking the dozen meters to his house; the crowd was only dispersed, after a nine-hour standoff, by seventy police officers hastily ferried in.[13] Twelve months later, following the town council's vote to invite Chugoku Electric investment in Kaminoseki, teams of between thirty and sixty islanders kept watch on a twenty-four-hour basis in order to prevent councillors Shimanaka, Hashimoto, and Kishita from returning to the island at all—a protest that lasted for forty days.[14]

Barricading the village to prevent the entry of officialdom was a traditional form of peasant protest in Japan,[15] and the reversion of late-twentieth-century villagers to this tactic highlighted the extent to which the power station plan had become an issue simply too big to be handled within the official frameworks of local politics. The island's politicians had allegedly been "bound" by the *nemawashi* tactics of Chugoku Electric;[16] thus, in Iwaishima (as in many other contentious cases throughout the country), the closure of political channels to the potential refugees of the nuclear plan became a catalyst for the development of grassroots citizen protest.[17] Significantly, given the vertical structure of political, social, and ritual relations in mid-twentieth-century Iwaishima, one might have expected ordinary villagers to follow their elites' lead in themselves being "bound" to the nuclear plan, but this did not happen. "It still astonishes me," one activist said in an interview, "that, in the nuclear dispute, the mute [*mono wo iwan hito*] 90 percent of islanders truly defied the powerful 10 percent and regained power."[18]

Thus it would be possible to view the antinuclear campaign on Iwaishima partly as an antielite movement, in which a democratic revolution from below transformed island politics. But when we examine the leadership of the antinuclear lobby on Iwaishima, the story becomes more complicated. The founder of the Loving Our Hometown Association was Kanata Toshio, who was sixty-one in November 1982 and was thus roughly a contemporary of Ujimoto Kuichi. Kanata's great-grandfather Jinjirō had donated 70 *sen* to the 1896 *kanmai,* indicating the household's relatively wealthy status on the island (see Figure 7.2). In the 1930s and 1940s, Kanata's father Fukuta had been the boss (*amimoto*) of the sardine nets owned by the Sakai company, and by 1948 he was ranked among the highest 2 percent of household taxpayers on the island; Fukuta also oversaw the construction of the *kanmai* temporary shrine for many of the island's postwar festivals.[19] Inheriting his father's engineering skills, Kanata Toshio himself owned a small construction company that won regular contracts from Kaminoseki town municipality. It would not, therefore, have been a surprise if Kanata had actually been pronuclear by inclination, just as Nagashima and Murotsu's dozen or so construction companies were also enthusiastic backers of the plan. Indeed, several people alleged to me that Kanata had secretly sought contracts from senior officials in the town office and that it was only when refused special treatment that he had decided to mobilize an antinuclear campaign.[20]

In an extraordinary newspaper interview given in 2001, shortly before he died, Kanata revealed his thinking at the beginning of the nuclear dispute some two decades earlier.

> *Why did you start the antinuclear campaign?*
> Because Chugoku Electric's communication was poor. They first contacted people who were inclined to oppose them, and for that reason I

> was told absolutely nothing. To cut a long story short, I was offended by losing face [*mentsu wo tsubusareta koto ni hanpatsu shite*], so I started the antinuclear movement. If supporters of the nuclear power station had come to me first, I would probably have raised the pronuclear flag. In addition, islanders who had experience of doing subcontractual work at nuclear power stations said, "Nuclear power is frightening." They cajoled me by saying, "Without you, we can't pull the movement together," and so I manfully became chair of the association [*otokogi wo dashite kaichō ni natta*]. In the old days, my household had been a fishing boss and I myself had a successful construction business, so I funded the antinuclear movement. People would listen to anything I said, so I raised the antinuclear flag. . . .
>
> *Did most islanders join the antinuclear organization?*
> Everyone followed the things I said; when I think of it now, it's almost unreal. I thought I was like a god [*jibun ga kami-sama mitai*], and I became reckless. My way of doing things was overbearing [*gōin*], and I feel responsible for the fact that the islanders got caught up in it. . . . But the mayor, the fishing cooperative, and even people in the construction world were afraid of me; nobody listened to me, reasoned with me, or admonished me. . . . [21]

There is doubtless an element of hyperbole in Kanata's words, and his motivations for giving the interview, in an obscure Yamaguchi newspaper, are unclear. Nevertheless, his remarkable mea culpa suggests that even if the antinuclear campaign on Iwaishima saw itself as an antielite movement, in which new constituencies were attempting to wrestle power from the elites, the behavior of its members still reflected older attitudes to politics—in particular, the assumption that money could buy power or that a strong male presence was synonymous with effective leadership. This last point is particularly important because environmental protest movements in postwar Japan have so often been associated with women—for example, the Suginami housewives' campaign to collect 20 million anti–atomic weapons signatures in the wake of the 1954 *Lucky Dragon* incident. However, as Margaret McKean notes, the *leadership* of antipollution campaign groups was actually almost always male—even if, as in the case of Iwaishima, some of the most forthright activists were female.[22]

As a result of Kanata's "reckless" ostracism tactics, islanders were forced to declare their opposition to the nuclear power plan or be branded "pronuclear":

there was no space for neutrality. But when island campaigners eventually became suspicious of Kanata's motives (if not of his tactics), they turned to a thirty-four-year-old man called Yamato Sadao to take over leadership of the movement. Yamato was university educated and had been a student activist during the 1970 demonstrations against the renewal of the US-Japan Security Treaty. Moreover, in the decade before his return to Iwaishima in September 1985, he had lived in the Japan Sea coastal city of Matsue, where he regularly engaged in protests against Chugoku Electric's nuclear power station in Shimane prefecture. But Yamato was also the eldest son of a significant farming household on Iwaishima—a family that had intermarried with important households such as the Ujimoto, Matsumoto, and Yakushi (see Chapter 5). In other words, the leadership of the antinuclear movement remained in the hands of an influential farming household even though its most vocal activists were fishermen and their wives.

Under Yamato's guidance, the antinuclear campaign in Kaminoseki gained its first significant political victory, increasing its representation in the February 1986 elections from one councillor to seven. Yamato's wife, Junko, was one of only three women to run as candidates for the first time in the town.[23] But a closer analysis of the antinuclear voting figures from Iwaishima revealed a remarkable breakdown: three island candidates had received, respectively, 230, 229, and 228 votes, with another 200 votes going to an antinuclear candidate in Kaminoseki itself.[24] Such a perfect division of votes raises suspicions that the traditional village practice of district leaders instructing their ward residents how to vote was still alive and well: an example, if true, of the fear of ostracism following ordinary islanders even into the private ballot booth.[25]

Thus the claim that the hitherto politically mute majority on Iwaishima suddenly "regained power" from the traditional elites is overly simplistic. Although it is true that some of the most influential households on the island—including some of those intimately bound up in the history of the *kanmai* festival—were pronuclear and consequently ostracized from island life, it is also the case that in terms of the style of leadership, the role of other elite households, and the way that voting appears to have been decided in advance, the anti campaign itself displayed a number of recognizably late-nineteenth-century characteristics.

The nuclear dispute exposed fault lines in island and town life over the extent to which the historical elites could continue to wield power and to which politics might be practiced according to custom. On the one hand, some people based their decisions about whether to be pro- or antinuclear not on issues of safety versus danger or on government subsidies versus environmental destruction, but rather on the fact that, say, their sister-in-law's brother was a pronuclear town councillor. In such cases, the webs of blood and marital loyalty took precedence over all else—although it is unclear to me whether the ultimate decision was made by the male household head alone or in consultation with his wife (perhaps based on her family ties). As one former councillor explained, the single most important factor in local politics is relatives: to "campaign" is thus to pay one's respects to every known relative you have and then to their extended family as well, thereby creating a set of social bonds similar to those that Chugoku Electric attempted to establish through study visits and alleged "laying the groundwork" socializing.[26]

On the other hand, in the same way that the normal channels of political communication had quickly become blocked by a lack of consultation during the earliest discussions on the nuclear proposal, so the enormous potential impact of the planned power station on the municipality caused division between households where family loyalty would once have suggested unity. Thus, on Iwaishima, the new leader of the antinuclear movement, Yamato Sadao, was actually the nephew of a leading pronuclear lobbyist, Ujimoto Kuichi: for fifteen years the two men allegedly didn't talk, despite their living only a stone's throw away from each other.[27] In Kaminoseki, meanwhile, the Kanō and Iwaki households were similarly divided. The former mayor's wife, Kanō Misuka, was originally from the Iwaki household—she was the daughter of Iwaki Kisaku (a Hawaiian returnee and a major political force in village life in the 1920s). In the town council elections of 1986, she stood as a candidate mainly, it is alleged, to split the family vote and thus to scupper the antinuclear campaign of her nephew, Iwaki Motonobu. Kanō was elected, but Iwaki ended up losing the election by only three votes.[28]

The Yamato-Ujimoto and Kanō-Iwaki examples were merely the headline cases in the mid-1980s: there were probably countless other ways in which nuclear politics became framed as family politics, and family arguments became nuclear arguments. Most people struggle to understand the vagaries of power relations within their own families, let alone those of outsiders. It is therefore impossible to judge the extent to which the nuclear plan exacerbated existing tensions within the community or provoked entirely new tensions. But this was a deeply traumatic period for the community as a whole and for Iwaishima in particular—a time in which political, social, and familial bonds from the past were tested under the rubric of the "nuclear problem" and often found wanting.[29] On top of that, certain individuals seem deliberately to have incited behavior that on the surface might be called "political protest" but that in some cases was no more than plain old-fashioned bullying. Examples included not only the intimidation of pronuclear households by some antinuclear activists on Iwaishima, but also the provocation of those same activists by the tactics and arrogance of certain pronuclear powerbrokers,[30] and of course the regular appearance in the town of trade union loudmouths and right-wing thugs. It was as if the traditional fabric of the hometown had been ripped apart—a community fissioned by nuclear power before the preliminary surveys had even begun.

Divided History

On the concrete outer wall of the Iwaishima Fishing Cooperative, facing back toward Kōmyōji temple and the port, is a large sign titled "Three *furusato* poems." Nobody seems to remember when the sign was erected, but it was first noted in the *Asahi shinbun* newspaper in the autumn of 1985, soon after Yamato Sadao had returned to lead the antinuclear movement.[31] Written by an elderly Iwaishima woman in *tanka* style, the poems read:

People call our village, "Hatoko's Sea,"
so why are the waves of the nuclear power station disturbing us?
My mother sent seaweed bearing the smell of the shore,
her affection in the taste of my *furusato*.
As spring approaches, my childhood days, playing in the shallows of the beach,
are still in my dreams.

The key imagery in the poems is of the sea, the shore, the beach. This is because if, as the media pointed out repeatedly in 1983, the power station were to be constructed, it would be the first nuclear plant within the Seto Inland Sea National Park. Thus through the language and imagery of what they called the "beautiful sea," antinuclear campaigners under the leadership of Yamato Sadao began to add an environmental angle to their case—an element that would later draw the support of Greenpeace.[32] At the same time, the campaign increasingly focused on fishermen, with Yamato himself subsequently elected head of the island's cooperative. This shift was tactical: once mayor Katayama had officially invited investment from Chugoku Electric, fishermen would be required to give permission for the next stage of the process, namely, the environmental survey of the site. They could thus delay the plan by refusing such permission, just as they could also refuse to enter into negotiations with the company over compensation packages for fishing rights that would be affected by the land reclamation in Tanoura Bay and by discharges of coolant water from the plant.[33]

But the first of the *furusato* poems goes further than simply depicting the sea in general terms: it speaks specifically of Hatoko's sea, thus taking a story irrevocably associated with Kaminoseki district (where the television series was both set and partly filmed) and appropriating it instead as an antinuclear image for Iwaishima. This pattern of appropriation and reappropriation is indicative of a hitherto understudied aspect of Japan's many postwar nuclear disputes: as the Kaminoseki example suggests, they were a battle not just over safety, inward investment, political power, historical leadership, and relations between individual households, but also over imagery and language. In Kaminoseki, respective visions of a future *furusato* were predicated on contested memories of the historical *furusato* in such a way that "history" itself became politicized—a phenomenon familiar to historians of issues such as Japanese war memories but much less commonly studied at a local level.

One catalyst for the historicization of the nuclear dispute was the formation, on 26 October 1991 (Nuclear Power Day), of the Kaminoseki Municipal Town-Making Liaison Committee, which grew out of the merger of the Association for Considering the Development of Kaminoseki and more than a dozen other pronuclear pressure groups from different districts of the town.[34] At the time of its formation in 1982, the Association for Considering the Development of Kaminoseki had characterized the town as having a "bright history": it was a strategic location (*yōshō*) in the Inland Sea, but, with the mechanization of modern life, the town had become depopulated and deprived of its old identity.[35] The new organization developed the theme of a bright historical identity by erecting eight striking billboards around the town. In keeping with the Liaison Committee's desire to emphasize the potential benefits of nuclear power for the wider local community rather than for Japan or for Chamber of Commerce–affiliated companies, two of the signs predicted, through the construction of a nuclear power station,

> Bright and rich *furusato*-making through a nuclear power station: [bringing] vitality to young people and comfort to the elderly. (Hetsu district)
>
> [Through nuclear power,] a *furusato* where young people gather and where we have heart-to-heart communication! (Shidai district)[36]

The emphasis on "young people" (*wakamono*) looked back to the predepopulation era, when the town was, to borrow the language of other Liaison Committee

Figure 11.1. "With nuclear power, charming town-making," Kamai, 2004

signs, "lively" (*katsuryoku*), "worth living in" (*ikigai*), and "prosperous" (*uruoi*). (There was, of course, no mention of overpopulation and poverty.) The signs thus framed the *furusato* not in terms of spatial distance, as in the *furusato* boom, but in terms of temporal distance—a *furusato* that was once prosperous and lively but that was now in trouble.[37] Through a brighter future, the nuclear power station offered townspeople the chance to return to the *furusato* of their past.

The nuclear power plant thus implicitly served as a bridge—from the Kaminoseki of the present to that of the future and equally from the promised "vision" of the future to the idealized memory of the past. Indeed, one of the three image-bearing billboards erected by the Liaison Committee depicted the Kaminoseki Great Bridge under the slogan "A lively and rich town through the nuclear power station," while a second showed elderly townspeople on one side of the bridge joyfully welcoming returning young workers as part of "charming town-making" (see Figure 11.1). One of the men who commissioned the billboards later explained, "Without the bridge, the billboards wouldn't have seemed characteristic of Kaminoseki [*Kaminoseki rashikunai*]."[38] Such a rationale seems also to have driven the public relations team at the new Kaminoseki offices of Chugoku Electric. Starting in 1986, the company published a monthly newsletter for the town called *Kakehashi* (The Bridge); as the head of the office recalled in a retrospective edition, *Kakehashi's the 20th Anniversary* [*sic*], the name represented "the bridge that links us to the townspeople."[39]

If the nuclear plant was to be a bridge linking both company and residents, future and past, then that "past" was more fully depicted in the Silk Road sign erected in September 1990 at the Nagashima end of Kaminoseki Bridge by the Kaminoseki town Youth and Young Men's Liaison Council (Kaminoseki-chō Seisōnen Renraku Kyōgikai)—an organization later affiliated with the Town-Making Liaison Committee (see Figure 1.1). Beneath images of Kaminoseki's "bright" pre-1868 history, a short explanatory text concluded: "Since the Meiji period, the role of Kaminoseki as an entrepôt (*chūkeichi*) has weakened owing to the development of land routes and the appearance of machine-powered boats. But even now, more than one thousand boats pass through the Kaminoseki straits every day, and everywhere in the town one can see traces of the past indicating great prosperity." At the bottom of the sign, there was a message from the Youth and Young Men's group written in boldface: "With this history as our backdrop, we are tackling a new town-making."

In light of the pronuclear Town-Making Liaison Committee billboards in every other Kaminoseki district, "new town-making" could be interpreted as referring to the nuclear power station plan. In this sense, the phrase "town-making" (*machi-zukuri*) and even the word "town" (*machi*) themselves became politicized terms. For their part, Iwaishima activists perceived that such rhetoric precluded their own alternative vision of a nonnuclear *furusato*.[40] To undermine the all-embracing pronuclear message, they created an alternative rhetorical space through the language not of "town-making" but rather of "island rejuvenation" (*shima okoshi*). Similarly, the alternative interpretation of the *furusato,* as expressed by the three poems, employed the word "village" (*sato*) rather than "town." Indeed, just as *furusato* became a contested term in the nuclear debate, so too did notions of "richness" and "young people," to name but two: the pronuclear "rich town" (*yutaka na machi*) versus the antinuclear "rich fishing grounds" (*yutaka na gyojō*); the "*furusato* where young people may gather" versus the need to stop the nuclear plan "for the sake of our children and grandchildren."

The Silk Road sign was but one example of the politicization of Kaminoseki's history within pronuclear rhetoric. A more egregious reframing of the past by pronuclear bureaucrats occurred with the establishment of the Suigun Matsuri festival. The Suigun Matsuri grew out of the Kaminoseki port festival, which had been held every summer since 1974 under the auspices of the Chamber of Commerce. In 1991, the town office applied for the first time to receive 75 percent of the festival budget under central government subsidies offered to municipalities that neighbor major power installations—in this case, Chugoku Electric's Liquified Natural Gas thermal power station in Yanai city, then under construction.[41] A committee was formed to consider the theme of the proposed new festival, and following the suggestion of one member it decided to focus on the Murakami Suigun, the maritime militia that had built a castle above Kaminoseki port in the sixteenth century (see Chapter 2). An early planning document explained the reasoning behind the choice: "We have decided on the image of 'Sea town Kaminoseki'—a town that, continuing the history of the Murakami Suigun, has prospered as a strategic port since the old days." But another document suggested that the significance of the Murakami image was not simply historical: the aim was also to use the festival in order to "image up" the town—"to use both the natural environment and our historical and cultural inheritances, and to bring together every group in the town . . . [so as to] widely appeal to tourists both inside and outside the prefecture." Thus history became a tool to bring people together and to improve the image of Kaminoseki, an image that had suffered, as one planner put it, from negative publicity surrounding the nuclear dispute.[42]

Together, the Town-Making Liaison Committee billboards, the Silk Road sign, and the Suigun Matsuri suggested a pronuclear interpretation of Kaminoseki's past, even though it was never explicitly articulated as such. Eliding the history of the port with the history of the wider town, this interpretation implied that just as "Kaminoseki" had prospered (*sakaeta*) in the past, so it would find profit (*uruoi*) in a nuclear-powered future. The Silk Road discourse in both the signs and the festival thus implicitly served as a bridge between the past and the future.

But despite the hope of Suigun Matsuri organizers that every group in the town might be brought together, the antinuclear lobby on Iwaishima had other ideas. They boycotted the new festival in 1991, and in 1992 they launched their own reinterpretation of the past.

Iwaishima's *kanmai* rites had been canceled in 1984 and 1988—a victim of *mura hachibu* ostracism, mutual resentment, and the fact that many islanders were too preoccupied with the antinuclear campaign to have time to undertake the festival's laborious preparations, which must be started in earnest at least six months in advance. Some villagers felt that now that the *kanmai* had been canceled twice, its longevity and cyclical place in people's lives had been irrevocably lost. By the winter of 1991–1992, however, the momentum to revive the festival, which had been apparent though unsuccessful four years previously, had gathered pace. At the turn of 1992, the island's ward heads (*kumichō*) finally voted to hold the rites in August of that year.[43]

There appear to have been two groups pushing the process of revival. On the one hand were history enthusiasts and islanders who simply wanted to preserve valuable traditions—people who saw it as their "responsibility" to continue the *kanmai* for the sake of future generations. Indeed, even in the summers of 1984 and 1988, a handful of islanders had held an informal morning ceremony high above the village at the Gyōja shrine built by Korean emigrant Matsuoka Toyozō in 1904. (Their chosen location was significant in light of the tensions between islanders and the priest of the main Miyato Hachimangū shrine.) On the other hand, and with considerably more political influence, was a group of antinuclear campaigners led by Yamato Sadao. A senior activist told me that one reason for reviving the rites was to give those campaigners—now in their tenth year of protest—"a change of focus that they could enjoy" (*tanoshimeru kibun tenkan*).

An even more important consideration was the image of Iwaishima that had spread in the media and governing circles in the 1980s as a result of the island's vigorous antinuclear campaign: that islanders wouldn't allow outsiders to approach, that its people were especially negative, and that the island was (the activist half-joked) "a pirate base." By contrast, the revival of the *kanmai* in 1992 was an opportunity to "appeal" both to tourists and to policy makers in regional and central government so as to "change the image" of the island from "closed" to "open." The revival of the *kanmai,* the activist continued, therefore became a manifestation of "island-rejuvenation"—the phrase that antinuclear campaigners use in lieu of "town-making."[44]

In terms of basic aims, the revival of the *kanmai* in 1992 can thus be compared to the creation of the Kaminoseki Suigun Matsuri the previous year: in both cases, activists were attempting to "use" history in order to improve their image to the outside world. The key difference was that the Suigun Matsuri had to be invented from scratch, whereas the *kanmai* had roots stretching back to at least 1168. Nevertheless, the very history of the *kanmai* presented antinuclear campaigners with certain difficulties. For a start, in 1992 the priest of the Iwaishima parish, which would host the *kagura* dancers from Imi Betsugūsha shrine in Kyushu, was Moritomo Nobuhiro (son of the late Hiromitsu). As the earliest surviving documents from the 1690s make clear, the Moritomo household had been intimately involved in the preparation of the festival for several centuries, yet the Moritomo household was also perceived to be pronuclear. Second, the rites were in part a celebration of the Miura Three households and of landowning elites on the island, yet the most important of the Miura Three was the household of Ujimoto Kuichi, leader of the pronuclear faction on the island. To hold the *kanmai* was to invite the participation of pronuclear households in community life.

The solution to these problems was straightforward. Yamato decided to "purge" both his uncle Kuichi and also Moritomo Nobuhiro from the 1992 festival: no Iwaishima priest welcomed the Imi priests, and the Miura Three in practice became the Miura Two.[45] The organizers—including both history enthusiasts and antinuclear campaigners—also produced new publicity for the festival, in which they offered an alternative dating of the *kanmai*'s origins: the rites had started in the year 886, they said, not 1168. The significance of the publicity materials was not that the 886 date was right or wrong; in fact, the date had been a source of serious contention between Iwaishima interpreters of the festival and their Imi counterparts well before the 1980s, along with other aspects of the rituals.[46] Instead, the problem was that the new interpretation flew in the face of the hitherto received "Iwaishima" view of the festival—a view which had been most passionately expounded by the Moritomo household. By denying the 1168 interpretation and instead adopting the 886 date (as proposed by the Imi shrine), the antinuclear campaigners signaled a refusal to accept that the pronuclear priest of the island's main shrine any longer spoke for the history of the festival. Moreover, the new origin of the *kanmai* rites predated the arrival of the Moritomo household on the island by several centuries and thus, in the eyes of leading antinuclear campaigners, justified the exclusion of the priest from the revived festival. Overturning decades of historiographical debate between Iwaishima and Imi, one activist concluded that the *kanmai* "is a festival of Imi Betsugūsha shrine [that] the people of Iwaishima receive."[47]

The appropriation of the Imi priests' interpretation of the *kanmai* in 1992 was part of a wider shift in which antinuclear campaigners disowned their own parish (*ujiko*). According to some islanders, this transformation had its roots in the 1970s, well before the nuclear plan was announced, when, after a number of alleged scandals, parishioners lost trust in then-priest Moritomo Hiromitsu. If true, this is a further example of entirely unrelated battles being fought through the framework of the nuclear dispute.[48] But regardless of what caused the original problem, the rupture between priest and parishioners found renewed expression in the nuclear dispute. The antinuclear majority of households started celebrating New Year rites not at the main Miyato shrine but rather at the Gyōja shrine built high above the village by Matsuoka Toyozō in 1904. Antinuclear islanders stopped making regular donations to the Miyato shrine, thus depriving the Moritomo household of a significant income stream (in response, Moritomo Nobuhiro went to live and work in Yanai). On the occasion of the Miyato shrine's summer festival, antinuclear islanders refused to participate and instead paid for the traditional paper hangings to be sent from the Imi Betsugūsha shrine in Kyushu.

The anthropologist Scott Schnell describes a festival in the mountains of central Japan in which participants used ritual both as an expression and as an instrument of political resistance—a "retribution for perceived injustices."[49] The same process can be seen in reverse in Iwaishima: antinuclear islanders used their nonparticipation in shrine rituals as a financial sanction to protest against an elite household that, in their view, had not only betrayed islanders by allegedly becoming bound up in Chugoku Electric's *nemawashi,* but that had also abused the trust of the parish in the 1970s. Even so, the rejection of their own shrine in favor of joining a parish fifty kilometers across the sea was an extraordinarily unusual step that even some antinuclear sympathizers judged to be "wrong" (*yoroshikunai*).[50] Others expressed their doubts to me through sardonic word-play. Every year since the beginning of the *kanmai,* a group of islanders have made pilgrimage to the Imi shrine as part of the *tane-modoshi* rites, whereby they "return the grains" as an expression of gratitude and goodwill.[51] Since the nuclear dispute erupted, however, islanders have additionally made regular offerings and occasional major donations to their new "parish" shrine—such as a one million yen contribution toward Imi shrine repairs in 1994. "So the *tane-modoshi* [returning the grains] has become a *kane-modoshi* [returning the money]," one man joked, while someone else played on Iwaishima's long history of out-migration labor by noting that the island now has *dekasegi kami-sama*—"out-migration deities."[52]

By the early 1990s, the nuclear dispute highlighted differing visions of the *furusato* within the Kaminoseki hometown. According to the billboards of the Town-Making Liaison Committee, *furusato* referred to the municipality as a whole—an area that included Iwaishima. But campaigners on Iwaishima constructed an alternative *furusato* that rejected the language of "town" and instead referred to "the island" or "the village." Yet "the island" did not include Iwaishima's Miyato shrine parish: instead, even the deities themselves became caught up in the nuclear dispute, so that the borders of the *furusato* extended, in ritual terms, to an entirely noncontiguous community in Kyushu. Just as pronuclear campaigners in Nagashima depicted the future plant as a bridge to their town's idealized past, so antinuclear campaigners in Iwaishima used their own historical bridge (to Imi and thereby to Kyushu) as an instrument of intense opposition to the future power station. This was a battle of the present engaged through alternative visions of the past and the future.

When we study postwar rural communities, we tend to employ atomic metaphors almost without thought: we write about the changing significance of the nuclear family, or the need for a critical mass of workers, or about the atomization of community life. In Kaminoseki, the intensity of the dispute made these metaphors real, as families found themselves divided by nuclear politics and as the "site fight" became also a fight over history, ritual, and the role of the historical elites in the town. At the most intense moments of conflict, civil society in Kaminoseki was replaced by uncivil society, as demonstrators screamed and officials schemed: a late-twentieth-century hometown, dying for survival.

12

The Silk Road of the Sea: An Ending

In the predawn darkness of 21 February 2011, six hundred employees and subcontractors of Chugoku Electric descended on Tanoura Bay. At 8:30 a.m., workers began dropping huge boulders into the sea from five of the thirty-two ships circling the site. The stones marked the first foundations of a 140,000-square-meter land reclamation project, part of the proposed 330,000-square-meter reactor complex. Around 130 antinuclear activists from Iwaishima and farther afield gathered to voice their protest. But after years of legal challenges and months of sea skirmishes between company security guards and Iwaishima fishermen, the construction of Japan's newest nuclear power plant was under way.[1]

On 11 March 2011, however, the worst earthquake in Japanese history struck the northeastern coast of the Tōhoku region. A devastating tsunami claimed 20,000 lives and flooded Tokyo Electric's aging Fukushima Daiichi nuclear power plant. In the days following the tsunami, the outer buildings of two reactors exploded; by April, amid widespread fears of reactor meltdown and radioactive release, 80,000 Fukushima residents had been evacuated from their homes.

The Fukushima crisis changed the Japanese nuclear landscape in ways nobody could have predicted. In Tanoura, construction was suspended almost immediately.[2] A few weeks later, in early May 2011, Prime Minister Kan Naoto ordered the temporary shutdown of Chubu Electric's controversial nuclear plant in Hamaoka, Shizuoka prefecture—controversial because of its location close to a major earthquake fault line. At a press conference, Kan then announced that Japan would go "back to the drawing board" over its future nuclear plans.[3] These plans, which included the goal of generating 50 percent of domestic electricity through nuclear power by 2030, were partly dependent on the completion of the two Kaminoseki reactors.[4] But on May 19, the governor of Yamaguchi prefecture announced that he would consider invalidating Chugoku Electric's land reclamation permit in Tanoura—at least until nuclear policy in Tokyo became clearer. "The myth of nuclear safety has collapsed," opined the regional newspaper. "It would be inconceivable to start land reclamation work without reexamining safety issues. Is this not an opportunity to call a halt and think again from square one?"[5]

Three decades after the nuclear plan was first broached, Kaminoseki thus finds itself at the center of national and even international attention.[6] As a "green" nuclear site (Japan's other proposed reactors would be built at existing nuclear plants), the town has become a test case for the future, post-Fukushima direction of Japanese energy and environmental policy. But anyone interested in this debate also needs to know how Kaminoseki came to the position of volunteering to host a nuclear power station in the first place and why—as this chapter discusses—influential townspeople maintained their support for nuclear power in the immediate aftermath of Fukushima. That stance seemed to be at cross-purposes to foreign media expectations of the Japanese response to the 2011 nuclear crisis. But with this issue as with many others discussed in this book, the apparently counterintuitive experiences of ordinary Kaminoseki townspeople offer an important additional perspective to our understanding of "Japan." Indeed, just as Kaminoseki has become a lens through which to reexamine Japan's future, so this book has argued that the history of Kaminoseki helps us reconsider our understanding of Japan's past. In particular, there are three story lines that throw new light on our study of modern Japan.

One story concerns the economic transformations that accompanied Japan's modernization. As the Chōshū domain's 1842 survey showed, the port economies of Murotsu and Kaminoseki had become highly commercialized in the years immediately preceding Japan's reengagement with the West. This was because by the mid-nineteenth century, crops and crafts throughout much of Japan were no longer produced merely for local consumption but as commodities to be sold to other domestic markets. With their fortuitous home on the main shipping routes of the Inland Sea, the residents of Murotsu and Kaminoseki ports could—with the help of significant investment from the Chōshū domain—gear their economic activities primarily toward the storage and resale of such commodities. Service industries then developed as a result of the many *kitamae*-ships and crews passing through the straits.

The economic success of the ports is suggested by the rapid population growth that occurred in the century after 1738, growth that may partly be explained by immigrant workers moving into the suburbs of the ports. Indeed, although neither Kaminoseki nor Murotsu villages boasted more than 2,500 people in 1842, the ports increasingly resembled urban centers—in function if not in scale. As in an urban center, mid-nineteenth-century shipping agents tailored their sale of commodities to the demands of external markets. Sensitivity to those markets depended on an ability to tap into the region's main communications network, the western circuit. Expanding commercial opportunities led to occupational diversification, especially in the service sector of the economy. New employment opportunities meant the arrival of new migrants from outside, and, as residents and immigrants alike turned away from full-time farming, there was a greater need to import food from other regions. In all these categories—external markets, communications, occupational diversity, inward migration, food imports—Kaminoseki and Murotsu in 1842 resembled what Maurice Agulhon has called, with reference to nineteenth-century French Mediterranean communities, "urbanized villages."[7]

The early-nineteenth-century history of Kaminoseki thus highlights the ways in which the economies of some regions in the late Edo period were both vibrant and growing, as identified by postwar "modernization" historians of Japan. But it is important not to press the extent of Kaminoseki's own modernization too far. David Howell has noted that the wage dependency of nominal "farmers" on outside markets—as opposed to community-based mutual dependency—is one characteristic of a capitalist economy.[8] In the case of Kaminoseki's outlying islands, this dependency on outside economic forces took the form of off-season migration to the sake breweries of Honshu or the whaling ships of the Japan Sea: farmers were physically drawn away from their hometowns as their labor was purchased by merchant capitalists. But labor-purchasing capitalists were not, so far as I can tell, to be found either in the islands or in the straits themselves. Even prosperous shipping agents, such as the Awa-ya household in Kaminoseki, or major landowners, such as the Yoshida household in Murotsu, probably employed only maids, porters, or shop assistants at the very most. Despite the extensive commercialization of the straits economies by the 1840s, we cannot characterize them as "capitalist" in terms of labor being locally bought and sold on a large scale.

Moreover, as Howell further argues, it is one thing to note that some regions in late Edo period Japan showed economic growth, but that in itself "says nothing directly about qualitative changes in the lives of the people involved in production."[9] While the qualitative evidence of two-story residences for shipping agents in downtown Kaminoseki and Murotsu suggests that some households prospered greatly from the commercialization of the local economy, the income differentials between the port areas and the outlying islands of the town—and indeed the fact that farmers in those outlying islands were forced to seek wage labor away from home in the first place—indicates that significant socioeconomic inequalities existed in the mid-nineteenth-century hometown. The concept of *kakusa shakai,* or the divergent society, which was debated by many Japanese commentators in the early 2000s as an apparent manifestation of the postbubble economy, is equally applicable to Kaminoseki in the 1840s: we must avoid the temptation to paint too colorful a picture of the breadth and smoothness of the mid-nineteenth-century "silk road."

These caveats notwithstanding, it is clear that the fortunes of the Kaminoseki and Murotsu economies changed for the worse in the decades after Japan's reengagement with the West as a trajectory of growth morphed into one of long-term economic decline. This metamorphosis forced greater numbers of townspeople to seek outside wage labor, leading eventually to population decline and to a corresponding sense of social and cultural decline, especially in the postwar community. In particular, some of the hardest times for ordinary townspeople appear to have occurred in the late 1880s and the late 1950s—two periods more usually associated, nationally, with the beginning of sustained economic growth. Thus, Kaminoseki's history conforms to our understanding that "proto" modernizing processes in one region do not necessarily lead to "modern growth" in that region.[10] On the contrary, there was a clear regression in Kaminoseki's case, from a highly commercialized community in the 1840s to a village from which impoverished "farmers" sought escape to Hawai'i and other parts of the Pacific Rim some fifty years later. Thomas C. Smith once argued that historians must find space for micronarratives of demographic growth within macronarratives of late Edo stagnation.[11] Equally, the history of Kaminoseki suggests that we must henceforth find greater space for studies of economic decline and associated hardship within wider narratives of Japan's modern growth. The story of a small town that became a "backwater"—an *ura Nihon* located in the one-time politically and economically "forward" regions of southwestern Japan—highlights the need to question our most basic binaries of growth-decline and forward-backward in modern Japanese history.

A second story concerns the ways in which ordinary townspeople experienced the world beyond Japan in the century and a half after Perry's arrival in 1853. Studying rural Japan, it is all too easy to project back the JET-program narrative of 1990s "internationalization"—the view that isolated villages in the late twentieth century should "import diversity," in the form of native English speakers, to come up to speed with the ways of the world.[12] But decades prior to the arrival of a JET teacher, Kaminoseki townspeople knew much about life beyond the borders of the Japanese state. Even before the first wave of overseas migration in the 1880s, residents of the ports communities welcomed foreigners passing through the straits during the two-hundred-year period when Japan was supposedly "closed" to the outside world. If individual townspeople did not see the Korean and Ryūkyū ambassadors or the Dutch traders with their own eyes—the arrival of foreigners in the Edo period was a far from everyday occurrence, even in Kaminoseki—then they would have heard stories about them from friends and parents, and they would have seen paintings such as that in the Chōsenji temple (Figure 2.3). As Ronald P. Toby reminds us of the Korean Embassies, these memories enabled foreign missions to gain a cultural currency in Edo Japan that went beyond the ephemeral quality of the event itself and that thus helped ordinary people to "articulate the very nature of their world, and their own place in it."[13]

By the turn of the twentieth century, the opportunity for ordinary townspeople to experience a world beyond Kaminoseki (and Japan) had shifted from the occasional arrival of exotic-looking foreigners to the chance to work abroad. The origins of this overseas diaspora lay partly in the deflationary crises of the mid-1880s, but the history of Kaminoseki suggests that other causes may also be found in the longer-term structural transformations that accompanied Japan's reengagement with the West—in particular the collapse of Edo period trading routes and the concomitant impact on coastal communities throughout both the Inland Sea and Japan Sea regions. Moreover, when viewed from the perspective of everyday history, the Japanese diaspora appears less an isolated episode in the history of Meiji and prewar Japan than part of an ongoing strategy by which individual townspeople sought outside income to ameliorate the difficulties of their daily lives. My analysis of individual Kaminoseki households over several generations thus underlines the need to integrate more fully the stories of overseas migrants into a general social or "people's" history of modern Japan—a history that embraces, as recent scholars have argued, both "local" and "global" aspects.[14]

To acknowledge that there was a connection between mid-nineteenth-century economic dislocations and the subsequent overseas diaspora has potentially profound implications for how we understand the social history of the Japanese empire. If we accept, as the evidence from Kaminoseki and Murotsu indicates, that the "push" factors motivating individual villagers to seek new lives overseas were largely the same regardless of whether those villagers ended up in the Americas or in Asia, then we must rethink the simplistic distinction that government officials at the turn of the twentieth century made between "emigrants" and "colonists." New scholarship is already questioning such distinctions in light of imperial and emigrant discourse in the 1930s and also as part of a sociological analysis of Japanese population movements to and between the prewar colonies (and indeed between America and Asia).[15] As Araragi Shinzō argues, established macrohistorical frames of Japanese imperialism are insufficient to explain the complex choices that lay behind the decision of individual workers and their families to move overseas.[16] The microhistorical framework of Chapters 6 and 7 may be one way to approach these problems anew. At the very least, the story of Kaminoseki's and Murotsu's migrants to Korea allows us "to populate the Japanese colonial landscape with living, acting individuals" and thus to address Mark Peattie's plea for more understanding of the "humanity, if not humaneness" of Japanese colonialism.[17]

This discussion of empire and everyday motivations brings us to a third story concerning the actions of ordinary people in the making of modern Japan. In the period covered by this book, some Kaminoseki townspeople exercised considerable agency both in their individual lives and in their contributions to community life. Village elites played an important and hitherto understudied role in the events that led up to the Meiji Restoration: their homes became a haven for leading Chōshū agitators, and they offered important backing to anti-Tokugawa militia groups. They did all this while also maintaining stable authority over hometown life in a period of great national unrest. Indeed, leading households institutionalized their personal authority over fellow villagers until the first decades of the twentieth century by manipulating local elections, monopolizing bureaucratic positions, and demonstrating their wealth and social largesse through the material culture of newly constructed schools, roads, rice fields, and so on. In these ways and many more, the Kaminoseki elites helped to shape the emerging Japanese state, as studies from other parts of Japan similarly conclude.[18]

But while the oligarchic structures that village elites established over hometown life—political, economic, ritual, and even marital—helped preserve the communal body, and thus avoid the political ructions of contemporary nineteenth-century villages in the Kantō and elsewhere,[19] such structures also closed off political opportunities to less wealthy villagers. One significance of the nuclear decision was that it revealed the continued exclusion of some village constituencies, such as ordinary fishermen, from political decision making even a century after the establishment of an elected village council. The personal and household authority of nearly all the Edo period elites may have waned by the 1980s, but a small group of men (always men) still combined the roles of political and civil society leadership much as their nineteenth-century counterparts had done.

Political agency in Kaminoseki was thus limited according to one's status in the community. By contrast, townspeople could exercise economic agency to a far greater extent. Indeed, some of the most striking stories in Kaminoseki's modern history are the examples of individual initiative and enterprise even against the backdrop of regional economic decline. As the cases of Kase Mihosuke and Katayama Hideyuki suggest, an entrepreneurial spirit, with a bit of luck and community support, could lead to an economic success story in mid-twentieth-century Kaminoseki similar to that of the shipping agents in the mid-nineteenth-century ports. But even the story of individual economic agency within the hometown goes only so far. For a young man from a non-elite household who wanted to succeed as a fishermen, the prewar structures of the sardine-fishing industry would for the most part have held him back rather than enabling him to fulfill his ambition. For a really ambitious young man—someone like Okada Usuke—economic agency could best be exercised outside the confines of the hometown. Other "success" stories in this book, such as Kōno Takenosuke and Awaya Torazuchi also made their money away from Kaminoseki, although they all gave generously to their hometown.

Ambition works at many levels. Everyone discussed in this book, no matter what the extent of their political activity or economic "success," was motivated by personal or household interest at the basest level: this is human nature. But I wonder if Kaminoseki townspeople did not also lead their lives with a sense that "work for the village is of primary importance," as a headman from the Kantō region wrote in 1869.[20] Work for the hometown, and the hometown will work for you; this, perhaps, was a second everyday motivation for many ordinary people in modern Japan. For example, in her analysis of the Chinese diaspora in the United States, Madeline Y. Hsu suggests that the hometown was a site of ambition for many successful emigrants who were thwarted from achieving success in America because of inherent racism in the host culture of the early twentieth century.[21] A similar formulation can be applied to the Kaminoseki townspeople for both residents and emigrants alike. Thus the hometown gave the Izutas and Kanōs a stage on which to exercise political influence unattainable at a national level. The hometown was a barometer by which businessmen such as Ogata Kenkurō and Katayama Hideyuki could gauge their success against that of their peers in terms of taller houses and bigger tankers. The hometown was a showpiece for expressions of loyalty and material largesse from men who had gone abroad, such as Matsubara Daikichi and Fujinaga Yosaku. And a hometown festival such as the *kanmai* offered a foundational narrative that gave hundreds of Iwaishima households a sense of structure in everyday relations—whether they were the beneficiaries of that structure or not. If we are to take seriously the *furusato* discourses of the nuclear dispute and see them as more than just rhetoric, then the ambition to save the hometown from threatening forces beyond one's control—foreigners, depopulation, corporate bullying—was perhaps another common thread that tied the political motivations of revolutionary oligarchs in the nineteenth century to those of pro- and antinuclear campaigners in the twentieth. As we attempt to patch the complex and contradictory lives of ordinary people into the historiography of modern Japan, this theme of hometown loyalty deserves a more extensive and empirical examination than it has received to date in the scholarly literature on postwar *furusato* discourse.

Such is the relevance of Kaminoseki's history for our understanding of nineteenth- and twentieth-century Japan. But themes of economic stagnation and population decline resonate in early-twenty-first-century Japan as well. In 2005, the overall population of Japan decreased for the first time in the postwar period. In 2010, it was announced that Japan had fallen behind China in economic strength, with respected media outlets warning that the former's economic status may become even more precarious in the near future.[22] Without doubt, it was easier for me to research Japanese decline in the 2000s than it would have been in the 1980s, when Suzanne Culter was questioned by fieldwork informants regarding why she was writing on a topic (managing decline in a northern mining community) that "did not fit the reality."[23] Nevertheless, I would argue that the story of Kaminoseki, although concerned with a particular time and space, speaks also to the reality of hundreds of other small communities throughout Japan, and indeed throughout the industrialized world—communities that have gone bankrupt or have voted for their own extinction,[24] that are in a "struggle for survival" or experiencing Main Street blues.[25] To understand how people lived with everyday decline in modern Kaminoseki is to begin to understand the hopes and hard times of small communities across the modern world.

In December 1948, French scientists working at their country's first experimental reactor conducted a successful nuclear reaction. Within months, they had isolated France's first milligram of plutonium, prompting a visit from President Vincent Auriol. "This achievement," the president announced, "will add to the radiance of France." Through his pun—*rayonnement* means both "radiance" and also "radiation"—the president articulated a relationship between nuclear technology and national grandeur that would become central to France's postwar identity, especially amidst the uncertainty of postwar decolonization and economic instability. Commentators described the new reactors as "concrete cathedral[s]" and "cathedrals of steel"—factories that launched themselves forward "like a *hymn* to the *glory* of industrial creation."[26]

In February 2011, as Chugoku Electric began construction work in Tanoura, it may have seemed to some townspeople that the radiance of Kaminoseki was at last being realized. Passing by bus through the town, one would have seen a transformed landscape. In front of the newly restored four-storied Shikairō, in the same bay where ships docked over the centuries, the sea has been reclaimed (see Figure 2.2, inset, and Figure 12.1). Nothing yet stands on the land reclamation site, but the 2011–2012 municipal budget promises a new cultural center here.[27] A short distance away, the Murotsu elementary school buildings have been razed and a new hot spring resort is under construction. Murotsu and Kaminoseki elementary schools have merged and are now housed in a state-of-the-art building on the Nagashima side of the straits. It is a light, airy space, all wood paneling and graceful curves—a fine successor to the Korean Hall and America-Hawai'i Hall of the 1910s. Just across from the new school, Jōyama Hill, site of a Murakami Suigun militia fort in the sixteenth century, has been partially flattened and relandscaped as a municipal park.

All these infrastructure developments—the land reclamation, the hot spring resort, the new elementary school, the park, even the restored Shikairō—come courtesy of central government subsidies paid out to municipalities that host (or plan to host) a nuclear power plant. Benefits from the subsidies are also felt in less concrete ways. Now that the Nagashima high school has closed down,

Figure 12.1. The Kaminoseki straits from Mt. Kamisakari, 2010, with the new elementary school and Kaminoseki Jōyama History Park in the foreground

the municipality subsidizes the bus fare of Kaminoseki students as they make their morning commute up the Murotsu peninsula to Yanai. The Kaminoseki-Yanai bus is even more heavily discounted for elderly residents. Parents with newborn babies receive 5,000 yen a month ($60) toward the cost of diapers. All townspeople receive a free influenza vaccination each fall. The list could go on.[28]

But there are several reasons to doubt whether Kaminoseki's new nuclear identity is really so radiant. First and most obvious, the Fukushima meltdown in March 2011 has raised fundamental questions about the management of the nuclear industry and of nuclear safety in Japan. The warning by Iwaishima antinuclear campaigners that islanders could become "nuclear refugees" in the event of an accident at Tanoura no longer seems like mere scaremongering to the pronuclear lobby. Indeed, a Fukushima-style twenty-kilometer exclusion zone around Kaminoseki's proposed nuclear plant would necessitate the evacuation of the entire town, not just of Iwaishima. Post-Fukushima, the refrain "nuclear power is scary" is heard even among nuclear supporters.[29]

Second, Kaminoseki's demographic travails continue unabated. In the twelve years after my first visit in the summer of 1998, the town's population decreased by another quarter, to 3,600 people. Forty-nine percent of those residents are aged sixty-five and above, and the situation is even more grim in Yashima and Iwaishima.[30] From these figures alone, it is difficult to view the history of modern Kaminoseki, or even of modern Japan, as a hymn to the glory of industrial creation. Even in the wake of Japan's most serious nuclear accident, these are the kind of statistics that prompted one town councillor to use the word "crisis" in reference to Kaminoseki, not Fukushima. "Given the crisis-like situation of our town," Sasaki Minoru wrote in April 2011, "in which the problems of depopulation and aging persist, we must bring the nuclear plant to fruition as soon as possible. The reality is that if we don't proceed with town-making [policies], the development of the town, and even its very existence, is at threat."[31]

But a third reason to question the town-making vision of men such as Sasaki concerns the historical foundations on which those policies, and thus the future hometown community, are being built. One man who had some prescient insights on the nature of hometown community and survival was the late Kaminoseki resident Ueda Kichisuke (1918–2006). In 1995, Ueda gave a lecture on Iwaishima's history at the invitation of the island's Women's Association. His opening words spoke of his concerns not only for Iwaishima, but also for Kaminoseki and even for Japan as a whole. This island, he began, has many precious historical inheritances.[32] To have an accurate understanding of historical facts, relics, and traditions is to cultivate fondness and pride in the hometown (*furusato*), which is more important than anything else. "In general, those of us who were born and brought up in a hometown do not know about its history and traditions. Even if we wanted to find out, we didn't have the time or energy to do so because of our great struggles with the hard times [*kurushimi*] of everyday life. But if someone does not tell these stories to our children and grandchildren and so bequeath them to a future generation, then one day we shall lose all knowledge of our hometowns."

In some ways, Ueda's own long life exemplified the kinds of stories that need to be told in order to gain better understanding of everyday history in the Japanese hometown. Born and raised on the island of Hawai'i, Ueda was the grandson of a wealthy Nagashima farmer who had donated money to the new Kaminoseki Village Office in 1896 (see Chapter 4).[33] When Ueda's parents returned to the village in 1932, they followed the pattern of other returnees in constructing a two-story house with the money they had saved from owning a bakery in Hilo. But the comfort of his new home could not make up for the bullying Ueda attracted from his younger classmates. In a school whose assembly hall had been built courtesy of donations from Hawai'i, the mainland United States, Korea, Taiwan, and Manchuria (Chapter 7), Ueda was mocked for his faltering Japanese and his perceived "praise of foreign countries" (*gaikoku raisan*). Nevertheless, by the end of the decade he was considered "Japanese" enough to be conscripted into the Imperial Army, and he spent the war years in China and Southeast Asia. Repatriated to Japan from a prisoner-of-war camp in March 1946, Ueda opened a small grocery shop in the family home, on the narrow hillside street connecting the port and inland areas of the old Kaminoseki district (Chapter 2). His growing standing in the community was reflected by his election as district head (*kuchō*) in 1961. During his term, Ueda raised money to pave district roads and to build a state-of-the-art gas crematorium: these were among his contributions to the postwar economic and cultural "improvement" of the municipality (Chapter 8).

Ueda's life thus threads its way through the many fabrics of Kaminoseki's—and Japan's—modern history. But Ueda's story is not the kind of *furusato* history that town administrators care about. Instead, they sponsor a very different vision of the past, one that I experienced firsthand in 2007, less than a year after Ueda's death, when I joined friends in attending the annual Suigun Matsuri festival. As it had been for several years, the Suigun Matsuri was held on the new land reclamation site in Murotsu. Hundreds of young people, mainly non-Kaminoseki residents, gathered in front of a temporary stage overlooking the straits. As the sun set, we listened to a taiko-drumming ensemble from the elementary school. The children wore *hachimaki* headbands bearing the Murakami Suigun ensign, while in the distance behind the stage stood the original Suigun fort, Jōyama Hill. Cooling ourselves with plastic fans provided by Chugoku Electric ("Toward a Bright Future: Kaminoseki Nuclear Power Plant, hand in hand with the local community"), we were reminded by an enthusiastic master of ceremonies that this was a festival of the town's "*furusato* history." But the irony, missed by most visitors, is that the earth and stones used to fill Murotsu's historical port actually come from the partially flattened Suigun militia base, now audaciously renamed Kaminoseki Jōyama History Park. We were thus trampling on the very Murakami history that the Suigun festival purported to celebrate.[34]

If central government subsidies continue and the nuclear power plant is one day completed in Kaminoseki, then a cultural center will eventually be built on this land—Kaminoseki's own concrete cathedral. The center will include an auditorium and a new library; there is even talk of moving the rediscovered village records from under their tarpaulin cover in the seafront warehouse to be stored here instead. But if the nuclear power station is not built in Kaminoseki as a consequence of a post-Fukushima policy change, then this site will remain a wasteland—a memorial to misplaced local optimism in the early twenty-first century. Either way, the future of the hometown does not look terribly bright, in my opinion, for by reclaiming the past at the expense of understanding it, Kaminoseki is building its future on unstable foundations. Regardless of the nuclear power debate, townspeople are in danger of continuing to live the hard times, waiting as of old for prosperous winds to blow.

ABBREVIATIONS

AS	*Asahi shinbun*
ASY	Asahi Shinbun Yamaguchi Shikyoku, *Kokusaku no yukue: Kaminoseki genpatsu no nijū nen* (2001)
BFC	Yamaguchi-ken Monjokan, *Bōchō fūdo chūshin'an,* vol. 6 (1963)
BJJ	Yamaguchi-ken Chihōshi Gakkai, *Bōchō jige jōshin,* vol. 1 (1978)
CS	*Chūgoku shinbun*
DRO	Diplomatic Record Office, Japanese Ministry of Foreign Affairs
JAS	*The Journal of Asian Studies*
KC	Kaminoseki Chōshi Hensan Iinkai, *Kaminoseki chōshi* (1988)
KK	*Kaminoseki kōhō*
KKS	Kaminoseki-chō Yakuba, *Kaminoseki-chō kaihatsu shindan* (1971)
KYM	Kaminoseki Yakuba monjo
MB	*Mura no bunka* (1948–1949)
MKCJSJ	Yamaguchi-ken Sōmubu Tōkeika, *Murotsu Kaminoseki chiku jūmin seikatsu jittai* (1957)
MN	*Monumenta Nipponica*
MYM	Murotsu Yakuba monjo
TD	*Tochi daichō*
YM	Yamaguchi Kenritsu Monjokan
YS	*Yomiuri shinbun*

NOTES

Chapter 1: The Silk Road of the Sea

1. Smith's essay, which originally appeared in the *Journal of Economic History*, 29, no. 4 (December 1969), was later republished in Smith, *Native Sources of Japanese Industrialization*, which is the version I use. The two quotations appear on p. 71 and p. 99.

2. Field, *In the Realm of a Dying Emperor*, p. 118.

3. Smith himself recognized this some years later, when he wrote, "in slighting much about the Japanese past that did not prove useful to the present, I have no doubt also slighted the cost of what occurred." Smith, *Native Sources*, p. 2.

4. Yasui, "Machi-zukuri, mura-okoshi to furusato monogatari," pp. 203–204. The Kamisakari Observatory Tower was completed in 1991.

5. I am grateful to Ann Waswo for giving me a photograph she took of this sign.

6. On political and economic history, see Craig, *Chōshū in the Meiji Restoration*; Huber, *The Revolutionary Origins of Modern Japan*; and Nishikawa, "The Economy of Chōshū on the Eve of Industrialization." On the leaders, see Hackett, *Yamagata Aritomo in the Rise of Modern Japan*; Iwata, *Ōkubo Toshimichi*; Hall, *Mori Arinori*; and Jansen, *Sakamoto Ryōma and the Meiji Restoration*.

7. Itō, *Itō Hirobumi*; Humphreys, *The Way of the Heavenly Sword*; Drea, *Japan's Imperial Army*. Two exceptions to this rule are the works of Kimura Kenji and Jonathan F. Dresner, to be discussed in Chapters 6 and 7.

8. I am indebted to Osamu Saitō for this formulation of the problem (personal correspondence, 2010).

9. Waters, *Japan's Local Pragmatists*; Bowen, *Rebellion and Democracy in Meiji Japan*.

10. Kimura Motoi, "Kyōdoshi, chihōshi, chiikishi kenkyū no rekishi to kadai." See also Ōkado, *Rekishi e no toi, genzai e no toi*, pp. 86–110.

11. Howell, *Capitalism from Within*; Wigen, *The Making of a Japanese Periphery*; Lewis, *Becoming Apart*; Furumaya, *Ura Nihon*.

12. This is not to say that there has been no research on southwestern Japan. One of the first community studies published in the English language focused on a village in central Kyushu: Embree, *Suye-mura*. There have also been studies of village life in Okayama (western Honshu), the Inland Sea, Shikoku, and northern Kyushu: see, respectively, Beardsley et al., *Village Japan*; Norbeck, *Takashima*; Robert J. Smith, *Kurusu*; and Kalland, *Shingū*. However, all these books focused on village life. By contrast, the books that have examined local and

regional history with a view to reframing paradigms of modern Japanese development have been overwhelmingly centered on central and northeastern Japan. The notable exception is Timothy George, who used the story of Minamata to highlight the darker side of Japan's modernity, especially that of postwar high growth: George, *Minamata*.

13. Lesbirel, *NIMBY Politics in Japan*.

14. Davis, *The Return of Martin Guerre*, p. 4.

15. Robert J. Smith, *Kurusu*, p. 231n.

16. Yamamuro, "Fiirudowāku ga 'jissenteki' de aru tame ni."

17. Bailey, *Ordinary People, Extraordinary Lives*, pp. 8–9.

18. Kaminoseki Chōshi Hensan Iinkai, *Kaminoseki chōshi*. Hereafter abbreviated as *KC*.

19. Overseas migration receives just twelve pages of analysis in the 230-page section of the *KC* that discusses the development of Kaminoseki and Murotsu villages between 1868 and 1945.

20. Partner, *Toshié*; Partner, *The Mayor of Aihara*; Bernstein, *Isami's House*.

21. Pratt, "Community and Conflict in Nineteenth-Century Japan," p. 12.

22. This was an example of my attempting to change what Tonkin calls the "genre" of the oral interview: Tonkin, *Narrating Our Pasts*, pp. 51–55.

23. Al Alvarez, "The Long Road Home," *The Guardian*, 11 September 2004, http://www.guardian.co.uk/books/2004/sep/11/fiction.philiproth, last accessed 12 October 2010.

24. Lüdtke, "Introduction: What Is the History of Everyday Life and Who Are Its Practitioners?" pp. 3–7. For an example of *Alltagsgeschichte* in practice, see Browning, *Ordinary Men*.

25. Herbert, "Good Times, Bad Times."

26. A similar point is made by Walthall, "Introduction: Tracking People in the Past," pp. xii–xiii.

27. Kerry Smith, *A Time of Crisis*.

28. See, for example, Waswo and Nishida, eds., *Farmers and Village Life in Twentieth-Century Japan*; Yamashita, *Leaves from an Autumn of Emergencies*; Partner, *Toshié*; Griffiths, "Need, Greed, and Protest in Japan's Black Market."

29. Lüdtke, "People Working," p. 90. This quotation appears in a section titled "The Patchwork of Practices."

30. Steele, "Edo in 1868"; Partner, *The Mayor of Aihara*; Kerry Smith, *A Time of Crisis*; Partner, *Toshié*; Dower, *Embracing Defeat*; Bailey, *Ordinary People, Extraordinary Lives*.

31. The phrase is from Ginzburg and Poni, "The Name and the Game," p. 6.

32. The complexities of fieldwork ethics in Japan are discussed in a collection of essays published in *Critical Asian Studies* 39, no. 4 (2007). For a discussion of the naming issue in particular, see Edwards, "An Ethics for Working Up?"

33. On the relationship between *Alltagsgeschichte* and microhistory, see Gregory, "Review: Is Small Beautiful?"

34. Ginzburg, *The Cheese and the Worms*, p. 21; Ginzburg and Poni, "The Name and the Game," pp. 2–3; Levi, "On Microhistory," p. 114; Peltonen, "Clues, Margins, and Monads," pp. 347–348.

35. Ginzburg and Poni, "The Name and the Game," p. 8.

36. Levi, "On Microhistory," p. 102.

37. Ginzburg, *The Cheese and the Worms*, p. 33.

38. Brown, "Microhistory and the Post-Modern Challenge," p. 18.

39. See Yamamura, "Toward a Reexamination of the Economic History of Tokugawa Japan," pp. 516–522, for an analytical division of Japan into two regions. Yamamura argues (p. 518) that Region I (including the Chūgoku region, of which Chōshū was a part) was "relatively more advanced" in terms of urbanization, transportation, communication, and "technical and institutional capabilities," than Region II (including northeastern Japan and parts of Kyushu).

40. For an example of "apparently humble residents [whose experiences] might often transcend, in quite spectacular ways, the bounds of street, neighbourhood, City Company, parish, county or even nation," see Boulton, "Microhistory in Early Modern London," p. 129.

Chapter 2: Edo Period Riches

1. Fortune, *Yedo and Peking*, p. 165.
2. Thunberg, *Japan Extolled and Decried: Carl Peter Thunberg and the Shogun's Realm, 1775–1776*, p. 127.
3. Suga, *The Man'yo-shu*, vol. 3, p. 28. The poem is in book 15, no. 3637.
4. Wigen, "Politics and Piety in Japanese Native-Place Studies," p. 492.
5. Fortune, *Yedo and Peking*, p. 166.
6. Kaempfer, *Kaempfer's Japan*, p. 421.
7. Thunberg, *Japan Extolled and Decried*, p. 127.
8. Craig, *Chōshū in the Meiji Restoration*, pp. 11–22.
9. *KC*, p. 214.
10. Ibid., pp. 218–20; Kanaya, *Kaizoku-tachi no chūsei*, p. 127 and passim; Yamaguchi-ken Kyōiku Zaidan, *Kaminoseki jōseki*; Shapinsky, "With the Sea as Their Domain."
11. Vaporis, *Breaking Barriers*, pp. 99–133.
12. *KC*, p. 864. Kaminoseki-chō Komonjo Kaidoku no Kai, *Hayashi-ke shozō shohikae*, pp. 226–227, 236–237.
13. Kaminoseki-chō Komonjo Kaidoku no Kai, *Kaminoseki go-bansho no kiroku*.
14. On the maritime route taken by the Chōshū lord on his way to alternate attendance in the first half of the Edo period, see Minamigata, "Hagi-han sankin kōtai no kōtei."
15. *KC*, p. 282.
16. Toby, *State and Diplomacy in Early Modern Japan*.
17. Chōsen Tsūshin-shi Shiryōkan Museum, Shōtōen, Shimo-Kamakari, Kure city (Hiroshima prefecture).
18. According to a domain survey in 1738, the total population of Kaminoseki's port and inland areas was 960, living in 146 households. Yamaguchi-ken Chihōshi Gakkai, *Bōchō jige jōshin*, vol. 1, pp. 453–454. Hereafter abbreviated as *BJJ*.
19. On the main street linking the *o-chaya* guest complex to the Miyato Hachimangū shrine, there were forty-three houses, of which thirty-six hosted at least one official (and sometimes up to four or five) in 1764. Kaminoseki-chō Kaidoku no Kai, *Hōreki-do Chōsen tsūshinshi*, pp. 12–21, 25–41.
20. Makino, *Kitamaebune no kenkyū*, pp. 19–21. One *koku* is equivalent to 180 liters, or 0.18 cubic meters; thus 80,000 *koku* was equivalent to 14,430 cubic meters, or roughly 5,100 gross tons. One reason that the overland routes were more expensive was because of the poor quality of roads, so that rice had to be carried by individual horses rather than in carriages.

Since one horse could only shoulder about one *koku,* five hundred horses would be needed to carry the equivalent of a large mid-seventeenth-century ship.

21. Metzger-Court, "From Kitchen to Workshop," p. 68n.

22. Jansen, *The Making of Modern Japan,* p. 133.

23. Thomas C. Smith, *Native Sources of Japanese Industrialization,* p. 74. In Kaminoseki county, striped cotton manufacture was concentrated in villages on the western side of the Murotsu peninsula.

24. Makino, *Kitamaebune no kenkyū,* p. 22.

25. McClain, "Failed Expectations," p. 432.

26. Wray, "Shipping," p. 269. Early in the Edo period the size of Japanese ships had been limited to 500 *koku,* but this rule was regularly breached by the second half of the eighteenth century.

27. Makino, *Kitamaebune no kenkyū,* p. 361.

28. This was the *buikukyoku* account: Craig, *Chōshū in the Meiji Restoration,* pp. 44–47. Other investments included land reclamations for new rice fields, improvement to Inland Sea port infrastructure, and the development of new salt fields. For an example from 1786 of salt field development in Hirao village, just north of Kaminoseki, see Sagara, "Kindai enden jinushi no seiritsu to sono seikaku," p. 11.

29. The following explanation is based on *KC,* pp. 275–281, and Ogawa, "Chōshū han ryūtsū seisaku to Kaminoseki koshini kaisho," pp. 20–26.

30. By the mid-1820s, one of the *koshini* branch's main expenditures in Kaminoseki was on "relief payments": in fact, these were loans extended to *kitamae*-ship owners in order to keep a flow of capital running through the system, and I suspect that similar loans were made to local shipping agents too.

31. The petition was written by Senior Headman Odamura, a Kaminoseki resident, and is reprinted in *KC,* p. 282.

32. See also Tanizawa, *Setouchi no machinami,* p. 73.

33. Anonymous interview 1; and interview with Harada Hiroyuki, 27 March 2008; Yamaguchi-ken Kyōiku Iinkai, *Yamaguchi-ken no minka,* p. 39.

34. Other households with regional names in 1865 included the Ōsaka-ya (surname Kase), Tosa-ya (Suzuki), Karatsu-ya (Katsura), plus the Sakai-ya (modern surname unknown): Tanizawa, *Setouchi no machinami,* pp. 73–75.

35. The *O-kyakuchō* and Awa-ya seals were kindly shown to me by Awaya Shigenori in January 2006 and June 2008. Compiled by Awaya Jiemon sometime after 1885 (Meiji 18), the register summarizes thousands of customer transactions between the 1830s and the 1880s.

36. Makino, *Kitamaebune no kenkyū,* p. 359.

37. Thunberg, *Japan Extolled and Decried,* p. 128.

38. *BJJ,* pp. 450, 454; Yamaguchi-ken Monjokan, *Bōchō fūdo chūshin'an,* vol. 6, pp. 241, 308. Hereafter abbreviated as *BFC.*

39. The only exception was the tiny hamlet of Hetsu (twenty-six households in 1842), whose population declined over the period.

40. These trends are described in Thomas C. Smith, "Pre-Modern Economic Growth."

41. *BJJ,* pp. 450, 454; *BFC,* pp. 240–241, 308–309. In the Murotsu inland area, the respective figures were 51 percent landless in 1738 and 88 percent in 1842.

42. The total number of farm households in Chōshū was 85,000, of which 27,000 were landless. Nishikawa, "The Economy of Chōshū on the Eve of Industrialization," p. 331.

43. For a more detailed discussion of imputed income, see Thomas C. Smith, *Native Sources of Japanese Industrialization,* pp. 78–81, 100–102; for a criticism of Smith's assumptions, see Saitō and Nishikawa, "Tokugawa Nihon no shotoku bunpu."

44. Thomas C. Smith, *Native Sources of Japanese Industrialization,* p. 86.

45. *BFC,* p. 456; *KC,* p. 271. Smith focused only on mainland (Honshu) communities and did not include *Reports* data from Nagashima, Yashima, or Iwaishima, despite their also being part of Kaminoseki county.

46. *BFC,* pp. 257–260.

47. The following data on income is taken from *BFC,* pp. 344–346. The number of prostitutes is given on p. 313. The annual reported income of the Kaminoseki port area was 400 *kan* 241 *monme;* that of Murotsu port was 292 *kan* 819 *monme.*

48. *KC,* p. 202.

49. On the significance of the *yobi-sen,* see Katō and Abumi, *Kitamaebune,* p. 43. Eight landless households in Murotsu port owned their own rowboats: *BFC,* p. 245.

50. The concentration of ships in a particular month seems to have depended on their provenance and thus, we might presume, on their cargo. Although the *Customer Register* records particular peaks in the spring (March, April) and autumn (September, October), ships were clearly docking in Kaminoseki throughout the calendar year.

51. For other historians who make this hypothesis, see Tanizawa, "Setonai no minato machi," p. 398, and Kimura Kenji, *Zaichō Nihonjin no shakaishi,* pp. 39–40.

52. Thomas C. Smith, "Pre-Modern Economic Growth," p. 140.

53. Wray, "Shipping: From Sail to Steam," p. 251.

54. *BFC,* p. 317.

55. Thomas C. Smith, *Native Sources of Japanese Industrialization,* p. 89.

56. *BFC,* p. 288. This is a description of Kaminoseki port and inland areas, but the same applied to Murotsu.

57. *BFC,* pp. 309, 344–346, 447.

58. Braudel, *The Mediterranean and the Mediterranean World in the Age of Philip II,* vol. 1, p. 117.

59. John W. Dower, "Black Ships and Samurai: Commodore Perry and the Opening of Japan (1853–1854)," http://ocw.mit.edu/ans7870/21f/21f.027/black_ships_and_samurai/bss_essay07.html, last accessed 12 October 2010.

60. The Awa-ya *Customer Register* records consistently large numbers of business transactions through the 1860s and 1870s.

61. By 1877, 2,827 miles of telegraph line had been installed. Jansen, *The Making of Modern Japan,* p. 374.

62. Wray, "Shipping: From Sail to Steam," p. 258.

63. Lewis, *Becoming Apart,* p. 136.

64. Furumaya, *Ura Nihon,* p. 33.

65. Kimura Kenji, *Zaichō Nihonjin no shakaishi,* pp. 37–43.

66. Ibid., p. 36; Sagara, "Kindai enden jinushi no seiritsu to sono seikaku," p. 12.

67. Makino, *Kitamaebune no kenkyū,* p. 363.

68. Furumaya, *Ura Nihon,* p. 33.

69. Yamaguchi Prefectural Archives (Yamaguchi Kenritsu Monjokan; hereafter YM), *Senzen A Keisatsu 47: shōgi kenkō shindan.* This is a petition by twelve licensed proprietors of "rooms to rent" (*kashizashiki*) concerning the need to open a health center for prostitutes in Murotsu.

70. Yamaguchi-ken, *Yamaguchi kenshi shiryōhen kindai 4,* pp. 942–943. The train line between Hiroshima and Shimonoseki was completed in 1901.

71. Furumaya, *Ura Nihon,* pp. 6–7 and passim.

Chapter 3: Murotsu and the Meiji Revolution, 1868

1. Accounts of the *Katoku-maru* attack are given in Tabuse Chōshi Hensan Iinkai, *Tabuse chōshi,* pp. 414–415, and in Ichisaka, *Chōshū kiheitai,* pp. 37–53.

2. The extent to which the Meiji Restoration was "made" or "came" is discussed in McClain, "Failed Expectations," pp. 403–404. See also Wilson, *Patriots and Redeemers in Japan,* pp. 4–6.

3. Fred G. Notehelfer outlines the general significance of the bottom-up approach and specifically asks for more research on "*gōnō* loyalism" in "Review: Meiji in the Rear-View Mirror," p. 217. An example of bottom up history in practice is Steele, "Edo in 1868": Steele argues that the commoners "muddled through the Restoration as best they could" and that the Restoration was experienced in terms of "good money, good work, good food, and good fun" (p. 153).

4. Kimura, *Zaichō Nihonjin no shakaishi,* p. 52.

5. Shūzō married the eldest daughter of the ninth-generation head, Yoshida Kenzō (see below). He officially became head of the Yoshida household in March 1879, but he may have been adopted into the household some years earlier. See Shibamura, *Yamaguchi-ken Kaminoseki Yoshida-ke shiryō to Yoshida-shi,* p. 103.

6. Bernstein, *Isami's House,* p. 22.

7. For the date of the Yoshida house, see Yamaguchi-ken Kyōiku Iinkai, *Yamaguchi-ken no minka,* p. 39. For historical details of the family, see Yamaguchi-ken Monjokan, *Yamaguchi-ken Monjokan shoka monjo mokuroku 6,* pp. 1–14.

8. The scrolls were only rediscovered in 1991, when the house was dismantled and moved to Shimo-Kamakari, Hiroshima prefecture. They are catalogued in Shibamura, *Yamaguchi-ken Kaminoseki Yoshida-ke no shiryō to Yoshida-shi.*

9. Craig, *Chōshū in the Meiji Restoration,* pp. 60–69.

10. Ibid., p. 111.

11. To avoid confusion, I refer to Yoshida as "Shōin" throughout this chapter.

12. Wakabayashi, "Opium, Expulsion, Sovereignty," pp. 17–23.

13. These and subsequent chronological details of Yoshida's life are taken from Hagi Hakubutsukan, *Yoshida Shōin to jukusei-tachi,* pp. 12–16.

14. Huber, *The Revolutionary Origins of Modern Japan,* pp. 45–51.

15. Drea, *Japan's Imperial Army,* p. 22.

16. Kawamura, *Furusato tanbō Kaminoseki,* vol. 2, pp. 24–25.

17. See Shibamura, *Yamaguchi-ken Kaminoseki Yoshida-ke no shiryō to Yoshida-shi,* pp. 105–108.

18. The Ogata household was listed as the *shōya* of Murotsu port in 1738: see *BJJ,* p. 450. Documents in the Yoshida-household collection in the Yamaguchi Prefectural Archives indicate that Ogata Ichiuemon (born 1806) was an elder of the port (*uradoshiyori*) in 1837; he may have served in that position again at the time of Shōin's 1853 and 1858 visits: Yamaguchi-ken Monjokan, *Yamaguchi-ken Monjokan shoka monjo mokuroku 6,* p. 22.

19. *KC,* p. 838. I am grateful to the late Ueda Kichisuke for translating the poem into modern Japanese.

20. Kido, *The Diary of Kido Takayoshi,* vol. 1, pp. 479–480.

21. See Totman, "Tokugawa Yoshinobu and Kobugattai."

22. Craig, *Chōshū in the Meiji Restoration,* pp. 167–178.

23. Ibid., pp. 72–73.

24. Hackett, *Yamagata Aritomo in the Rise of Modern Japan,* pp. 18–19.

25. Nish, "Politics, Trade and Communications in East Asia."

26. The Mito domain, for example, was one of the first to start establishing peasant militia groups in the 1830s. See Bolitho, "The Tempō Crisis," p. 137.

27. Tabuse Chōshi Hensan Iinkai, *Tabuse chōshi,* p. 404.

28. *KC,* pp. 273–274. The five were Sanjō Sanetomi, Sanjō Nishisuetomo, Mibu Motonaga, Saijō Tahanta, and Nishiki no Kōji Yorinori. Kawamura, *Furusato tanbō Kaminoseki,* vol. 1, p. 43.

29. On funding, see Craig, *Chōshū in the Meiji Restoration,* p. 271.

30. Hirao Chōshi Hensan Iinkai, *Hirao chōshi,* p. 732.

31. Tabuse Chōshi Hensan Iinkai, *Tabuse chōshi,* p. 415.

32. The Yoshida household genealogical records note Kenzō's donations both to the Giyūtai and also to a Yamaguchi-based branch of the Nōheitai (called the Kōjōgun) billeted in Murotsu in 1865. Shibamura, *Yamaguchi-ken Kaminoseki Yoshida-ke shiryō to Yoshida-shi,* p. 102. Documents relating to Kenzō's work as an accountant for the Kōjōgun are also catalogued in Yamaguchi-ken Monjokan, *Yamaguchi-ken Monjokan shoka monjo mokuroku 6.*

33. Murotsu Yakuba Monjo (hereafter MYM) 1076 (2).

34. Kaminoseki-chō Komonjo Kaidoku no Kai, *Hayashi-ke shozō shohikae,* pp. 40–41.

35. The Ogata gravestone.

36. Itō, *Itō Hirobumi,* pp. 37–39.

37. Ibid., pp. 50–53. See also Sidney DeVere Brown, "Nagasaki in the Meiji Restoration: Chōshū loyalists and British Arms Merchants," http://www.uwosh.edu/home_pages/faculty_staff/earns/meiji.html, last accessed 12 October 2010.

38. Katō and Abumi, *Kitamaebune,* p. 50.

39. Hirao Chōshi Hensan Iinkai, *Hirao chōshi,* p. 734.

40. The *bakufu* attack on Murotsu is described in three sources: a report by a domain official in Kaminoseki, a diary by a soldier in the Second Kiheitai, and the diary of Atsuki's Ura Yukie. See, respectively, Yamaguchi-ken, *Yamaguchi kenshi shiryōhen Bakumatsu ishin 4,* pp. 261, 299, and *Yamaguchi kenshi shiryōhen Bakumatsu ishin 3,* p. 909.

41. On the *Heiin-maru,* see Yamaguchi-ken, *Yamaguchi kenshi shiryōhen kindai 4,* pp. 1006–1008.

42. Kaminoseki-chō Komonjo Kaidoku no Kai, *Hayashi-ke shozō shohikae,* pp. 54–55.

43. Craig, *Chōshū in the Meiji Restoration,* p. 267.

44. Yamaguchi-ken Monjokan, *Yamaguchi-ken Monjokan shoka monjo mokuroku 6,* p. 2.

45. MYM 112. For Ogata's ranking in 1865, see Hirao Chōshi Hensan Iinkai, *Hirao chōshi,* p. 734. Such promotions were common in the late Tokugawa period as a way of rewarding rich peasants for their contribution to domain finances; see Pratt, *Japan's Protoindustrial Elite,* p. 24.

46. John W. Dower, "Black Ships and Samurai: Commodore Perry and the Opening of Japan (1853–1854), http://ocw.mit.edu/ans7870/21f/21f.027/black_ships_and_samurai/bss_essay03.html, last accessed 12 October 2010.

47. Indeed, many of these elites were educated at the Seikyō Sōdō, the school established in Tōzaki village (present-day Yanai city) by Gesshō in 1848: the school's twenty-five students, according to the onsite museum, were a mixture of samurai retainers, priests, and farming elites from southeastern Chōshū, plus a few students from farther afield.

48. I am influenced here by George M. Wilson's argument that in 1868 "many restorations occurred, not just one": Wilson, *Patriots and Redeemers in Japan,* p. 48.

49. Kano, *Torishima wa haitteiru ka,* pp. 1–6.

50. The best book on the *gōnō* in English is Pratt, *Japan's Protoindustrial Elite.* On village elites as cultural conduits in the late Edo period, see Walthall, "Peripheries," p. 383; Platt, "Elegance, Prosperity, Crisis," p. 69.

Chapter 4: The Political Culture of the Meiji Village

1. Irokawa, *The Culture of the Meiji Period,* pp. 44–45.
2. Ibid., pp. 18, 13.
3. Gluck, "The People in History," p. 32.
4. On democracy, see Irokawa, "Japan's Grass-Roots Tradition."
5. Irokawa, *The Culture of the Meiji Period,* p. 197.
6. Waters, *Japan's Local Pragmatists,* pp. 4–8.
7. Gluck, "The People in History," p. 45.
8. Irokawa, *The Culture of the Meiji Period,* p. 151.
9. Kaminoseki-chō Kyōiku Iinkai Kyōiku Bunkaka, *Yamaguchi-ken shitei bunkazai.*
10. Details of Ogata's stipend are given on his gravestone.
11. Yamaguchi-ken Monjokan, *Yamaguchi-ken Monjokan shoka monjo mokuroku 6,* p. 6. Ogata Kenkurō's involvement in the company is briefly noted in *KC,* p. 839.
12. In addition to the newly introduced local taxes, local levies (*kyōgihi*) raised 120 yen; education (*kyōikuhi*), 151.50 yen; and festivals (*saitenhi*), 36 yen. *KC,* p. 335.
13. Kaminoseki-chō Kyōiku Iinkai Kyōiku Bunkaka, *Yamaguchi-ken shitei bunkazai,* p. 7. In 1883, seventeen of the twenty-seven services from Osaka to Shimonoseki and beyond were scheduled to stop at Kaminoseki (which presumably means Kaminoseki and/or Murotsu): see Yamaguchi-ken, *Yamaguchi kenshi shiryōhen kindai 4,* pp. 1035–1036.
14. On the *chihōzei,* see Baxter, *The Meiji Unification through the Lens of Ishikawa Prefecture,* pp. 186–193. In Murotsu, the exact level of the household tax appears to have changed each six-month period in which it was levied, and it is unclear whether the tax was based on land value, income, or a mixture of both. As a result, the records tell us about individual household prosperity more in relative terms than in absolute ones.
15. MYM 95. The total amount paid by Murotsu's 538 households in October 1891 was 101.144 yen.
16. Of seventy-seven individuals who paid business taxes in 1887, twenty were brokers (*nakagai*) and five were shipping agents (*ton'ya*).
17. MYM 93 (1887) and 112 (1893).
18. Yamaguchi-ken, *Yamaguchi kenshi shiryōhen kindai 4,* pp. 1013–1015.
19. On the decline of the Higoya, see *KC,* pp. 273–274.
20. MYM 112. I have based these calculations on the amount of national land tax that leading Murotsu families paid, a figure that I have multiplied by forty (land tax was levied at 2.5 percent after 1877). Only those households that qualified to vote in prefectural assembly elections by paying land tax at 10 yen or more are recorded in this document.
21. The exact figure was 49.86 yen: Meiji Bunken Shiryō Kankōkai, *Yamaguchi-ken nōji chōsasho,* p. 3. The average annual income for a farming household in Yamaguchi prefecture was 67.31 yen. Kumage county had the second-lowest average in the prefecture, after Ōshima county (39.73 yen).

22. Partner, *The Mayor of Aihara*, pp. 74–75.

23. MYM 1076, parts 1 and 2. These cover the port area of Murotsu and the inland hamlets to the east; data on the hamlets to the north is presumably included in part 3, which has not survived.

24. Nagatsuka, *The Soil*.

25. Baxter, *The Meiji Unification through the Lens of Ishikawa Prefecture*, pp. 188, 193.

26. Gluck, *Japan's Modern Myths*, p. 166.

27. Figures for local donations are compiled from an unfiled document in MYM titled *Kifu-bo: Murotsu-son yakuba*.

28. Kaminoseki Yakuba monjo (hereafter KYM) 66.

29. *KC*, pp. 369–370.

30. This is based on a total household count of 608 in 1884 (*KC*, p. 335) and 529 in 1893 (MYM 112). Although 228 household heads were enfranchised for village assembly elections in Murotsu, only twelve household heads were eligible to vote in the 1889 prefectural elections in Murotsu and only four in the 1894 general election.

31. MYM 93, 112. The occupation of two councillors, Yagi Torakichi and Matsuoka Rihei, is unclear, but from their known addresses we can surmise that they were not merchants and thus were almost certainly farmers.

32. By 1877, there were twenty such boats in the Kaminoseki area. *KC*, p. 412.

33. MYM 1061.

34. *KC*, p. 450.

35. Ibid., p. 412.

36. KYM 69.

37. Okano and Kanaya, "Kaminoseki-chō Iwaishima no yagō," p. 33.

38. Interview with Hashibe Yoshiake, 18 December 2007.

39. The presence of hundreds of Edo period loan receipts in the surviving documents of the Yoshida household attests to such networks in Murotsu.

40. Interview with Shigemura Sadao, the last surviving grandchild of Masakichi, 28 June 2004.

41. Anonymous interview 2.

42. Ministry of Justice Legal Affairs Bureau, Yanai branch (Hōmukyoku Yanai Shutchōsho): *Tochi daichō* (hereafter *TD*) (Nagashima).

43. The following analysis of elections is based on KYM 63. Izuta was also chief electoral officer in 1892.

44. *KC*, pp. 369–370.

45. MYM 63.

46. *KC*, pp. 371–372.

47. Nagatsuka, *The Soil*, p. 189.

48. *KC*, pp. 378–379. The Kaminoseki mayor was Sakuraya Seihachirō.

49. *TD* (Murotsu).

50. Tanizawa, *Setouchi no machinami*, p. 80.

51. The so-called despised classes (*senmin*) were excluded from the *BFC*, although the survey does record 54 female prostitutes and 5 male "shop-clerks" (*tedai*) in Kaminoseki's three teahouses (p. 243) and 111 itinerant people (effectively *chasen* or *hinin*—entertainers and beggars) in nineteen households in Murotsu (p. 313). Based on extensive research in domain archives, Kitagawa has made the thirty-two-household calculation for *eta* in Kaminoseki county: Kitagawa, *Bōchō fūdo chūshin'an to dōwa mondai*, p. 10.

52. *KC*, p. 365.

53. Partner, *The Mayor of Aihara,* p. 24.
54. See Hane, *Peasants, Rebels, Women, and Outcastes,* pp. 138–171.

Chapter 5: Ritual Culture and Political Power

1. *KC,* pp. 855–858.
2. The document was written on the twenty-eighth day of the seventh month in the imperial year Genroku 10 (1697) and is signed by Priest Moritomo of the Iwaishima Miyato Hachimangū shrine and the island's three headmen. It is kept in the private collection of the Moritomo household and is reprinted in Kaminoseki-chō Kyōiku Iinkai, *Suō-Iwaishima no kanmai gyōji,* p. 79. A document from 1698 in the Ujimoto household (ibid., p. 120) is almost identical in content; it adds only the detail that the Imi priests were returning from the Iwashimizu Hachimangū shrine in Kyoto when they anchored in Miura.
3. From an anthropological perspective, the *kanmai* oral traditions are open to many other symbolic interpretations; here I focus only on the political implications of the foundational narratives.
4. Kaminoseki-chō Kyōiku Iinkai, *Suō-Iwaishima no kanmai gyōji,* p. 68. A similar point was made to me many times in advance of the 2004 *kanmai:* "If you think of Iwaishima, you think of the *kanmai*" (*Iwaishima to ieba, kanmai*).
5. Shapiro, *Oberammergau,* p. 104.
6. Okano and Kanaya, "Kaminoseki-chō Iwaishima no yagō," pp. 32, 38.
7. Kaminoseki-chō Kyōiku Iinkai, *Suō-Iwaishima no kanmai gyōji,* p. 68.
8. Unless otherwise specified, the following discussion of the Ujimoto household is based on two interviews with the late Ujimoto Kuichi, on 22 July and 24 August 2004.
9. For 1896, see Kaminoseki-chō Kyōiku Iinkai, *Suō-Iwaishima no kanmai gyōji,* pp. 149–154 (see also Figure 7.2 below). The 1948 tax figures are from KYM 17. One *sen* is one-hundredth of a yen.
10. *BJJ,* p. 466; *BFC,* p. 429. In total, the number of Iwaishima households increased from 123 to 273 in this period.
11. See also Chapter 11 for the significance of the 1168 date.
12. Interview with Mita Tsutomu, nephew of Matsuoka Jinta, 27 September 2004.
13. Unless otherwise stated, the following discussion is based on a survey of the *kabu-uchi* carried out by Iwaishima native Izuta Masaji between 1923 and 1927, which is summarized in Kaminoseki-chō Kyōiku Iinkai, *Suō-Iwaishima no kanmai gyōji,* pp. 70–72.
14. Interview with Hashibe Yoshiake, 18 December 2007.
15. Fueto estimated in 1953 that the *kabu-uchi* system finished "two generations ago": Fueto, "Yamaguchi-ken Kumage-gun Kaminoseki-son Iwaishima no hōshakaigakuteki kenkyū," p. 49.
16. There were in fact two Matsubara households in the Matsuya *kabu-uchi,* making a total of six households in all.
17. The following discussion is based on an interview with Matsumoto Takeji, grandson of Bukichi, 23 December 2004.
18. *KC,* pp. 523–524. Matsumoto Takeji told me that the union members borrowed 3,000 yen (although I suspect it was more) from the Suō Bank in Hirao.
19. Such bonds are in contrast to the "vertical model" of village relations: for discussion of both the vertical model and the so-called egalitarian model, see Johnson, "Status Changes in Hamlet Structure Accompanying Modernization."
20. All figures are from Fueto, "Yamaguchi-ken Kumage-gun Kaminoseki-son Iwaishima no hōshakaigakuteki kenkyū," p. 56.

21. Anonymous interview 3.

22. A total of 347 individuals made donations toward the cost of the 1896 *kanmai*.

23. Anne Walthall also notes that Edo period unions linked households of similar status and class so that marriage "tended to reinforce economic divisions and social distinctions." Walthall, "The Life Cycle of Farm Women in Tokugawa Japan," pp. 53–54.

24. *KC*, pp. 242–244. The *tateura-haura* division crossed the post-Meiji administrative boundaries of southeastern Yamaguchi. Iwaishima, for example, was a *haura* to the *tateura* of Murozumi (present-day Hikari city), while Murotsu was a *tateura* to several ports in Ōshima county.

25. *KC*, p. 418. In 1913, the catch was 131,250 kg (out of a total fishing catch of 795,840 kg); the following year, it was 100,807 kg (out of 585,147 kg). As Norbeck noted, fishermen are in general notorious for underdeclaring their earnings and thus paying less tax. Norbeck, *Takashima*, p. 41.

26. Interview with the late Nakamura Shin, 16 March 2005.

27. A third structure, lineage-based nets, was found by Kalland in Kyushu but appears not to have occurred in Kaminoseki. Kalland, *Shingū*, pp. 114–118.

28. On Iwaishima, for example, two of the *amimoto*—Matsuno Shigekichi in 1882 and Shimizu Aizō in 1904—were responsible for "discovering" and then developing lucrative sardine-fishing grounds around the island. *KC*, p. 428.

29. *KC*, p. 435. In one of the communities studied by Margaret McKean, the division was 70 percent to 30, meaning that an *amimoto* boss took home seventy times the catch of one of his thirty employees: McKean, *Environmental Protest and Citizen Politics in Japan*, p. 84.

30. KYM 17; the Yoshida and Ujimoto households were the top two taxpayers out of 564 households.

31. KYM 60; *KC*, pp. 393, 434.

32. On favors, see Kalland, *Shingū*, p. 126. On the role of *amimoto* as political bosses in the nearby coastal communities of northeastern Kyushu, see Broadbent, *Environmental Politics in Japan*, pp. 192–196.

33. The undated list, passed down to Ebesu Tadao (born 1929) by his great-great-grandfather, Gonshichi, details 240 households on the island: four had surnames (*sei*), 125 had household names (*yagō*), and the rest merely had given names (*jinmei*). For comparative purposes, the Chōshū domain's *BFC* survey listed 269 households on Iwaishima in 1842.

34. There are no surviving documents relating to the land reforms in Kaminoseki village, but elderly people do not remember vast tracts of land changing hands at this time.

35. Primary industry data courtesy of Kaminoseki town office.

Chapter 6: Overseas Migration at the Turn of the Twentieth Century

1. MYM 411. This letter is also reprinted in *KC*, p. 461.

2. Doi, *Yamaguchi-ken Ōshima-gun Hawai iminshi*, pp. 60–61.

3. Miyamoto and Okamoto, *Tōwa chōshi*, p. 647.

4. United Japanese Society of Hawai'i, *Hawai Nihonjin iminshi*, p.78.

5. Moriyama, *Imingaisha*, pp. 15–16.

6. On the *Chūgai bukka shinpō*, which became the *Nihon keizai shinbun* in 1946, see Doi, *Yamaguchi-ken Ōshima-gun Hawai iminshi*, p. 22. On the founding of the *Bōchō shinbun*, see Dresner, "Emigration and Local Development," pp. 60, 112.

7. Moriyama, *Imingaisha*, p. 16; Dresner, "Emigration and Local Development," p. 76.

8. Doi, *Yamaguchi-ken Ōshima-gun Hawai iminshi*, p. 34.

9. Dresner, "Emigration and Local Development," p. 76. The highest population density was in Akamagaseki (Shimonoseki), followed by Ōshima county.

10. Quoted by kind permission of Mr. Saneo Okada, son of Usuke and chairman of U. Okada and Company, Ltd., Honolulu.

11. For more on the Niikawa household, see the Kaminoseki-chō Sakuraya-ke monjo (nos. 25–33), YM Archives.

12. This letter was in the private collection of the late Ueda Kichisuke. He kindly gave me a handwritten copy that he had made of the letter, but he did not show me the original.

13. Doi, *Yamaguchi-ken Ōshima-gun Hawai iminshi,* p. 16.

14. Moriyama, *Imingaisha,* pp. 18, 188.

15. Ibid., pp. 26–27.

16. *KC,* p. 462.

17. On these networks, see Murayama, "Information and Emigrants."

18. Moriyama, *Imingaisha,* p. 4; Pratt, *Japan's Protoindustrial Elite,* p. 38. For salt, see Dresner, "Emigration and Local Development," p. 66.

19. Nationwide figures for 1904 are from Murayama, "Information and Emigrants," pp. 130–131. For Kumage county, see Kimura, *Zaichō Nihonjin no shakaishi,* p. 45.

20. Meiji Bunken Shiryō Kankōkai, *Yamaguchi-ken nōji chōsasho,* p. 3.

21. See, for example, Miyamoto and Okamoto, *Tōwa chōshi,* p. 649; Ishikawa, "Yamaguchi-ken Ōshima-gun Tōwa-chō ni okeru deimin no rekishi chirigakuteki kōsatsu," pp. 7–8.

22. Database of Ōshima's Museum of Japanese Emigration to Hawai'i, itself compiled from *Nippon jinmin Hawaikoku e dekasegi ikken; dekaseginin meibo no bu,* Diplomatic Record Office (hereafter DRO) 3.8.2.5–14.

23. For a number of reasons, Shirahama does not appear in *BFC,* but if it had appeared, it would have been an inland area. The district of Shiraura appears as both "inland" and "port" in 1842, but given its geographical location, my guess is that it too should be considered "inland."

24. Moriyama, *Imingaisha,* p. 52.

25. DRO 3.8.2.38–1. Even in the rare cases that local records remain, they are fragmentary. DRO statistics indicate that there were at least thirteen more Hawaiian emigrants from Kaminoseki village in the second half of 1894 than are listed in the village office records, and there were probably even more when we consider that not all emigration companies listed the addresses of their customers. The local archives also have no record of emigrants to Canada, of whom there were at least eight from Murotsu and four from Kaminoseki in 1894.

26. By 1903, Yamaguchi and Hiroshima prefectures boasted the highest number of emigration companies—twenty each—engaged in recruitment: Moriyama, *Imingaisha,* p. 72. DRO records suggest that at least seven of these companies were active in Kaminoseki and Murotsu by 1902.

27. MYM 412.

28. DRO 3.8.2.38–12,13,13B. Nationwide, there were peaks in private emigration in 1899, 1902, and 1905–1907. A pattern of intense company recruitment similar to that seen in Murotsu is also implied by the Nagashima figures from 1898 (see Table 6.2): 31 of Nagashima's 42 emigrants in that year had their applications processed in a three-week period between December 13 and 31.

29. KYM 60.

30. A similar observation is made by Miyamoto of Tōwa town in Ōshima county: Miyamoto and Okamoto, *Tōwa chōshi,* p. 670.

31. Kimura, *Zaichō Nihonjin no shakaishi,* pp. 11, 14.

32. Kōno Naozō was also active in Murotsu politics in the late 1870s: *KC,* p. 328. For the Kōno household's tax status, see MYM 93, 95; for the number of houses, MYM 1076 (1 and 2). Unless otherwise stated, biographical details for the following section are from Izeki, *Gendai Bōchō jinbutsu-shi,* pp. 39–47.

33. Duus, *The Abacus and the Sword,* p. 262.

34. There may be some hyperbole in these figures. According to Duus (ibid., p. 254), in the 1870s, one *koku* of rice bought in Korea for 40 to 45 *sen* could be sold in Japan for 8 *yen*—an increase of twenty times, whereas Kōno apparently made profits at a factor of 330.

35. On the construction industry in Incheon, see Kimura, *Zaichō Nihonjin no shakaishi,* p. 17.

36. The comment was made in 1896 and is quoted in Duus, *The Abacus and the Sword,* p. 291; see also Henderson, "Japan's Chōsen."

37. MYM 298 is the list of those contacted in 1910. For documents relating to the appeal and to the construction of the school, see MYM 773.

38. The petition is reprinted in full in *KC,* p. 450.

39. The land area of the Awaya residence in Kaminoseki was roughly 55 *tsubo* (including the warehouse). In 1913, the average amount of cultivated land per Kaminoseki village household was 8.9 *tan,* or around 0.9 hectares: *KC,* p. 340.

40. On the 1827 donation, see Tanizawa, *Setouchi no machinami,* p. 73. Building receipts for the Korean farmhouse were kindly shown to me by Awaya Shigenori, grandson of Torazuchi. The stone engraving marking Torazuchi's 100-yen donation is so faded that the date is unreadable, but the priest of the shrine, Murata Kageaki, remembers it to have been 1937 (interview, 21 January 2005).

41. Interview with Awaya Kayoko, granddaughter of Torazuchi, 17 January 2005.

42. Ho, "Colonialism and Development," pp. 363–373; Duus, *The Abacus and the Sword,* p. 309.

43. Natsume, *Kokoro,* p. 245.

Chapter 7: The Transnational Hometown

1. The phrase is from Oguma, *"Nihonjin" no kyōkai.*

2. Irokawa, *The Culture of the Meiji Period,* pp. 300–305.

3. Interview with Mifuji Kōichi, 18 March 2005. According to Hashibe Yoshiake (interview, 18 December 2007), Toyozō married the daughter of Okabe Tahei, one of the richest households on the island in 1896: this may have explained his ability to invest in Korea in 1900.

4. Kimura, *Zaichō Nihonjin no shakaishi,* pp. 55–56.

5. Ibid., pp. 37–43.

6. Toyozō sold the ancestral home in July 1902 but had made other sales in 1900. *TD* (Iwaishima).

7. The increase was from 6,249 to 18,481. Duus, *The Abacus and the Sword,* p. 293.

8. On the brewing industry in western Japan, see Pratt, *Japan's Protoindustrial Elite,* p. 72.

9. MYM 412.

10. MYM 1127. This document contains two lists: Murotsu villagers resident in Hawai'i and the United States (undated), and villagers resident in both the Americas and the Japanese empire in 1927. For a number of reasons, I calculate the undated list to be c. 1915. If anything,

both lists underestimated the numbers of villagers abroad: Mineishi Magoichi, Kawamoto Shōkichi, Maeda Hikoemon, and Maeda Yoshimi were all still living in Hawai'i in the late 1940s (MYM 300, 620, 679) but were not recorded in the 1927 list.

11. Hori Masaaki, "Taiheiyō wo wattata umibito-tachi," *Mainichi shinbun,* 22 June 2004.

12. For the full table, see Dusinberre, "Unread Relics of a Transnational 'Hometown,'" p. 314.

13. See Chapter 6.

14. Webster, "Transnational Journeys and Domestic Histories," p. 651.

15. Interview with the late Mifuji Masako and her husband, Kōichi, 18 March 2005.

16. Young, *Japan's Total Empire,* p. 64n.

17. Moriyama, *Imingaisha,* p. 25; Dresner, "Emigration and Local Development," pp. 101–109, 130. See also Dresner, "International Labour Migrants' Return to Meiji-era Yamaguchi and Hiroshima."

18. Kamegorō then remarried on 24 February 1897—the day that he and his new wife applied to return to Hawai'i as private emigrants. This was his third marriage, at the age of twenty-nine. MYM 412.

19. *TD* (Iwaishima).

20. Morris-Suzuki, "Northern Lights," pp. 251, 255. After 1905, the Japanese government attempted to lure settlers to Sakhalin through offers of free land, houses, tools, tax exemptions, competitive loans, and so on. Duus, *The Abacus and the Sword,* p. 297.

21. Interview with Mifuji Kōichi, 18 March 2005.

22. Okada Kōichi later became the adopted son of the Mifuji household and changed his name. Kōichi remembered that the monthly pay in Sakhalin was 30 yen, compared to 24 to 25 yen at breweries on the mainland (*naichi*). But according to wage data from 1936 (the year that Kōichi started in Toyohara), even the most junior brewing assistant from Iwaishima was paid 120 yen for 129 days work in a mainland brewery. This works out to monthly pay of just under 28 yen—a smaller differential than Kōichi remembered: *KC,* p. 455.

23. Interviews with Isozaki Hisao, 16 March 2005, and the late Nishiyama Hiroshi, 8 January 2005.

24. Interview with Mifuji Kōichi, 18 March 2005.

25. Although the employment patterns of the Matsuoka brewery in Busan are unknown, Toyozō (and later Jinta) is known to have employed the specialist brewmasters from Iwaishima. At its peak, the Matsuoka brewery employed around twenty workers (interview with Mita Tsutomu, grandson of Toyozō, 27 September 2004).

26. The *Bōchō Kaigai Kyōkai kaihō* (edn. 4 [1922] and 12 [1926]) is held in the Kaminoseki-chō Sakuraya-ke monjo (ref. 49–50), YM Archives.

27. *Kifu-bo,* numbered MYM 30 but not catalogued.

28. Bernstein, *Isami's House,* pp. 6–7; Pratt, *Japan's Protoindustrial Elite,* p. 2.

29. For guarantors, see MYM 412. For the Bōchō Overseas Association, see the *Bōchō Kaigai Kyōkai kaihō* (edn. 4 [1922] and 12 [1926]) in the Kaminoseki-chō Sakuraya-ke monjo (ref. 49–50), YM Archives. Kaminoseki's other representatives included Kanō Kurazō, second son of one of the village's oldest and most successful shipping agents.

30. Moriyama, *Imingaisha,* pp. 59–62.

31. KYM 63; *KC,* p. 841; anonymous interview 4.

32. The number of villagers who could vote in local elections increased steadily in the 1910s (KYM 69); Japan introduced universal manhood suffrage for all elections in 1925.

33. Interview with Nishida Tomiko, daughter-in-law of Mansaku, 18 March 2008.

34. Concepts of mutual need and social capital are discussed in Hsu, "Migration and Native Place," pp. 311–312, 323, and passim.

35. MYM 891; Yamaguchi-ken Sōmubu Tōkeika, *Murotsu Kaminoseki chiku jūmin seikatsu jittai*, pp. 10–11. Hereafter abbreviated as *MKCJSJ*.

36. MYM 620. As in Kaminoseki village, the 1946–1947 land reforms seem to have had little impact on farming in Murotsu.

37. Murotsu villagers in Hawai'i and the United States made two group donations to the school, in 1952 and 1955 respectively: MYM 300 and MYM, *Murotsu chūgakkō dai niji kōji kifu meibo* (1955, not catalogued).

38. A small corps of soldiers was billeted in Kaminoseki for defense purposes from April 1945 on. *KC*, p. 537.

39. At the end of the Allied Occupation, in April 1952, there were twenty-two Koreans, or seven households, resident in Murotsu village (MYM 428). Older residents of Kaminoseki village recall that there were a number of Koreans who lived in Nagashima and Iwaishima as well.

40. Interview with Ishimaru Hiroko, 28 December 2004.

41. Ibid.

42. Hikari Shishi Hensan Iinkai, *Hikari shishi*, pp. 776–778; interview with Ebesu Tadao, a survivor of the attack, 20 December 2004.

43. *KC*, pp. 845–859.

44. *Mura no bunka*, May 1949 (edn. 7): Gordon W. Prange Collection microfiche M621, Modern Japanese Political History Materials Room, National Diet Library. Hereafter abbreviated as *MB*.

45. Dower, *Embracing Defeat*.

46. The contest was held on 12 December 1948, and Shimanaka's speech was printed in *MB*, February 1949 (edn. 4).

47. *MB*, July 1949 (edn. 9).

Chapter 8: Bridging the Postwar Divide

1. *Kaminoseki kōhō*, 20 April 1969. Hereafter abbreviated as *KK*.

2. MYM 909—5 October 1956, 5 November 1956, 5 February 1957; KYM 71.

3. *KK*, 10 August 1959, 15 February 1966, 15 October 1968, 20 March 1969.

4. *KK*, 30 June 1969.

5. On the rhetoric of the "bright life," see Partner, *Assembled in Japan*, especially pp. 137–139.

6. http://www.showanomachi.com/index.php, last accessed 17 May 2008.

7. *Always—sanchōme no yūhi* was based on a long-running manga by Saigan Ryōhei. The film sequel was released in 2007.

8. The self-conscious comparison of the present with the Shōwa Thirties is apparent both in Bungo Takada's Shōwa Town and in the opening words of a book that accompanied the Those Were the Days exhibition: see Machida, *Chikakute natsukashii Shōwa ano koro*, p. 3.

9. Broadbent, *Environmental Politics in Japan*, p. 36.

10. Machida, *Chikakute natsukashii Shōwa ano koro*, p. 37.

11. The comment was made by the chairman of the nuclear power commission on 13 February 1961. Aldrich, *Site Fights*, p. 123.

12. The best discussion of the mercury-poisoning scandal is George, *Minamata*.

13. http://www.showanomachi.com/index.php, last accessed 17 May 2008; Machida, *Chikakute natsukashii Shōwa ano koro*, p. 50.

14. *KK*, 10 December 1960.

15. *KK*, 15 February 1961.

16. *MKCJSJ*, pp. 12, 19.

17. For a wider discussion of this law, the *seikatsu hogohō*, see Garon, *Molding Japanese Minds*, pp. 217–221.

18. *MKCJSJ*, p. 28. In fact, there appear to be two figures for the number of households on welfare assistance: 165 (cited in the preface) and 186 (p. 30). I have consistently taken the lower figure in making calculations. Given that the report covered both Murotsu and Kaminoseki villages, for the sake of convenience I use the phrase "the town," even though the two villages did not merge until 1958.

19. *MKCJSJ*, pp. 10–11; MYM 891.

20. Data from the Kaminoseki town office.

21. *MKCJSJ*, p. 14. One hectare is roughly equivalent to one *chō* in Japanese, and one *chō* comprises ten *tan*; thus half a hectare is roughly equivalent to five *tan*.

22. *MKCJSJ*, p. 22.

23. Partner, *Assembled in Japan*, p. 166.

24. The figure of 43 percent was given by the authors of *MKCJSJ*, p. 23. Central government figures, by contrast, suggest that the average Japanese household only spent 34 percent of total expenditures on food in 1957: Partner, *Assembled in Japan*, p. 251.

25. *MKCJSJ*, pp. 22–23. Table 39 (p. 23) incorrectly calculates the average food expenditure for nonwelfare households as 49.6 percent of total income, rather than 50.7 percent. The figure I have given (51.5 percent) includes both welfare-receiving and non-welfare-receiving households.

26. The extremely high proportion of children to the adult population in 1950s Kaminoseki suggests that abortion was not as widely practiced in the town as in the rest of Japan, where the ratio of abortions to births was considerably higher than 50 percent by the mid-1950s. Gordon, "Managing the Japanese Household," p. 254.

27. In Japanese, *Akarui yutakana machi-zukuri*: see *KK*, 15 January 1961.

28. The historical ambiguity of the phrase "town-making" is noted in an urban context by Watanabe, "*Machizukuri* in Japan," p. 128.

29. *KK*, 10 March 1958, 5 June 1958; MYM 909—6 June 1950.

30. MYM 909—5 January 1954, 10 July 1952; *KK*, 15 February 1958. Emphasis added.

31. *MB*, January 1949 (edn. 3).

32. *MKCJSJ*, p. 26.

33. Thus the concept of "culture" embraces two broad, contrasting meanings: "culture" as a horizontal construct, analogous to upward social mobility, and "culture" as a vertical construct, a way of distinguishing the people of one nation (regardless of their social status) from another. See Wallerstein, "Culture as the Ideological Battleground of the Modern World-System."

34. *Danpō* (Group Report), 28 February 1947. Emphasis added. An original copy of this document was shown to me by Shigemura Sadao in 2004. Ishimaru, the head priest of Iwaishima's Kōmyōji temple, was mayor of Kaminoseki village between November 1942 and November 1946. *KC*, p. 378.

35. MYM 909—1 November 1955; see also 5 October 1956.

36. MYM 909—1 February 1955.

37. MYM 909—5 January 1956.

38. At Murotsu junior high school in 1952, only 22 percent of graduates went directly into employment, compared to 54 percent continuing their education—a proportion that highlights the relative proximity of high schools in Yanai to the village. MYM 909—1 August 1953.

39. *KK*, 10 May 1960.

40. *KK*, 15 December 1963, 15 February 1962.

41. Nationwide, for example, 88.7 percent of all households owned a black-and-white television by 1963, compared to only 5.1 percent in 1957. Partner, *Assembled in Japan*, p. 247.

42. MYM 909—15 January 1969.

43. All postwar data is provided by the Kaminoseki town office.

44. The photograph shows the departure of two girls and five boys. In general, however, the proportion of female to male leavers was more equal across the town: the number of women declined by 30.3 percent between 1960 and 1975, compared to 36.1 percent for men.

45. A survey published in 1971 suggested that 73 percent of workers who had left Nagashima (excluding Kaminoseki district), Yashima, and Iwaishima had no intention of returning with their families to the town: Kaminoseki-chō Yakuba, *Kaminoseki-chō kaihatsu shindan*, p. 20. Hereafter abbreviated as *KKS*.

46. *KKS*, p. 52.

47. *KKS*, p. 1.

Chapter 9: *Furusato* Boom, Kaminoseki Bust

1. Narita, *"Kokyō" to iu monogatari*, pp. 18–23.

2. See, for example, Robertson, "*Furusato* Japan."

3. Tsurumi, *A Cultural History of Postwar Japan*, pp. 148–149. According to Tsurumi's figures, *Hatoko's Sea* was regularly viewed by 21 million viewers, making it the most popular of NHK's morning dramas in the 1970s.

4. Samuels, *The Business of the Japanese State*, p. 73.

5. *KC*, p. 479.

6. These general points are made by Sasaki et al., "Kihansengyō no shuyō chiiki no jittai chōsa," pp. 50–51.

7. *KC*, pp. 479–480.

8. Nagayama, *The Connoisseur's Book of Japanese Swords*, p. 287.

9. Harris and Ogasawara, *Swords of the Samurai*, p. 115.

10. Interview with Kase Sadao, the only surviving grandson of Chūnoshin, 23 January 2005.

11. Doi, *Yamaguchi-ken Ōshima-gun Hawai iminshi*, p. 16.

12. *TD* (Nagashima) shows that Kase Mihosuke bought a house in Kaminoseki in 1905.

13. Interview with the late Nishiyama Hiroshi, the youngest son of Yōichi, 8 January 2005.

14. KYM 60, 17. Mihosuke died circa 1932.

15. *TD* (Nagashima). Nishiyama bought the land from Iwaishima's Izuta household (see Chapter 4).

16. Unless otherwise noted, the biographical details on the Katayama household are based on anonymous interviews (number 5).

17. Samuels, *The Business of the Japanese State*, p. 88.

18. In the towns of Kurahashi and Ondo, Hiroshima prefecture, the first engines were attached to wooden cargo ships in 1918. Sasaki et al., "Kihansengyō no shuyō chiiki no jittai chōsa," p. 45.

19. Ibid., p. 45.

20. *KC*, p. 480.

21. *KC*, p. 853.

22. Sasaki et al., "Kihansengyō no shuyō chiiki no jittai chōsa," p. 38.

23. Ibid., p. 53. On the number of ships in Shiraida in 1955, see *KC*, p. 481.

24. Data from *MKCJSJ*, pp. 17–18.

25. Samuels, *The Business of the Japanese State*, p. 88.

26. Sasaki et al., "Kihansengyō no shuyō chiiki no jittai chōsa," p. 40. The precise figures are, respectively, 25,550; 6,646; 5,567; and 2,218.

27. Ibid., p. 48.

28. *KK*, 20 February 1970; 5 March 1974.

29. The following synopses of *Hatoko no umi* are based on my viewing of the 22 surviving episodes (out of 312) in the NHK Archives and on Hayashi, *Hatoko*, vol. 1.

30. Harvey, "*Nonchan's Dream*," pp. 134–136.

31. *Yomiuri shinbun*, 28 May 2004.

32. Morris-Suzuki, *Re-inventing Japan*, p. 132.

33. Video Research Ltd., http://www.videor.co.jp/index.htm, last accessed 31 May 2008.

34. The first image is printed on the front cover of Ōkado et al., *Sengo keiken wo ikiru*. The second image is described in Creighton, "Consuming Rural Japan," p. 246.

35. Fujioka, *Disukabā Japan*, p. 40.

36. Tanigawa, "*Furusato* to iu yōkai."

37. Hayashi, *Hatoko*, vol. 2, p. 310.

38. Aldrich, *Site Fights*, p. 132.

39. The figures are for 1975: Federation of Electric Power Companies of Japan, *Electricity Review Japan 2003–2004*, previously available from http://www.fepc.or.jp. Last accessed 24 October 2004.

40. For a more extended discussion of the nuclear allergy, see Dusinberre and Aldrich, "Hatoko Comes Home."

41. Hein, *Fueling Growth*, pp. 298–309.

42. The LPG controversy is summarized in *KC*, pp. 580–581. Somewhat surprisingly, I found no articles devoted to the issue in *Chūgoku shinbun* between 1976 and 1979.

43. Federation of Electric Power Companies of Japan, *Electricity Review Japan 2003–2004*, previously available from http://www.fepc.or.jp. Last accessed 24 October 2004.

44. *KK*, 5 July 1978.

45. The memorandum, shown to me anonymously, is dated 31 August 1979.

46. *KC*, p. 559.

Chapter 10: Nuclear Decision

1. Chūgoku Denryoku Kabushiki Gaisha, *Chūgoku Denryoku 50–nenshi*, pp. 186, 380–381.

2. For the role of the state in siting decisions, see Aldrich, *Site Fights*, and Samuels, *The Business of the Japanese State*. For the role of utility companies, see Lesbirel, *NIMBY Politics in Japan*.

3. As was common practice among elite families, all sons bore the same official name, passed down from generation to generation; they also had a personal given name. Thus documents shown to me state that Kanō Kenzō was postmaster between 1901 and 1905, and we might presume that this Kenzō was the same "Sauemon" who was village councillor in the 1890s (KYM 63). For tax, see KYM 60.

4. Given the date of Kanō's return, it is possible that this land sale was a rare example of the Occupation land reforms having a major impact on one Kaminoseki household, but unfortunately there is no evidence to back up this hypothesis.

5. Anonymous interview 6.

6. This claim is disputed by some of Kanō's former political opponents: anonymous interview 7.

7. *KK,* 5 January 1979.

8. *KK,* 5 January 1980.

9. Aldrich, *Site Fights,* p. 126.

10. Lesbirel, *NIMBY Politics in Japan,* pp. 35–38.

11. Aldrich, *Site Fights,* p. 127.

12. Lesbirel, *NIMBY Politics in Japan,* p. 31.

13. Aldrich, *Site Fights,* p. 136.

14. Quoted in Lesbirel, *NIMBY Politics in Japan,* p. 23.

15. *CS,* 14 November 1982, p. 2; 30 June 1984, p. 2; 16 October 1984, p. 1.

16. Lesbirel, *NIMBY Politics in Japan,* p. 108; Federation of Electric Power Companies of Japan, *Electricity Review Japan 2003–2004,* previously available at http://www.fepc.or.jp, last accessed 24 October 2004.

17. *CS,* 2 July 1977, p. 7.

18. *CS,* 19 January 1978, p. 2. With Hōhoku's designation, there were now 22 such sites nationwide, of which half were either completed (8) or proposed (3) nuclear sites.

19. *CS,* 28 August 1977, p. 22.

20. *CS,* 15 May 1978, p. 1.

21. *CS,* 8 May 1981, p. 2; Hirao Chōshi Hensan Iinkai, *Hirao chōshi,* p. 1320. Satō Eisaku was prime minister from 1964 to 1972.

22. Anonymous interview 8.

23. Matsunaga was vice-governor from 1976 to 1984. For his comments about Hōhoku, see *CS,* 7 February 1978 (evening edition), p. 1; 15 May 1978, p. 2.

24. Anonymous interviews 9.

25. These exchanges were reported in the evening edition of *Asahi shinbun* (hereafter *AS*), 30 September 1981: see Asahi Shinbun Yamaguchi Shikyoku, *Kokusaku no yukue,* p. 16. Hereafter abbreviated as ASY.

26. Anonymous interview 10.

27. Anonymous interview 11.

28. ASY, p. 19.

29. Lesbirel, *NIMBY Politics in Japan,* pp. 61–79.

30. *KC,* pp. 581–582.

31. Aldrich, *Site Fights,* p. 15 and passim.

32. ASY, p. 26.

33. Anonymous interview 12.

34. *KK,* 15 May 1962, 15 July 1963, 15 August 1965; *KC,* p. 579.

35. For Nishimoto and the Kaminoseki *kuchō,* see *KK,* 15 May 1962, 15 July 1963, 15 August 1965, and 15 August 1967; also *KC,* p. 391.

36. Goldman, *Doing Business with the Japanese,* pp. 155–156.

37. See, for example, *CS,* 25 October 1982, p. 1; 5 May 1983, p. 6; 16 March 1984, p. 2. During this period, the regional media also reported that Chugoku Electric had given a 400-million-yen donation to Yamaguchi prefecture, although both parties denied that the money had anything to do with the ongoing search for a new nuclear site. *CS,* 30 September 1982, p. 1.

38. *CS,* 22 September 1982, p. 2. This was a line he had first taken during the council session in June 1982, when he had said, "I think that the construction of nuclear power stations is essential considering [Japan's] energy problems": ASY, p. 18.

39. MYM 909—5 March 1955, 5 January 1956.

40. Kanō Shin, as quoted in *CS,* 25 October 1982, p. 1.

41. Quoted in *CS,* 15 December 1982, p. 6.

42. ASY, pp. 20–21. See also *CS,* 30 September 1982, p. 1.

43. *CS,* 22 September 1982, p. 2; 25 October, p. 1; 18 November, p. 2.

44. Donnelly, "Japan's Nuclear Energy Quest," p. 196.

45. Anonymous interviews 13.

46. Anonymous interviews 14.

47. *CS,* 18 December 1982, p. 22

48. Aldrich, "The Limits of Flexible and Adaptive Institutions," p. 120.

49. Zonabend, *The Nuclear Peninsula,* p. 22.

50. Quoted in ibid., p. 22.

51. Anonymous interview 15.

52. *CS* estimated 1,000 participants by October 1982 (25 October, p. 1); the *Asahi* gave a number of 900 by November: ASY, p. 24.

53. *CS,* 25 October 1982, p. 1; ASY, pp. 21, 25. According to a report in *CS,* 17 July 1984 (p. 18), a spokesperson for Chugoku Electric further admitted, "Observation visits are necessary in order [for townspeople] to understand nuclear power stations. It's natural [*tōzen*] for [Chugoku Electric] to shoulder the expenses." The only visit explicitly paid for by the town itself was when Kaminoseki's eight district heads (*kuchō*) went on a trip; this was so they might be seen as making a "fair judgment." ASY, pp. 24–25.

54. Broadbent, *Environmental Politics in Japan,* p. 190.

55. *CS,* 19 March 1988, p. 30; 27 March 1988, p. 23; 6 June 1989, p. 22; ASY, pp. 58–62. The deputy speaker from March 1986 was Komura Yoshinori, who succeeded Shimanaka Hiroshi.

56. Aldrich, *Site Fights,* p. 138.

57. *CS* estimated 1,200 protesters, while the police estimated 800: 27 October 1986, p. 18. Nuclear Power Day was first designated in 1964, the eighth anniversary of Japan's having joined the International Atomic Energy Agency. Aldrich, *Site Fights,* p. 125.

58. *KK,* 5 February 1987.

59. *AS,* 27 April 1987, p. 2.

60. *CS,* 30 June 1984, p. 2. The *Asahi shinbun* described the town's approach as "rare": ASY, p. 41. The June 1984 vote is not mentioned in Chugoku Electric's official history.

61. *CS,* 28 September 1985, p. 1.

62. *CS,* 22 December 1985, p. 7.

63. Surrounding an elected chamber was one common form of environmental protest in the postwar period; see, for example, McKean, *Environmental Protest and Citizen Politics in Japan,* p. 91.

64. Anonymous interview 16; *KC,* p. 586; *CS,* 23 October 1984, p. 6; 25 October 1984, p. 19; 28 February 1983, p. 2. Teachers played an important role in many environmental protests both as educators and as intermediaries through which local disputes could be more widely publicized. See McKean, *Environmental Protest and Citizen Politics in Japan,* pp. 30–31.

65. Anonymous interview 17.

66. *CS,* 28 February 1983, p. 2. The Japanese read, *"Machi no hatten wa wareware no te de yarō!"*

Chapter 11: Atomic Power, Community Fission

1. *CS,* 18 November 1982, p. 22.
2. *CS,* 28 February 1983, p. 2; ASY, p. 25.
3. Zonabend, *The Nuclear Peninsula,* pp. 29–30.
4. "Genpatsu nanmin" (The Refugees of the Nuclear Power Plant) was a song performed at the Iwaishima "Motherland Concert" series, starting in 1988; it was later recorded on an antinuclear CD, *Iwaishima sanka* (The Songs of Iwaishima).
5. *Danpō (Group Report),* 1947 (month illegible). See Chapter 8, note 34.
6. Between 1960 and 1980, the population of Iwaishima fell by 50 percent. The highest decrease was on Yashima (64 percent), whereas Kaminoseki, Hetsu, and Murotsu recorded decreases of between 25 and 29 percent.
7. *CS,* 19 September 1983 (evening edition), p. 2.
8. *CS,* 22 January 1983, p. 2.
9. Steiner, *Local Government in Japan,* p. 212.
10. The following examples of *mura hachibu* are based on eight separate interviews (Anonymous interviews 18). Similar *mura hachibu* tactics in the hamlet of Kazanashi, Usuki city (Kyushu) are described in McKean, *Environmental Protest and Citizen Politics in Japan,* p. 85. McKean notes that both sides of the dispute had different arrangements for fire protection—an extension of the traditional eight-part frame.
11. *CS,* 19 September 1983 (evening edition), p. 2.
12. *CS,* 2 October 1985, p. 21.
13. *CS,* 3 October 1984, p. 21; ASY, p. 40.
14. ASY, p. 50.
15. During the Tode protests over tenancy rights in Toyama prefecture in 1877, for example, farmers barricaded their village to keep out prefectural officials. See Lewis, *Becoming Apart,* p. 132.
16. *CS,* 19 September 1983 (evening edition), p. 2.
17. See also Apter and Sawa, *Against the State,* p. 7; McKean, *Environmental Protest and Citizen Politics in Japan,* pp. 225–228.
18. Anonymous interview 19.
19. KYM 17. Kaminoseki-chō Kyōiku Iinkai, *Suō-Iwaishima no kanmai gyōji,* pp. 33, 39.
20. Anonymous interviews 20.
21. Anonymous, "Hantai undō wa machigai datta," *Nippon jiji hyōron,* 19 January 2001. The newspaper is published in Yamaguchi city.
22. McKean, *Environmental Protest and Citizen Politics in Japan,* p. 127.
23. *KK,* 5 March 1986; *CS,* 5 February 1986, p. 1.
24. ASY, p. 54.
25. Steiner, *Local Government in Japan,* p. 213.

26. Anonymous interview 21. For a classic description of such social bonds at work in local politics, see Dore, *Shinohata*, pp. 228–249.

27. Anonymous interview 22.

28. Anonymous interview 23. Rather than running against each other in particular wards, candidates run on a list across the whole of the town constituency, with the highest-ranking eighteen candidates declared the winners. Iwaki Motonobu was ranked nineteenth out of twenty-five candidates in 1986, just three votes behind the eighteenth-placed candidate: ASY, p. 70.

29. Margaret McKean identifies the "trauma" and "emotional crisis" caused particularly by participating in protest movements: McKean, *Environmental Protest and Citizen Politics in Japan*, pp. 130, 195.

30. One of the few reported cases of such provocation was when a pronuclear fishing boat from Iwaishima deliberately crossed a sardine net being trawled by antinuclear fishermen, provoking an argument that culminated in the arrest of one pronuclear supporter. *CS*, 3 September 1983, p. 23.

31. ASY, p. 49.

32. *CS*, 4 May 1983, p. 6; 19 September 1983 (evening edition), p. 2.

33. This was part of an increasingly sophisticated strategy that relied not only on ostracism but on political, legal, and media mechanisms to oppose the plan. For example, antinuclear campaigners bought land around the planned site in Tanoura and then recouped some of that investment by selling individual trees to fellow campaigners: Aldrich, *Site Fights*, p. 59. For the kinds of negotiating power wielded by fishermen, see Befu, "Political Ecology of Fishing in Japan." As of 2011, the Iwaishima fishing cooperative has refused to accept the compensation package on offer from Chugoku Electric.

34. One reason for the Liaison Committee's formation may have been the fact that Mayor Katayama Hideyuki won reelection in April 1991 by a lower-than-expected margin—only 54 percent to Koyanagi Akira's 46 percent. See ASY, pp. 78–82.

35. *CS*, 15 December 1982, p. 6.

36. One man told me that the Development Association (organized by the Chamber of Commerce) had been perceived to be interested merely in "sales," whereas the new organization wished to consider the "harmony" (*yūwa*) of the townspeople (anonymous interview 24).

37. The temporal and spatial aspects of *furusato* are discussed by Kuraishi, "Toshi seikatsusha no furusato-kan," p. 18.

38. Anonymous interview 25.

39. Chūgoku Denryoku Kabushiki Gaisha, *Kakehashi's the 20th Anniversary* [*sic*] (2005).

40. Anonymous interview 26.

41. The thermal power plant began operation in December 1992.

42. Anonymous interview 27.

43. Anonymous interview 28.

44. Anonymous interview 29. Regardless of the specific ferocity of the nuclear dispute in 1980s Iwaishima, the island's negative image can partly be explained in terms of general prejudice against the perceived "bizarre" behavior of Japanese environmental protesters. McKean, *Environmental Protest and Citizen Politics in Japan*, pp. 26–27.

45. Anonymous interviews 30.

46. For the Imi interpretation of the origins of the rites, see Irie, *Umi wo wataru matsuri*. Moritomo Hiromitsu wrote a long, unpublished rebuttal to Irie's book, and the Iwaishima/

Moritomo interpretation of the rites was later formalized in Kaminoseki-chō Kyōiku Iinkai, *Suō-Iwaishima no kanmai gyōji.*

47. Anonymous interview 31.

48. During interviews, I heard repeated allegations that Moritomo Hiromitsu, late father of the current priest, had stolen money from the Fishing Cooperative (of which he had been head in the 1960s and 1970s) and that he had also misused the financial offerings (*saisen*) of his parishioners.

49. Schnell, "Ritual as an Instrument of Political Resistance in Rural Japan."

50. Anonymous interview 32.

51. Kaminoseki-chō Kyōiku Iinkai, *Suō-Iwaishima no kanmai gyōji*, p. 53.

52. Anonymous interviews 33.

Chapter 12: The Silk Road of the Sea

1. *AS*, 21 February 2011, http://www.asahi.com, last accessed 17 March 2011. For a detailed examination of one of the legal disputes, concerning common land on Nagashima, see Nomura, "Jinjachi no kizoku to iriaiken." Protests by Iwaishima fishermen at Tanoura were declared illegal by the Hiroshima high court in September 2010. *CS*, 16 September 2010, p. 24.

2. *CS*, 17 March 2011, http://www.chugoku-np.co.jp, last accessed 17 March 2011.

3. http://www.kantei.go.jp/jp/kan/statement/201105/10kaiken.html, last accessed 12 May 2011.

4. Ministry of Economy, Trade and Industry, Japan, *The Strategic Energy Plan of Japan* (revised June 2010), http://www.meti.go.jp/english/press/data/pdf/20100618_08a.pdf, last accessed 9 October 2010.

5. *CS*, 20 May 2011, http://www.chugoku-np.co.jp, last accessed 20 May 2011.

6. "Japan islanders oppose proposed nuclear plant, year after year," *Los Angeles Times*, 5 May 2011: http://www.latimes.com/news/nationworld/world/la-fg-japan-nuclear-protest-20110504,0,6852596,full.story, last accessed 14 May 2011.

7. Agulhon, *The Republic in the Village*, pp. 7–10.

8. Howell, *Capitalism from Within*, pp. 7–8.

9. Ibid., p. 6

10. See, for example, Wigen, *The Making of a Japanese Periphery*, pp. 294–295, and passim.

11. Thomas C. Smith, "Pre-Modern Economic Growth."

12. See McConnell, *Importing Diversity*.

13. Toby, "Carnival of the Aliens," pp. 421, 456.

14. Kawanishi, Namikawa, and Steele, *Rōkaru hisutorii kara gurōbaru hisutorii e*.

15. See, for example, Azuma, "'Pioneers of Overseas Japanese Development'"; Araragi, *Nihon teikoku wo meguru jinkō idō no kokusai shakaigaku*.

16. Araragi, *Nihon teikoku wo meguru jinkō idō no kokusai shakaigaku*, p. xxxiv.

17. Peattie, "Introduction," p. 52.

18. See, for example, Partner, *The Mayor of Aihara*; Waters, *Japan's Local Pragmatists*.

19. Howell, "Hard Times in the Kantō."

20. Quoted in Steele, "The Ishizaka of Notsuda," p. 63.

21. Hsu, "Migration and Native Place," p. 323.

22. "Japan as Number Three: Watching China Whizz By," *The Economist*, 19 August 2010: http://www.economist.com/node/16847828?story_id=16847828, last accessed 9 October 2010.

23. Culter, *Managing Decline,* p. 22.

24. Seaton, "Depopulation and Financial Collapse in Yūbari"; "Where Have All the Young Men Gone?" *The Economist,* 26 August 2006, pp. 47–48.

25. "Slow Death of a Small German Town as Women Pack Up and Head West," *The Guardian,* 27 January 2008: http://www.guardian.co.uk/world/2008/jan/27/germany.jasonburke, last accessed 2 February 2010; Davies, *Main Street Blues.*

26. Hecht, *The Radiance of France,* pp. 2, 214–215. Emphasis in original.

27. *KK,* 14 April 2011.

28. Ibid.

29. This observation is based on informal conversations with many townspeople during a visit to Kaminoseki in April 2011.

30. Kaminoseki figures as of 1 September 2010 (compared to 1 September 1998). In 2010, the town's dependency ratio was 123 nonworkers to every 100 workers—considerably worse than in the 1950s and more than double the national ratio of 57:100.

31. *Kaminoseki gikai dayori,* 22 April 2011 (no. 114).

32. Ueda's lecture appears in an unpublished ten-page pamphlet, "Iwaishima no rekishi" (The History of Iwaishima), dated February 1995.

33. Interviews with the late Ueda Kichisuke, 15 and 28 March 2005.

34. The tension between the *furusato* as a site of the "imagined homeplace" and the destruction of physical traces of the historical past by "the bulldozer and the wrecking ball" is discussed in Siegenthaler, "Development *for* Preservation," p. 332.

BIBLIOGRAPHY

Archives

Diplomatic Record Office (Gaikō Shiryōkan), Ministry of Foreign Affairs. Records relating to overseas migration, class 3.8.2.

Kaminoseki Town Office (Kaminoseki-chō Yakuba). Kaminoseki Yakuba monjo (Documents of the Kaminoseki Village Office) and Murotsu Yakuba monjo (Documents of the Murotsu Village Office). Both numbered according to *Kaminoseki-chō shiryō mokuroku,* 1972.

Ministry of Justice Legal Affairs Bureau, Yanai branch (Hōmukyoku Yanai Shutchōsho). *Tochi daichō* (Land Records). Organized by municipality.

National Diet Library, Modern Japanese Political History Materials Room, Gordon W. Prange Collection.

Yamaguchi Prefectural Archives (Yamaguchi Kenritsu Monjokan).

Printed Primary Materials

Asahi shinbun 朝日新聞.

Asahi Shinbun Yamaguchi Shikyoku 朝日新聞山口支局. *Kokusaku no yukue: Kaminoseki genpatsu no nijū nen* 国策の行方 上関原発の二十年. Kagoshima: Nanpō Shinsha, 2001.

Chūgoku Denryoku Kabushiki Gaisha 中国電力株式会社. *Chūgoku Denryoku 50-nenshi: anata to tomoni, chikyū to tomoni* 中国電力50年史 あなたとともに、地球とともに. Hiroshima: Chūgoku Denryoku Kabushiki Gaisha, 2001.

Chūgoku shinbun 中国新聞.

Fortune, Robert. *Yedo and Peking: A Narrative of a Journey to the Capitals of Japan and China.* London: John Murray, 1863.

Hayashi Hidehiko 林秀彦. *Hatoko* 鳩子. 3 vols. Tokyo: Nippon Hōsō Shuppan Kyōkai, 1974–1975.

Izeki Kurō 井関九朗. *Gendai Bōchō jinbutsu-shi (ji)* 現代防長人物史 地. Tokyo: Hattensha, 1917.

Kaempfer, Engelbert. *Kaempfer's Japan: Tokugawa Culture Observed.* Trans. Beatrice M. Bodart-Bailey. Honolulu: University of Hawai'i Press, 1999.

Kaminoseki-chō Komonjo Kaidoku no Kai 上関町古文書解読の会. *Hayashi-ke shozō sho-hikae: Bakumatsu kara Meiji shoki made no Chōshū han ni kansuru sho-kiroku* 林家所蔵諸控: 幕末から明治初期までの長州藩に関する諸記録. Kaminoseki: Kaminoseki-chō Kyōiku Iinkai, 1999.

———. *Hōreki-do Chōsen tsūshinshi: shinshi raichō(ge) kihan(chū) Kaminoseki kiroku* 宝暦度朝鮮通信使 信使来朝(下)帰帆(中)上関記録. Kaminoseki: Kaminoseki-chō Kyōiku Iinkai, 2003.

———. *Kaminoseki go-bansho no kiroku* 上関御番所の記録. Kaminoseki: Kaminoseki-chō Kyōiku Iinkai, 1997.

Kaminoseki-chō Yakuba. 上関町役場. *Kaminoseki-chō kaihatsu shindan* 上関町開発診断. Kaminoseki: Kaminoseki-chō Yakuba, 1971.

Kaminoseki kōhō 上関広報.

Kido, Takayoshi. *The Diary of Kido Takayoshi.* Trans. Sidney D. Brown and Akiko Hirota. 3 vols. Tokyo: University of Tokyo Press, 1983.

Meiji Bunken Shiryō Kankōkai 明治文献資料刊行会. *Yamaguchi-ken nōji chōsasho (Meiji 24 nen)* 山口県農事調査書(明治二十四年). Tokyo: Meiji Bunken Shiryō Kankōkai, 1966.

Nagatsuka, Takashi. *The Soil: A Portrait of Rural Life in Meiji Japan.* Trans. Ann Waswo. Berkeley: University of California Press, 1989 [1910].

Natsume, Sōseki. *Kokoro.* Trans. Edwin McClellan. London: Peter Owen, 1968 [1914].

Oe, Kenzaburo. *Hiroshima Notes.* Trans. David Swain and Toshi Yonezawa. New York: Grove Press, 1996 [1965].

Shibamura Keijirō 柴村敬次郎. *Yamaguchi-ken Kaminoseki Yoshida-ke shiryō to Yoshida-shi* 山口県上関吉田家資料と吉田氏. Hiroshima: Shimo Kamakari-chō, 2000.

Suga, Teruo. *The Man'yo-shu: A Complete English Translation in 5-7 Rhythm.* Vol. 3. Kanda Institute of Foreign Languages; Kanda University of International Studies, 1991.

Thunberg, Carl Peter. *Japan Extolled and Decried: Carl Peter Thunberg and the Shogun's Realm, 1775–1776.* Trans. Timon Screech. London: Curzon, 2005.

Yamaguchi-ken 山口県. *Yamaguchi kenshi shiryōhen Bakumatsu ishin 3* 山口県史史料編幕末維新3. Yamaguchi: Yamaguchi-ken, 2007.

———. *Yamaguchi kenshi shiryōhen Bakumatsu ishin 4* 山口県史史料編幕末維新4. Yamaguchi: Yamaguchi-ken, 2010.

———. *Yamaguchi kenshi shiryōhen kindai 4* 山口県史史料編近代4. Yamaguchi: Yamaguchi-ken, 2003.

Yamaguchi-ken Chihōshi Gakkai 山口県地方史学会. *Bōchō jige jōshin* 防長地下上申. Vol. 1. Yamaguchi: Matsuno Shoten, 1978.

Yamaguchi-ken Monjokan 山口県文書館. *Bōchō fūdo chūshin'an* 防長風土注進案. Vol. 6. Yamaguchi: Yamaguchi Kenritsu Yamaguchi Toshokan, 1963.

———. *Yamaguchi-ken Monjokan shoka monjo mokuroku 6: Kaminoseki-chō Yoshida-ke monjo* 山口県文書館諸家文書目録6 上関町吉田家文書. Yamaguchi: Yamaguchi-ken Monjokan, 2002.

———. *Yamaguchi-ken Monjokan shoka monjo mokuroku 7: Kaminoseki-chō Kuniyuki-ke monjo, Sakuraya-ke monjo, Yoshizaki-ke monjo* 山口県文書館諸家文書目録7 上関町国行家文書・佐倉谷家文書・吉崎家文書. Yamaguchi: Yamaguchi-ken Monjokan, 2005.

Yamaguchi-ken Sōmubu Tōkeika 山口県総務部統計課. *Murotsu Kaminoseki chiku jūmin seikatsu jittai* 室津・上関地区住民生活実態. Yamaguchi: Yamaguchi-ken Sōmubu Tōkeika, 1957.

Yomiuri shinbun 読売新聞.

Secondary Materials

Agulhon, Maurice. *The Republic in the Village: The People of the Var from the French Revolution to the Second Republic.* Trans. Janet Lloyd. Cambridge: Cambridge University Press, 1982.

Aldrich, Daniel P. "The Limits of Flexible and Adaptive Institutions: The Japanese Government's Role in Nuclear Power Plant Siting over the Postwar Period." In *Managing Conflict in Facility Siting,* edited by S. Hayden Lesbirel and Daigee Shaw, pp. 111–136. Northampton, MA: Edward Elgar, 2005.

———. *Site Fights: Divisive Facilities and Civil Society in Japan and the West.* Ithaca, NY: Cornell University Press, 2008.

Apter, David E., and Nagayo Sawa. *Against the State: Politics and Social Protest in Japan.* Cambridge, MA: Harvard University Press, 1984.

Araragi Shinzō 蘭信三, ed. *Nihon teikoku wo meguru jinkō idō no kokusai shakaigaku* 日本帝国をめぐる人口移動の国際社会学. Tokyo: Fuji Shuppan, 2008.

Azuma, Eiichiro. "'Pioneers of Overseas Japanese Development': Japanese American History and the Making of Expansionist Orthodoxy in Imperial Japan." *JAS* 67, no. 4 (2008): 1187–1226.

Bailey, Jackson H. *Ordinary People, Extraordinary Lives: Political and Economic Change in a Tōhoku Village.* Honolulu: University of Hawai'i Press, 1991.

Baxter, James C. *The Meiji Unification through the Lens of Ishikawa Prefecture.* Cambridge, MA: Council on East Asian Studies, Harvard University, 1994.

Beardsley, Richard K., John W. Hall, and Robert E. Ward. *Village Japan.* Chicago: University of Chicago Press, 1959.

Befu, Harumi. "Political Ecology of Fishing in Japan: Techno-Environmental Impact of Industrialization in the Inland Sea." *Research in Economic Anthropology* 3 (1980): 323–347.

Bernstein, Gail Lee. *Isami's House: Three Centuries of a Japanese Family.* Berkeley: University of California Press, 2005.

Bolitho, Harold. "The Tempō Crisis." In *The Cambridge History of Japan,* vol. 5, edited by Marius B. Jansen, pp. 116–167. Cambridge: Cambridge University Press, 1989.

Boulton, Jeremy. "Microhistory in Early Modern London: John Bedford (1601–1667)." *Continuity and Change* 22, no. 1 (2007): 113–141.

Bowen, Roger W. *Rebellion and Democracy in Meiji Japan: A Study of the Commoners in the Popular Rights Movement.* Berkeley: University of California Press, 1980.

Braudel, Fernand. *The Mediterranean and the Mediterranean World in the Age of Philip II.* Trans. Sian Reynolds. 2 vols. London: Harper and Row, 1972.

Broadbent, Jeffrey. *Environmental Politics in Japan: Networks of Power and Protest.* Cambridge: Cambridge University Press, 1998.

Brown, Richard D. "Microhistory and the Post-Modern Challenge." *Journal of the Early Republic* 23, no. 1 (2003): 1–20.

Browning, Christopher R. *Ordinary Men: Reserve Police Battalion 101 and the Final Solution in Poland.* London: Penguin, 2001.

Craig, Albert M. *Chōshū in the Meiji Restoration.* Cambridge, MA: Harvard University Press, 1961.

Creighton, Millie. "Consuming Rural Japan: The Marketing of Tradition and Nostalgia in the Japanese Travel Industry." *Ethnology* 36, no. 3 (1997): 239–254.

Culter, Suzanne. *Managing Decline: Japan's Coal Industry Restructuring and Community Response.* Honolulu: University of Hawai'i Press, 1999.

Davies, Richard O. *Main Street Blues: The Decline of Small-Town America.* Columbus: Ohio State University Press, 1998.

Davis, Natalie Zemon. *The Return of Martin Guerre.* Cambridge, MA: Harvard University Press, 1983.

Doi Yatarō 土井弥太郎. *Yamaguchi-ken Ōshima-gun Hawai iminshi* 山口県大島郡ハワイ移民史. Tokyo: Matsuno Shoten, 1980.

Donnelly, Michael W. "Japan's Nuclear Energy Quest." In *Japan's Foreign Policy after the Cold War: Coping with Change,* edited by Gerald L. Curtis, pp. 179–201. Armonk, NY: M. E. Sharpe, 1993.

Dore, Ronald P. *Shinohata: A Portrait of a Japanese Village.* Berkeley: University of California Press, 1994.

Dower, John W. *Embracing Defeat: Japan in the Wake of World War II.* New York: Norton, 1999.

Drea, Edward J. *Japan's Imperial Army: Its Rise and Fall, 1853–1945.* Lawrence: University of Kansas Press, 2009.

Dresner, Jonathan F. "Emigration and Local Development in Meiji-era Yamaguchi." Ph.D. diss., Harvard University, 2001.

———. "International Labour Migrants' Return to Meiji-Era Yamaguchi and Hiroshima: Economic and Social Effects." *International Migration* 46, no. 3 (2008): 65–94.

Dusinberre, Martin. "Unread Relics of a Transnational 'Hometown' in Rural Western Japan." *Japan Forum* 20, no. 3 (2008): 305–335.

Dusinberre, Martin, and Daniel P. Aldrich. "Hatoko Comes Home: Civil Society and Nuclear Power in Japan." *JAS* 70, no. 3 (2011): 683–705.

Duus, Peter. *The Abacus and the Sword: The Japanese Penetration of Korea, 1895–1910.* Berkeley: University of California Press, 1995.

Edwards, Elise. "An Ethics for Working Up? Japanese Corporate Scandals and Rethinking Lessons about Fieldwork." *Critical Asian Studies* 39, no. 4 (2007): 561–582.

Embree, John F. *Suye-mura: A Japanese Village.* Chicago: University of Chicago Press, 1939.

Field, Norma. *In the Realm of a Dying Emperor.* New York: Pantheon Books, 1991.

Fueto Toshio 不破勝敏夫. "Yamaguchi-ken Kumage-gun Kaminoseki-son Iwaishima no hōshakaigakuteki kenkyū: sonraku kōzō, kazoku seido, gyogyōken seido wo chūshin toshite" 山口県熊毛郡上関村祝島の法社会学的研究　村落構造、家族制度、漁業権制度を中心として. *Yamaguchi keizaigaku zasshi* 4, nos. 5–6 (1953): 48–82.

Fujioka Wakao 藤岡和賀夫. *Disukabā Japan: karei naru shuppatsu* ディスカバー・ジャパン華麗なる出発. Tokyo: Mainichi Shinbun, 1972.

Furumaya Tadao 古厩忠夫. *Ura Nihon: kindai Nihon wo toinaosu* 裏日本 近代日本を問いなおす. Tokyo: Iwanami Shoten, 1997.

Garon, Sheldon M. *Molding Japanese Minds: The State in Everyday Life.* Princeton, NJ: Princeton University Press, 1997.

George, Timothy S. *Minamata: Pollution and the Struggle for Democracy in Postwar Japan.* Cambridge, MA: Harvard University Asia Center, 2001.

Ginzburg, Carlo. *The Cheese and the Worms: The Cosmos of a Sixteenth-Century Miller.* Trans. John Tadeschi and Anne Tadeschi. London: Penguin, 1992.

Ginzburg, Carlo, and Carlo Poni. "The Name and the Game: Unequal Exchange and the Historiographic Marketplace." In *Microhistory and the Lost Peoples of Europe,* edited by Edward Muir and Guido Ruggiero, pp. 1–10. Baltimore: The Johns Hopkins University Press, 1991.

Gluck, Carol. *Japan's Modern Myths: Ideology in the Late Meiji Period*. Princeton, NJ: Princeton University Press, 1985.

———. "The People in History: Recent Trends in Japanese Historiography." *JAS* 38, no.1 (1978): 25–50.

Goldman, Alan. *Doing Business with the Japanese: A Guide to Successful Communication, Management, and Diplomacy*. Albany: State University of New York Press, 1994.

Gordon, Andrew. "Managing the Japanese Household: The New Life Movement in Postwar Japan." *Social Politics* 4, no. 2 (1997): 245–283.

Gregory, Brad S. "Review: Is Small Beautiful? Microhistory and the History of Everyday Life." *History and Theory* 38, no. 1 (1999): 100–110.

Griffiths, Owen. "Need, Greed, and Protest in Japan's Black Market, 1938–1949." *Journal of Social History* 35, no. 4 (2002): 825–858.

Hackett, Roger F. *Yamagata Aritomo in the Rise of Modern Japan, 1838–1922*. Cambridge, MA: Harvard University Press, 1971.

Hagi Hakubutsukan 萩博物館. *Yoshida Shōin to jukusei-tachi* 吉田松陰と塾生たち. Hagi: Hagi Hakubutsukan, 2007.

Hall, Ivan Parker. *Mori Arinori*. Cambridge, MA: Harvard University Press, 1973.

Hane, Mikiso. *Peasants, Rebels, Women, and Outcastes: The Underside of Modern Japan*. 2nd ed. Oxford: Rowman and Littlefield, 2003.

Harris, Victor, and Nobuo Ogasawara. *Swords of the Samurai*. London: British Museum Publications, 1990.

Harvey, Paul A. S. "*Nonchan's Dream:* NHK Morning Serialized Television Novels." In *The Worlds of Japanese Popular Culture: Gender, Shifting Boundaries, and Global Cultures*, edited by D. P. Martinez, pp. 133–151. Cambridge: Cambridge University Press, 1998.

Hecht, Gabrielle. *The Radiance of France: Nuclear Power and National Identity after World War II*. Cambridge, MA: MIT Press, 1998.

Hein, Laura E. *Fueling Growth: The Energy Revolution and Economic Policy in Postwar Japan*. Cambridge, MA: Council on East Asian Studies, Harvard University, 1990.

Henderson, Gregory. "Japan's Chōsen: Immigrants, Ruthlessness and Developmental Shock." In *Korea under Japanese Colonial Rule: Studies of the Policy and Techniques of Japanese Colonialism*, edited by Andrew C. Nahm, pp. 261–269. Kalamazoo: Center for Korean Studies, Western Michigan University, 1973.

Herbert, Ulrich. "Good Times, Bad Times." *History Today* 36, no. 2 (1986): 42–48.

Hikari Shishi Hensan Iinkai 光市史編纂委員会. *Hikari shishi* 光市史. Hikari: Hikari-shi, 1975.

Hirao Chōshi Hensan Iinkai 平生町史編纂委員会. *Hirao chōshi* 平生町史. Hirao: Hirao-chō Yakuba, 1978.

Ho, Samuel Pao-san. "Colonialism and Development: Korea, Taiwan, and Kwantung." In *The Japanese Colonial Empire, 1895–1945*, edited by Ramon H. Myers and Mark R. Peattie, pp. 347–398. Princeton, NJ: Princeton University Press, 1984.

Hori Masaaki 堀雅昭. *Hawai ni watatta kaizoku-tachi: Suō Ōshima no iminshi* ハワイに渡った海賊たち 周防大島の移民史. Fukuoka: Genshobō, 2007.

Howell, David L. *Capitalism from Within: Economy, Society, and the State in a Japanese Fishery*. Berkeley: University of California Press, 1995.

———. "Hard Times in the Kantō: Economic Change and Village Life in Late Tokugawa Japan." *Modern Asian Studies* 23, no. 2 (1989): 349–371.

Hsu, Madeline Y. "Migration and Native Place: Qiaokan and the Imagined Community of Taishan County, Guangdong, 1893–1993." *JAS* 59, no. 2 (2000): 307–331.

Huber, Thomas M. *The Revolutionary Origins of Modern Japan.* Stanford, CA: Stanford University Press, 1981.

Humphreys, Leonard A. *The Way of the Heavenly Sword: The Japanese Army in the 1920's.* Stanford, CA: Stanford University Press, 1995.

Ichisaka Tarō 一坂太郎. *Chōshū kiheitai: shōsha no naka no haisha-tachi* 長州奇兵隊 勝者のなかの敗者たち. Tokyo: Chūōkōron Shinsha, 2002.

Irie Hidechika 入江英親. *Umi wo wataru matsuri: Iwaishima to Kunisaki Betsugūsha no kanmai* 海を渡る祭 祝島と国東別宮社の神舞. Tokyo: Keiyūsha, 1975.

Irokawa, Daikichi. *The Culture of the Meiji Period.* Translation edited by Marius B. Jansen. Princeton, NJ: Princeton University Press, 1985 [1970].

———. "Japan's Grass-Roots Tradition: Current Issues in the Mirror of History." *Japan Quarterly* 20, no. 1 (1973): 78–86.

Ishikawa Tomonori 石川友紀. "Yamaguchi-ken Ōshima-gun Tōwa-chō ni okeru deimin no rekishi chirigakuteki kōsatsu" 山口県大島郡東和町における出移民の歴史地理学的考察. *Nihon imin no chirigakuteki kenkyū* 34 (1991): 1–21.

Itō Yukio 伊藤之雄. *Itō Hirobumi: kindai Nihon wo tsukutta otoko* 伊藤博文 近代日本を創った男. Tokyo: Kōensha, 2009.

Iwata, Masakazu. *Ōkubo Toshimichi: The Bismarck of Japan.* Berkeley: University of California Press, 1964.

Jansen, Marius B. *The Making of Modern Japan.* Cambridge, MA: Harvard University Press, 2000.

———. *Sakamoto Ryōma and the Meiji Restoration.* Princeton, NJ: Princeton University Press, 1961.

Johnson, Erwin H. "Status Changes in Hamlet Structure Accompanying Modernization." In *Aspects of Social Change in Modern Japan,* edited by Ronald P. Dore, pp. 153–183. Princeton, NJ: Princeton University Press, 1967.

Kalland, Arne. *Shingū: A Japanese Fishing Community.* London: Curzon, 1981.

Kaminoseki-chō Kyōiku Iinkai 上関町教育委員会. *Suō-Iwaishima no kanmai gyōji* 周防祝島の神舞行事. Kaminoseki: Kaminoseki-chō Kyōiku Iinkai, 1978.

Kaminoseki-chō Kyōiku Iinkai Kyōiku Bunkaka 上関町教育委員会教育文化課. *Yamaguchi-ken shitei bunkazai: Shikairō hozon shūri kōji hōkokusho* 山口県指定文化財 四階楼保存修理工事報告書. Kaminoseki: Kaminoseki Kyōiku Iinkai, 2002.

Kaminoseki Chōshi Hensan Iinkai 上関町史編纂委員会. *Kaminoseki chōshi* 上関町史. Kaminoseki: Kaminoseki-chō Yakuba, 1988.

Kanaya Masato 金谷匡人. *Kaizoku-tachi no chūsei* 海賊たちの中世. Tokyo: Yoshikawakō Bunkan, 1998.

Kano Masanao 鹿野政直. *Torishima wa haitteiru ka: rekishi ishiki no genzai to rekishigaku* 「鳥島」は入っているか 歴史意識の現在と歴史学. Tokyo: Iwanami Shoten, 1988.

Katō Teijin 加藤貞仁 and Abumi Keiki 鐙啓記. *Kitamaebune: kikōchi to kōeki no monogatari* 北前船 寄港地と交易の物語. Akita: Mumeisha, 2002.

Kawamura Toshiyuki 河村利幸. *Furusato tanbō Kaminoseki* ふるさと探訪かみのせき. 2 vols. Kaminoseki: Kaminoseki-chō no Hatten wo Kangaeru Kai, 1984, 1986.

Kawanishi Hidemichi 河西英通, Namikawa Kenji 浪川健治, and M. William Steele, eds. *Rōkaru hisutorii kara gurōbaru hisutorii e: tabunka no rekishigaku to chiikishi* 『ローカルヒストリーからグローバルヒストリーへ』多文化の歴史学と地域史. Tokyo: Iwata Shoin, 2005.

Kimura Kenji 木村健二. *Zaichō Nihonjin no shakaishi* 在朝日本人の社会史. Tokyo: Miraisha, 1989.

Kimura Motoi 木村礎. "Kyōdoshi, chihōshi, chiikishi kenkyū no rekishi to kadai" 郷土史、地方史、地域史研究の歴史と課題. In *Iwanami kōza Nihon tsūshi betsumaku 2: chiikishi kenkyū no genjō to kadai,* edited by Kimura Motoi et al., pp. 3–31. Tokyo: Iwanami Shoten, 1994.

Kitagawa Ken 北川健. *Bōchō fūdo chūshin'an to dōwa mondai* 防長風土注進案と同和問題. Yamaguchi: Yamaguchi-ken Monjokan, 1983.

Kuraishi Tadahiko 倉石忠彦. "Toshi seikatsusha no furusato-kan" 都市生活者の故郷観. *Nihon minzokugaku* 206 (1966), Special Feature: "Furusato wo tō," 12–24.

Lesbirel, S. Hayden. *NIMBY Politics in Japan: Energy Siting and the Management of Environmental Conflict.* Ithaca, NY: Cornell University Press, 1998.

Levi, Giovanni. "On Microhistory." In *New Perspectives in Historical Writing,* edited by Peter Burke, pp. 97–119. Cambridge: Cambridge University Press, 1991.

Lewis, Michael. *Becoming Apart: National Power and Local Politics in Toyama, 1868–1945.* Cambridge, MA: Harvard University Asia Center, 2000.

Lüdtke, Alf. "Introduction: What Is the History of Everyday Life and Who Are Its Practitioners?" In *The History of Everyday Life: Reconstructing Historical Experiences and Ways of Life,* edited by Alf Lüdtke, pp. 3–40. Princeton, NJ: Princeton University Press, 1995.

———. "People Working: Everyday Life and German Fascism." *History Workshop Journal* 50 (2000): 74–92.

Machida Shinobu 町田忍. *Chikakute natsukashii Shōwa ano koro* 近くて懐かしい昭和あのころ. Tokyo: Toei Co., 1999.

Makino Ryūshin 牧野隆信. *Kitamaebune no kenkyū* 北前船の研究. Tokyo: Hōsei Daigaku Shuppankyoku, 1989.

McClain, James L. "Failed Expectations: Kaga Domain on the Eve of the Meiji Restoration." *The Journal of Japanese Studies* 14, no. 2 (1988): 403–447.

McConnell, David L. *Importing Diversity: Inside Japan's JET Program.* Berkeley: University of California Press, 2000.

McKean, Margaret A. *Environmental Protest and Citizen Politics in Japan.* Berkeley: University of California Press, 1981.

Metzger-Court, Sarah. "From Kitchen to Workshop: The Commercial and Industrial Transformation of Osaka in the Late Nineteenth Century." In *Japan's Socioeconomic Evolution: Continuity and Change,* edited by Sarah Metzger-Court and Werner Pascha, pp. 66–75. Folkestone, UK: Japan Library, 1996.

Minamigata Takeshi 南方長. "Hagi-han sankin kōtai no kōtei: Setonaikai tsūkō kara Chūgokuro tsūkō e no ikō" 萩藩参勤交代の行程 瀬戸内海通行から中国路通行への移行. *Yamaguchi Kenritsu Monjokan kenkyū kiyō* 29 (2002): 29–50.

Miyamoto Tsuneichi 宮本常一 and Okamoto Sadamu 岡本定. *Tōwa chōshi* 東和町誌. Tōwa: Tōwa-chō Yakuba, 1982.

Moriyama, Alan Takeo. *Imingaisha: Japanese Emigration Companies and Hawaii, 1894–1908.* Honolulu: University of Hawai'i Press, 1985.

Morris-Suzuki, Tessa. "Northern Lights: The Making and Unmaking of Karafuto Identity." In *Race, Ethnicity and Migration in Modern Japan,* edited by Michael Weiner, pp. 251–279. London: Routledge, 2004.

———. *Re-inventing Japan: Time, Space, Nation.* New York: M. E. Sharpe, 1998.

Murayama, Yuzo. "Information and Emigrants: Interprefectural Differences of Japanese Emigration to the Pacific Northwest, 1880–1915." *The Journal of Economic History* 51, no. 1 (1991): 125–147.

Nagayama, Kōkan. *The Connoisseur's Book of Japanese Swords.* Trans. Kenji Mishina. Tokyo: Kodansha International, 1997.

Narita Ryūichi 成田龍一. *"Kokyō" to iu monogatari: toshi kūkan no rekishigaku* 「故郷」という物語 都市空間の歴史学. Tokyo: Yoshikawakō Bunkan, 1998.

Nish, Ian. "Politics, Trade, and Communications in East Asia: Thoughts on Anglo-Japanese Relations, 1861–1907." *Modern Asian Studies* 21, no. 4 (1987): 667–678.

Nishikawa, Shunsaku. "The Economy of Chōshū on the Eve of Industrialization." *The Economic Studies Quarterly* 38, no. 4 (1987): 323–337.

Nomura Yasuhiro 野村泰弘. "Jinjachi no kizoku to iriaiken: Kaminoseki genpatsu yōchi wo sozai toshite" 神社地の帰属と入会権 上関原発用地を素材として. *Shimane Kenritsu Daigaku sōgō seisaku ronsō* 14 (2008): 43–75.

Norbeck, Edward. *Takashima: A Japanese Fishing Community.* Salt Lake City: University of Utah Press, 1954.

Notehelfer, F. G. "Review: Meiji in the Rear-View Mirror: Top Down vs. Bottom Up History." *MN,* 45, no. 2 (1990): 207–228.

Ogawa Kuniharu 小川国治. "Chōshū han ryūtsū seisaku to Kaminoseki koshini kaisho" 長州藩流通政策と上関越荷会所. *Yamaguchi Daigaku Kyōikugakubu kenkyū ronsō* 25, no. 1 (1976): 17–35.

Oguma Eiji 小熊英二. *"Nihonjin" no kyōkai: Okinawa, Ainu, Taiwan, Chōsen shokuminchi shihai kara fukki undō made* 「日本人」の境界 沖縄、アイヌ、台湾、朝鮮 植民地支配から復帰運動まで. Tokyo: Shin'yōsha, 1998.

Ōkado Masakatsu 大門正克. *Rekishi e no toi, genzai e no toi* 歴史への問い、現在への問い. Tokyo: Azekura Shobō, 2009.

Ōkado Masakatsu 大門正克, Yasuda Tsuneo 安田常雄, and Amano Masako 天野正子. *Sengo keiken wo ikiru* 戦後経験を生きる. Tokyo: Yoshikawakō Bunkan, 2003.

Okano Nobuko 岡野信子 and Kanaya Masato 金谷匡人. "Kaminoseki-chō Iwaishima no yagō" 上関町祝島の屋号. In *Yamaguchi kenshi minzokubukai hōkokusho 2: Yamaguchi-ken no iena, kadona, yagō* 山口県史民俗部会報告書第二号 山口県の家名・門名・屋号, edited by Yamaguchi Kenshi Hensan Minzoku Bukai, pp. 30–41. Yamaguchi: Yamaguchi Kenshi Hensanshitsu, 1995.

Partner, Simon. *Assembled in Japan: Electrical Goods and the Making of the Japanese Consumer.* Berkeley: University of California Press, 1999.

———. *The Mayor of Aihara: A Japanese Villager and His Community, 1865–1925.* Berkeley: University of California Press, 2009.

———. *Toshié: A Story of Village Life in Twentieth-Century Japan.* Berkeley: University of California Press, 2004.

Peattie, Mark R. "Introduction." In *The Japanese Colonial Empire, 1895–1945,* edited by Ramon H. Myers and Mark R. Peattie, pp. 3–52. Princeton, NJ: Princeton University Press, 1984.

Peltonen, Matti. "Clues, Margins, and Monads: The Micro-Macro Link in Historical Research." *History and Theory* 40 (2001): 347–359.

Platt, Brian W. "Elegance, Prosperity, Crisis: Three Generations of Tokugawa Village Elites." *MN* 55, no. 1 (2000): 45–81.

Pratt, Edward E. "Community and Conflict in Nineteenth-Century Japan: A Reconsideration." *Early Modern Japan* 8, no. 2 (2000): 5–13.

———. *Japan's Protoindustrial Elite: The Economic Foundations of the Gōnō.* Cambridge, MA: Harvard University Asia Center, 1999.

Robertson, Jennifer. "*Furusato* Japan: The Culture and Politics of Nostalgia." *Politics, Culture and Society* 1, no. 4 (1988): 494–518.

Sagara Eisuke 相良英輔. "Kindai enden jinushi no seiritsu to sono seikaku: Hirao enden no baai" 近代塩田地主の成立とその性格 平生塩田の場合. *Yamaguchi-ken chihōshi kenkyū* 26 (1971): 11–19.

Saitō Osamu 斉藤修, and Nishikawa Shunsaku 西川俊作. "Tokugawa Nihon no shotoku bunpu" 徳川日本の所得分布. *Keizai kenkyū* 58, no. 4 (2007): 289–301.

Samuels, Richard J. *The Business of the Japanese State: Energy Markets in Comparative and Historical Perspective.* Ithaca, NY: Cornell University Press, 1987.

Sasaki Hiroshi 佐々木弘, Shinohara Yōichi 篠原陽一, Amemiya Yōji 雨宮洋司, Bujō Masanaga 武城正長, and Doi Yasunori 土居靖範. "Kihansengyō no shuyō chiiki no jittai chōsa: sono hatten no ruikei ni chūmoku shite" 機帆船業の主要地域の実態調査 その発展の類型に注目して. *Tōkyō Shōsen Daigaku kenkyū hōkoku jinbun kagaku* 30 (1980): 33–85.

Schnell, Scott. "Ritual as an Instrument of Political Resistance in Rural Japan." *Journal of Anthropological Research* 51, no. 4 (1995): 301–328.

Seaton, Philip. "Depopulation and Financial Collapse in Yubari: Market Forces, Administrative Folly, or a Warning to Others?" *Social Science Japan Journal* 13, no. 2 (2010): 227–240.

Shapinsky, Peter D. "With the Sea as Their Domain: Pirates and Maritime Lordship in Medieval Japan." In *Seascapes: Maritime Histories, Littoral Cultures, and Transoceanic Exchanges,* edited by Jerry H. Bentley, Renate Bridenthal, and Kären Wigen, pp. 221–238. Honolulu: University of Hawaiʻi Press, 2007.

Shapiro, James. *Oberammergau: The Troubling Story of the World's Most Famous Passion Play.* London: Little, Brown and Company, 2000.

Siegenthaler, Peter. "Development *for* Preservation: Localizing Collective Memory in 1960s Kanazawa." In *The Power of Memory in Modern Japan,* edited by Sven Saaler and Wolfgan Schwentker, pp. 319–336. Folkestone: Global Oriental, 2007.

Smith, Kerry. *A Time of Crisis: Japan, the Great Depression, and Rural Revitalization.* Cambridge, MA: Harvard University Asia Center, 2001.

Smith, Robert J. *Kurusu: The Price of Progress in a Japanese Village, 1951–1975.* Folkestone, UK: Dawson, 1978.

Smith, Thomas C. *Native Sources of Japanese Industrialization, 1750–1920.* Berkeley: University of California Press, 1988.

———. "Pre-Modern Economic Growth: Japan and the West." *Past and Present* 60 (1973): 127–160.

Steele, M. William. "Edo in 1868: The View from Below." *MN* 45, no. 2 (1990): 127–155.

———. "The Ishizaka of Notsuda: A Family in Transition." In *The Human Tradition in Modern Japan,* ed. Anne Walthall, pp. 61–76. Wilmington, DE: SR Books, 2002.

Steiner, Kurt. *Local Government in Japan.* Stanford, CA: Stanford University Press, 1965.

Tabuse Chōshi Hensan Iinkai 田布施町史編纂委員会. *Tabuse chōshi* 田布施町史. Tabuse: Tabuse-chō Yakuba, 1990.

Tanigawa Ken'ichi 谷川健一. "*Furusato* to iu yōkai" 「ふるさと」という妖怪. *Dentō to gendai* 55 (1978): 15–24.

Tanizawa Akira 谷沢明. *Setouchi no machinami: minato machi keisei no kenkyū* 瀬戸内の町並み 港町形成の研究. Tokyo: Shōgakukan, 1991.

———. "Setouchi no minato machi" 瀬戸内の港町. In *Umi to rettō bunka 9: Setouchi no ama bunka* 海と列島文化9 瀬戸内の海人文化, pp. 387–420. Tokyo: Shōgakukan, 1991.

Toby, Ronald P. "Carnival of the Aliens: Korean Embassies in Edo-Period Art and Popular Culture." *MN* 41, no. 4 (1986): 415–456.

———. *State and Diplomacy in Early Modern Japan: Asia in the Development of the Tokugawa Bakufu*. Stanford, CA: Stanford University Press, 1984.

Tonkin, Elizabeth. *Narrating Our Pasts: The Social Construction of Oral History*. Cambridge: Cambridge University Press, 1992.

Totman, Conrad. "Tokugawa Yoshinobu and Kobugattai: A Study of Political Inadequacy." *MN* 30, no. 4 (1975): 393–403.

Tsurumi, Shunsuke. *A Cultural History of Postwar Japan, 1945–1980*. London: KPI, 1987.

United Japanese Society of Hawai'i. *Hawai Nihonjin iminshi* ハワイ日本人移民史. Honolulu: United Japanese Society of Hawai'i, 1964.

Vaporis, Constantine Nomikos. *Breaking Barriers: Travel and the State in Early Modern Japan*. Cambridge, MA: Council on East Asian Studies, Harvard University, 1994.

Wakabayashi, Bob Tadashi. "Opium, Expulsion, Sovereignty: China's Lessons for Bakumatsu Japan." *MN* 47, no. 1 (1992): 1–25.

Wallerstein, Immanuel. "Culture as the Ideological Battleground of the Modern World-System." *Theory, Culture and Society* 7, no. 2 (1990): 31–55.

Walthall, Anne. "Introduction: Tracking People in the Past." In *The Human Tradition in Modern Japan*, edited by Anne Walthall, pp. xi–xx. Wilmington, DE: SR Books, 2002.

———. "The Life Cycle of Farm Women in Tokugawa Japan." In *Recreating Japanese Women, 1600–1945*, edited by Gail Lee Bernstein, pp. 42–70. Berkeley: University of California Press, 1991.

———. "Peripheries: Rural Culture in Tokugawa Japan." *MN* 39, no. 4 (1984): 371–392.

Waswo, Ann, and Yoshiaki Nishida, eds. *Farmers and Village Life in Twentieth-Century Japan*. Abingdon, Oxon: RoutledgeCurzon, 2003.

Watanabe, Shun'ichi J. "*Machizukuri* in Japan: A Historical Perspective on Participatory Community-Building Initiatives." In *Cities, Autonomy and Decentralization in Japan*, edited by C. Hein and P. Pelletier, pp. 128–138. London: Routledge, 2006.

Waters, Neil L. *Japan's Local Pragmatists: The Transition from Bakumatsu to Meiji in the Kawasaki Region*. Cambridge, MA: Council on East Asian Studies, Harvard University, 1983.

Webster, Wendy. "Transnational Journeys and Domestic Histories." *Journal of Social History* 39, no. 3 (2006): 651–666.

Wigen, Kären. *The Making of a Japanese Periphery, 1750–1920*. Berkeley: University of California Press, 1995.

———. "Politics and Piety in Japanese Native-Place Studies: The Rhetoric of Solidarity in Shinano." *positions* 4, no. 3 (1996): 491–517.

Wilson, George M. *Patriots and Redeemers in Japan: Motives in the Meiji Restoration*. Chicago: University of Chicago Press, 1992.

Wray, William D. "Shipping: From Sail to Steam." In *Japan in Transition: From Tokugawa to Meiji,* edited by Marius B. Jansen and Gilbert Rozman, pp. 248–270. Princeton, NJ: Princeton University Press, 1988.

Yamaguchi-ken Kyōiku Iinkai 山口県教育委員会. *Yamaguchi-ken no minka: Shōwa 47 nendo minka kinkyū chōsa hōkoku* 山口県の民家 昭和47年度民家緊急調査報告. Yamaguchi: Yamaguchi-ken Kyōiku Iinkai, 1972.

Yamaguchi-ken Kyōiku Zaidan 山口県教育財団. *Kaminoseki jōseki: Kaminoseki shinchi chiku kyūkeishachi hōkai taisaku jigyō ni tomonau hakkutsu chōsa hōkoku* 上関城跡 上関新地地区急傾斜地崩壊対策事業に伴う発掘調査報告. Yamaguchi: Yamaguchi-ken Maizō Bunkazai Sentā, 1999.

Yamamura, Kozo. "Toward a Reexamination of the Economic History of Tokugawa Japan, 1600–1867." *The Journal of Economic History* 33, no. 3 (1973): 509–546.

Yamamuro Atsushi 山室敦嗣. "Fiirudowāku ga 'jissenteki' de aru tame ni: genshiryoku hatsudensho kōhochi no genba kara" フィールドワークが「実践的」であるために 原子力発電所候補地の現場から. In *Shakaigakuteki fiirudowāku,* edited by Yoshii Hiroaki and Miura Kōkichirō, pp. 132–166. Kyoto: Sekai Shisōsha, 2004.

Yamashita, Samuel Hideo. *Leaves from an Autumn of Emergencies: Selections from the Wartime Diaries of Ordinary Japanese.* Honolulu: University of Hawai'i Press, 2005.

Yasui Manami 安井眞奈美. "Machi-zukuri, mura-okoshi to furusato monogatari" 町づくり、村おこしとふるさと物語. In *Matsuri to ibento,* edited by Komatsu Kazuhiko, pp. 201–226. Tokyo: Shōgakukan, 1997.

Young, Louise. *Japan's Total Empire: Manchuria and the Culture of Wartime Imperialism.* Berkeley: University of California Press, 1998.

Zonabend, Françoise. *The Nuclear Peninsula.* Trans. J. A. Underwood. Cambridge: Cambridge University Press, 1993.

INDEX